SPEECH COMMUNICATION IN SOCIETY

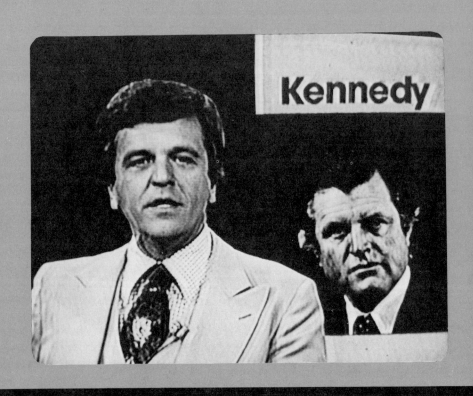

CHARLES R. GRUNER
CAL M. LOGUE
DWIGHT L. FRESHLEY
RICHARD C. HUSEMAN
THE UNIVERSITY OF GEORGIA

ALLYN AND BACON, INC.
BOSTON   LONDON   SYDNEY   TORONTO

SPEECH COMMUNICATION IN SOCIETY

SECOND EDITION

Library of Congress Cataloging in Publication Data

Main entry under title:

Speech communication in society.

    Includes bibliographical references and indexes.
    1. Oral communication.   I. Gruner, Charles R.
PN4121.S753   1977   301.14   76-47527

ISBN 0-205-05732-2

Photos by Bobbi Carrey.

The authors and publisher wish to thank those who granted permission for the use
of the photographs in this book: cover, George Fenneman and "The Donny and Marie
Osmond Show"; pages 2 and 3, from "All in the Family," Tandem Productions, all
rights reserved; pages 12 and 13, from "Dr. Kildare," courtesy of NBC; page 23, from
"Search for Tomorrow," Procter & Gamble Productions; pages 26 and 27, NBC News;
page 48, Patricia Dixon/"All My Children," ABC, Inc.; pages 52 and 53, Billy Graham;
page 65, WBZ-TV, Boston, and Pat Mitchell; pages 68 and 69, from "The Jeffersons,"
Tandem Productions, all rights reserved; page 88, courtesy of The Coca-Cola Company; pages 92 and 93, courtesy WNAC-TV, Boston; page 123, © Allen Products Co.,
Inc.; pages 128 and 129, from "Search for Tomorrow," Procter & Gamble Productions;
page 148, from CBS Sports, Sonny Jurgensen and Don Criqui; pages 154 and 155,
from the "Good-Day!" show, and Santina Curran, "Supper Shopper"; page 184,
WNAC-TV, Boston; pages 188 and 189 (left) WCVB-TV and Richard Burdick, and
(right) WBZ-TV, Boston; pages 218 and 219, WBZ-TV, Boston, and Tony Pepper and
Jack Williams; and pages 240 and 241, from "Mugsie," courtesy of NBC.

CONTENTS

PREFACE

This book is intended for use in what is typically called the "first course" or the "basic course" in speech communication at the college level. We hope that the book shows evidence of certain principles we have tried to keep in mind.

During the past generation, the role of college and university training has shifted from a philosophy of training and enriching an "educated elite" who will become society's leaders and teachers to one of *mass* education. It is recognized that, with the population growth, large numbers of educated, articulate citizens will be needed to run the industrial, governmental, and social agencies of this complicated culture. Fully 75 percent of our waking hours are spent in some sort of communication, and we realize that the very act of communication is vastly complex.

The first edition of this book was intended to fit the kind of beginning speech communication course which a survey showed to be prevalent at the time ("The First Course in Speech: A Survey of U.S. Colleges and Universities," *Speech Teacher,* 19, January, 1970). That survey showed the basic course to be primarily a public speaking course but with a tendency to include "communication theory" and "interpersonal communication" more and more frequently.

This second edition is a response to a later survey ("A Re-examination of the First Course in Speech at U.S. Colleges and Universities," *Speech Teacher,* 23, September, 1974) which indicated that more and more beginning speech communication courses were stressing communication theory and interpersonal communication. In recognition of this trend, we think we have made several changes and additions to provide the necessary background to help the student become more sensitive to and adept at interpersonal communication skills.

Chapter 1, for instance, is a new chapter stressing the importance of communication in every aspect of United States life. Chapter 2 is new, also, and includes a communication model we devised to represent *graphically* the various stages of the communicative *process*. Chapter 3 shows in more detail the critical factor of psychological *selectivity* that takes place in speaking and listening. Chapter 4 now includes new material explaining the symbolic process in interpersonal communication. Added to Chapter 5 is new material on the role of nonverbal communication in interpersonal relations. Chapter 7 is expanded to include material on "conversation," as well as greater stress on the all-important activity of employment interviewing. Chapter 11 retains its former theoretical rigor concerning communicating in small groups, and is supplemented by specific prescriptions of how groups can go about the step-by-step operations of solving problems through the give and take of group discussion.

The increasing interest of modern-day United States with the mass media, especially the influence of television,[1] has prompted the authors of this text to include Chapter 10 on Mass Communication. It is our hope that this chapter will bring greater understanding and more profitable consumption of our media of mass communication to the students who use this text. And, finally, placed at strategic spots throughout the text, are "Activities" for the student to apply the content or theory just preceding them in the text.

But "public speaking" has hardly been banished from the first course in speech communication. The latest national survey of that course, mentioned above, concluded that, more often than not, the basic speech communication course contained numerous assignments of a public speaking nature regardless of the *name* given the course. And so, this book retains the prescriptive advice of the first edition on how to prepare and present public speeches of various kinds, updated and in a somewhat different format.

For instance, Chapter 4 still prescribes how to attain proper language and style in public addresses. Chapter 6 describes how to find good supporting materials and what kinds are most useful (for public speaking *or* interpersonal communication). Chapter 8 explains how one should analyze an audience and then organize material in order to best *inform* that audience; Chapter 9 does the same to show how best to *persuade.*

We are neither surprised nor disappointed that the latest survey indicates strong interest in public speaking assignments. For we believe that instruction in public speaking remains important for the individual in society. We feel that Brigance had a good point when he stated that public speaking should have many of the qualities of "enlarged conversation."[2]

We hope that the students using this book have ample opportunity to use the principles herein to improve their "public speaking." For we strongly feel that the educated citizen has not only the right, but the *duty* to be a responsible and vocal citizen. We feel that democracy is not served best by the well-intentioned and yet silent citizen who does not raise his or her voice. And we believe that some concerned people do not rise to speak at PTA meetings, political rallies, school bond or re-zoning ordinance hearings, and business or professional conferences because they fear that they *cannot* speak well enough. Training in public speaking should ensure that more informed men and women will be heard.

Further, we believe, with Aristotle, that the study of public speaking

1. For instance, the Autumn 1975 issue of the *Journal of Communication* contained an *eleven*-article symposium on television's effects on children and adolescents.
2. William Norwood Brigance, *Speech: Its Techniques and Disciplines in a Free Society,* 2nd ed. (New York: Appleton-Century-Crofts, 1961), pp. 26–27.

is justifiable even if the student does not subsequently practice the craft actively—since he needs to know the craft in order to defend himself against it as used by the politician, the salesman, and the advertiser.

We are concerned with *analysis* as a basis of serious communication. Central to this concept is the idea that a person, before starting to look for a way to inform or persuade, must understand the subject matter, must know how and where to find useful and enlightening materials, must perceive the issues inherent in the topic, and yet may still fail unless he or she has correctly analyzed the target audience.

Finally, we believe that the assignments in a speech course should be approached as genuine opportunities for *real* communication. We recognize that there is a kind of "laboratory-ness" to assignments in speaking and discussing in the typical speech communication course; they are not "real" speeches in the sense that a president makes a State of the Union Address, a lawyer makes an appeal to a jury, or a jury deliberates the facts in the case just presented to them. In this sense, all of college is a "laboratory" and not "real." But we hope that each student will consider each assignment in every speech course an opportunity to impart meaningful information and ideas, to learn more about oneself as a communicating human being, to educate oneself in the ways auditors respond to communications, and to receive lay and expert guidance for improvement in preparing, delivering, receiving, and evaluating spoken messages.

Appendix A suggests that there are universal criteria for the evaluation of all speeches, whether "real-life" or "laboratory" speeches. The only difference between evaluating these two kinds of speeches is that the latter must usually be *graded;* we do not hear the president, our congressman, or the guest speaker at the Lions or Rotary Club and give that speaker an A, B, C, or a 93 or an 86. We *do* evaluate the speech, although we assign grades only to classroom speeches. This simple difference in evaluation, however, should not be taken as an excuse for assuming that "laboratory" speeches are a genre apart from "real" speeches. We feel that the student who strives for excellence in communicating and in learning how to improve at communicating will benefit far more than will that student who approaches each classroom exercise as *only* an "assignment," considering a good grade as the major goal. The truly educated are those who have made the *effort* to learn. As Oscar Wilde put it in *The Critic as Artist,* "Education is an admirable thing, but it is well to remember from time to time that nothing that is worth knowing can be taught."

C. R. G.
C. M. L.
D. L. F.
R. C. H.

1□

COMMUNICATION: A VITAL PROCESS

1 ⌐⌐

The ability to communicate with others through a complicated system of abstract symbols is a most distinctively human accomplishment. Of course, "lower" animals communicate also. A honeybee, for example, uses a complicated "dance" to point out to the rest of the hive the direction and distance to a new source of food. Through various vocal and visual displays different animals can communicate aggression, submissiveness, possession of territory, common danger, and willingness to mate. While such communicating is important to the individual animal and to its species for survival, ability to communicate through such a display is severely limited. In fact, the maximum number of such displays available to the most communicative species other than humans probably does not exceed forty:[1]

> It may be that the maximum number of messages any animal needs in order to be fully adaptive in any ordinary environment, even a social one, is no more than 30 or 40. Or it may be . . . that each number represents the largest amount of signal diversity the particular animal's brain can handle efficiently in quickly changing social interactions.

Only humans among the animals are able to think and dream of the future through symbol systems. Washoe, a chimpanzee, through a highly artificial and stimulating training program, has been taught to "speak" in the symbols of sign language, but her conversations remain centered on the here-and-now. Washoe does not use sign language to communicate with herself (that is, to *think*) about "graduating" at some future time from her training program; she cannot dream of attaining promotions, honor, wealth; and she cannot know in advance that at the end of her life she must die.

Whereas apes and baboons probably live today the exact same way they did a hundred generations ago, humans have been able to accumulate knowledge and to create cultures. Today people do not live as they did ten or twenty years ago, yet they can think and talk and write about faraway times and places.

The importance of communication

It is impossible to overstress the importance of the role communication plays in our daily life. Too often communication is taken for granted. Stop and reflect occasionally about just how communication dominates everyday life.

First of all, consider how much *time* we spend communicating. A recent survey of adult communication activities by Samovar and his colleagues[2] indicates that people spend, on the average, nearly three-fourths (72.8 percent) of their waking hours engaged in some sort of communication. About three-quarters of our time not spent sleeping is spent communicating! And this is a conservative figure, since people were not asked to list time spent writing, listening to the radio, or attending movies.

Samovar and his colleagues analyzed their data to determine what activities predominated in communicating. Based on percentage of waking hours, the rank order of activities in terms of average amount of time engaged in them was:

1. conversation, 24.1 percent
2. speaking, 15.2 percent
3. listening, 13.1 percent
4. television, 12.2 percent
5. reading, 11.1 percent

The writers conclude from their study that, since approximately two-thirds (64.6 percent) of human waking hours seem to be given to activities that require speaking or listening abilities, considerable attention should be paid to developing these skills in school.

All too often educators overlook the fact that we are an oral-communicating society. You probably began talking before the age of two and have been talking naturally without much formal training for years. Your schooling was more likely to have stressed learning to communicate in a more "unnatural" way: reading and writing. Hopefully, this book and the course you are taking will restore the balance in communication training and make you more effective at both speaking and listening, for these are the two major skills of speech communication.

Let us briefly consider in what areas increased skill in speech communication will benefit you.

Making a living. Can any other skill than effective speech communication be more useful in earning a living? The occupational value of interacting with fellow workers, with supervisors, and with subordinates is an accepted fact. One of the authors was once part of a discussion group in which a number of students were trying to think of an occupation in which skill in oral communication would make no substantial difference in one's performance. The only job they could come up with was teaching sign language to the deaf and mute. However, it was pointed out by some in the group that even a sign-language teacher would have to communicate with superiors, other teachers, building custodians, and persons from whom supplies need to be ordered. Also, nonverbal communication ability (gestures and expressions) would be important even to one who never spoke to students in words. And such nonverbal communication as gestures, facial expressions, or posture is part of speech communication, as will be shown in later chapters. Furthermore, included in communication skills are the processes of attention, perception, retention, and symbolization; and increased skill in these elements of communication would be useful in any kind of job, whether you talked and listened much or not.

Socializing. Human beings are socially more diversified than other animals. As social animals, humans must learn to communicate within groups. Any one person may be a member of a family, a profession, several social clubs, a bridge club, an office clique, a high school graduating class, a fraternity, and an old Army squad. In addition to group memberships each person has individual social relations with individuals. A woman may be a mother to her child, a friend and lover to her husband, a best friend to one or two other women, a supervisor of several workers, an old friend to key sorority sisters, and a chum to some youngsters who live nearby. The major ingredient in developing and maintaining the myriad social relationships the modern American must manage is probably that of communication—mostly *speech* communication—for it is only through personal contact with others that we become social beings. An "inventory of scientific findings of human behavior" concluded after a survey of relevant scientific research: "Normal adult human behavior develops only through the stimulation of other people."[3] That stimulation means mostly face-to-face speech communication.

Exercising citizenship. Harry Emerson Fosdick once wrote that, "Democracy is based upon the conviction that there are extraordinary possibilities in ordinary people." Our society benefits from a number of uncommon exercises of personal citizenship, for instance, volunteer teachers in public schools and in Sunday schools and synagogues; volunteer workers in hospitals and social organizations such as the USO, the Red Cross, United Fund, and in various community groups; and volunteers who make it possible for the Girl Scouts and Boy Scouts, Boys' Clubs, and other youth organizations to make their contributions to our communities. In these volunteer jobs the ability to communicate well is highly important. Each citizen ought to contribute some time and energy to the improvement of the world. Hopefully this book and this course will contribute to your effectiveness in doing so.

Another duty of the good citizen in a democracy is to do what is necessary to improve the political process. You may not decide to run for office, but you can still play a part in the political life of your community as an officer or a committee member of your neighborhood association, for instance. At the very least, you should take upon yourself to become a citizen well informed on candidates and on the issues of political life, and to speak out for what you believe best for your community, your nation, and the world. Improving your communication skill should make you more politically involved.

Achieving self-actualization. "Self-actualization" has been defined as "the processes of developing one's capacities and talents, of understanding and accepting oneself, of harmonizing or integrating one's motives; or the state resulting from these processes."[4] Achieving self-actualization is considered the "highest" need of humans by psychologist Abraham Maslow.[5] Of course, one hardly worries about self-actualization or esteem unless physiological needs have been met. For instance, a person who is starving or in grave physical danger assigns little importance to self-actualizing or to personal esteem from others. But once basic biological needs are satisfied, each of us at least occasionally asks such questions as: Who am I? What am I? What do I want out of life? What should I be doing to attain my goals? What *are* my goals? Young people especially are apt to say they are "trying to find themselves." This means merely that they are trying to figure themselves out, to develop concepts of *self.*

To "figure one's self out," is not a simple task. First, you must do your best to determine what *other* people think of you. How other people respond to you (or, how you *perceive* others' responses to you) has a great deal to do with what you think of yourself. How you perceive yourself and the objective world about you also plays a large part in developing your self-concept. As we shall see in this book, how we perceive and think are vital aspects of communication with the self and will help determine our self-concepts.

Eisenson, Auer, and Irwin in their popular text insist that "speech and personality parallel one another and that personality is directly expressed in speech." They add, "This generalization holds both for well adjusted individuals and for those whose problems of adjustment direct them to psychotherapists for help."[6]

In further explanation of their thesis of the link between speech behavior and personality, Eisenson and his colleagues go on to contrast the speech behavior of the normal, or well-adjusting, personality to that of the not-so-well-adjusting personality. For instance, the well-adjusting individual chooses words carefully, mindful at all times of their impact on listeners. This person selects words, or re-selects them if necessary, for what he or she anticipates the listeners will understand. The good speaker, as well as the well-adjusted person, is constantly "listener-centered."

Likewise, according to these authors, a person's voice and gestures are not manipulated to please oneself, but to communicate with the listener. "The voice of the well-adjusting person *reveals* rather than betrays his intentions about what he is saying." And "The well-adjusting person shows no concern about his gestures unless he finds that they are giving the listener-observer cause for concern."

In other words, the well-adjusting person is open, communicative, listener-centered, self-revealing. In order to be this kind of person one must both have positive self-concepts and be a skilled communicator. We hope this book will improve your self-concepts (or your perceptions of them), and make you a better thinker, speaker, and listener.

Communication: Intentional and unintentional

Books on communication often make distinctions between communication that is intentional and that which is unintentional, usually pointing out that the emphasis will be on *intentional* communication. This book, too, is primarily concerned with communication which is intentional, for it is the care and attention that we pay to our deliberate communicative acts with friends, relatives, acquaintances, customers, and others that can most improve our communicative effectiveness. However, this book also stresses the importance of *un*intended communicative acts, for they can play a large role in your dealings with people.

In the first place, in human society it is almost impossible *not* to communicate. You may *wish* not to communicate, but you cannot help yourself. Were you ever asked a question by a teacher for which you had no acceptable answer? Your silence, perhaps your squirming posture and unwilliness to make eye contact with your questioner would communicate something! Consider an exercise included in a speech projects textbook: you are sitting in the back of a classroom and your teacher asks you to stand, walk to the front of the classroom, look at your "audience" briefly, then return to your seat. Included in the instructions is this admonition: "Do not communicate anything to your audience." Do you think you could fulfill this task without communicating anything to your audience? Or consider a cigarette smoker who puffs away in a closed room without asking permission of others present. Isn't something communicated to the others in the room, namely, "I am completely indifferent as to whether I offend your breathing apparatus"?

Suppose you are giving a speech in class, and you intend to communicate your concern over the destruction of our natural environment, but you are "shaking like a leaf" from stage fright (or "communication apprehension"). What you are unintentionally communicating to your audience is your own discomfort. This unintentional communication is important, since it will interfere with what you *intend* to communicate.

Stage fright or communication apprehension is not the only nonverbal communication that may interfere with or contradict your verbal message. Facial expression, gestures, bodily posture, and the like may say one thing while your words say another. At least one psychiatrist even videotapes patients while they discuss their psychological material and then plays back these sessions to them. He reports that frequently the patient recognizes the "body talk" that was contradicting what he was saying and "confesses" that he was being less than candid with the psychiatrist.[7]

It is also possible that your words may unintentionally stir up in your listeners meanings that are contrary to what you intended. This can be especially true if you use abstract or figurative language. One unfortunate incident of this involved Earl Butz, U. S. Secretary of Agriculture, in 1974. During a discussion with reporters over the general area of world population, world food resources, and birth control, "Butz repeated an old joke he had heard during the recent food conference in Rome. The story had to do with the Italian mother who was told that when she used birth control she was disobeying the Pope: 'He's-a no playa da game. He's-a no make'a da rules.' "[8] Secretary Butz apparently intended merely to add some humor to an otherwise serious discussion. But when the remarks got into the newspapers, his jest communicated to many Italians and other Catholics disrespect for their ethnic background and for their religion. A furor erupted that included demands for Secretary Butz's resignation.

We have tried to stress the uniqueness of the human ability to communicate using oral and visual symbols and the importance of this ability for earning a living, socializing with our fellows, exercising our roles as citizens, and achieving satisfactory self-actualization through skillful use of speech communication. Finally, we indicated that we all communicate intentionally and unintentionally, and we hope this book helps you improve your intentional communication and to avoid communication of unintended messages.

Activity

These two activities should give you behavioral proof that speech communication is a highly important human activity.

1. Keep a diary of your communication activities for three days in a row. Try to record how many minutes and hours you spend in each of the communication activity classifications used by Samovar et al. in this chapter. After three days, add up your times, convert them into percentages, and check the percentages with those the researchers found.

2. During initiation into the Order of the Arrow (an honor camper organization related to the Boy Scouts of America) candidates must work one complete day without talking—without saying *one word.* Try to go through an entire day without talking. Write down instances where the urge to talk was almost overwhelming. Keep a record of difficulties you encountered because you decided not to talk. Make a record of others' reactions that you noticed in particular.

QUESTIONS FOR THOUGHT
AND DISCUSSION
CHAPTER 1

1. What communicative advantages do humans have over other animals?
2. Why do people invest so much of their time communicating?
3. What role does communication play in making a living?

4. What social role does communication serve among human beings?
5. Why is communication particularly important for a democratic society?
6. How do individuals use communication to help determine their own self-identity?
7. To what degree is communication on your campus "intentional?"

EXERCISES · ASSIGNMENTS | *CHAPTER 1*

1. Keep a diary of the amount of time you spend during one entire day in various types of communication: speaking, listening, writing, and so on.
2. Observe persons communicating in some situation on campus and report on the extent to which their communications were intentional and unintentional. How could you tell?
3. Evaluate communication in various situations (dorm, apartment, classroom, student union, office) and judge to what degree there exists a free atmosphere for candid talk.
4. Interview a local business person and ask what role communication plays in his or her work?

ENDNOTES | *Chapter 1*

1. Edward O. Wilson, "Animal Communication," in *Communication* (San Francisco: W. H. Freeman, 1972), p. 32. Quoted by permission of *The Scientific American* and the publisher.
2. Larry A. Samovar, Robert D. Brooks, and Richard E. Porter, "A Survey of Adult Communication Activities," in *A Reader in Speech Communication,* edited by James W. Gibson (New York: McGraw-Hill, 1971), pp. 129–134.
3. Bernard Berelson and Gary A. Steiner, *Human Behavior: An Inventory of Scientific Findings* (New York: Harcourt, Brace and World, 1964), p. 65.
4. Horace B. English and Ava C. English, *A Comprehensive Dictionary of Psychological and Psychoanalytical Terms* (New York: Longmans, Green, 1958), p. 485.
5. Abraham H. Maslow, *Motivation and Personality* (New York: Harper and Row, 1954).
6. Jon Eisenson, J. Jeffery Auer, and John V. Irwin, *The Psychology of Communication* (New York: Appleton-Century-Crofts, 1963), p. 340.
7. "Video Therapy," *Time,* February 26, 1973: 58.
8. James Kilpatrick, "Kicking Earl Butz Around," *Athens (Ga.) Daily News,* December 7, 1974, p. 6.

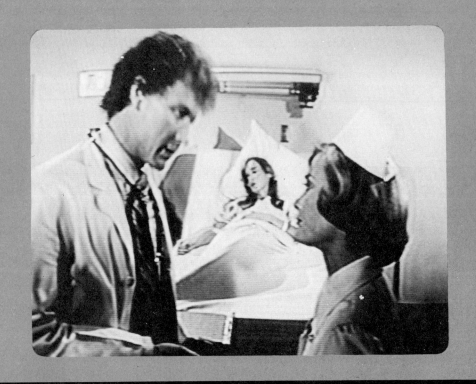

2

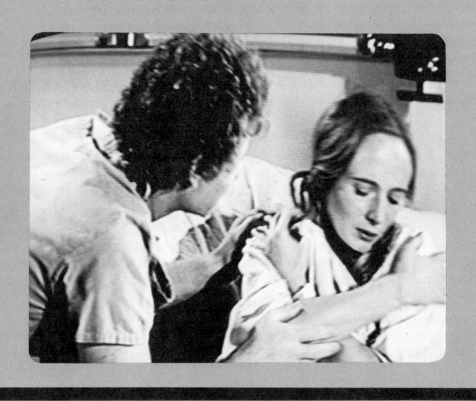

COMMUNICATION: DYNAMIC PROCESS

Defining just what "communication" is has occupied the time and effort of many scholars. Although no two definitions we know agree word for word, definers of "communication" tend to concur that it is a *process*. For instance:

> Communication: The transmission of information, ideas, emotions, skills, etc., by the use of symbols—words, pictures, figures, graphs, etc. It is the *act* or *process* of transmission that is usually called communication.*
>
> Communication consists in the communicator's selecting and arranging symbols that have a certain meaning to him and his audience's sensing those symbols and inferring their intended meaning.†
>
> Speech communication is a dynamic process, in which the speaker's encoding and the listener's decoding of a message is affected by his attitudes, skills, knowledge, and interest. The process requires the use of a code so that the speaker can represent his thoughts and feelings in words. It takes place within an environment—an immediate environment (occasion) and a broad social context.§

* Bernard Berelson and Gary A. Steiner, *Human Behavior: An Inventory of Scientific Findings* (New York: Harcourt Brace and World, Inc., 1964), p. 527.
† Wayne C. Minnick, *The Art of Persuasion* (Boston: Houghton Mifflin Company, 1957), p. 70.
§ Ronald F. Reid, "The Process of Speech Communication," in *Introduction to the Field of Speech,* edited by Ronald F. Reid (Chicago: Scott, Foresman & Company, 1965), p. 12.

Communication: Dynamic process

Defining communication as a *process* (as opposed to a *thing*) implies that it is an ongoing, changing, non-static, and, thus, highly complicated activity. And a complicated activity is difficult to define in just a few words. The definitions above are very much akin to what scientists call a *state description,* one that describes an object at any one time. For instance, a state description of a house would indicate that it is split-level, with three bedrooms, a den, two bathrooms, family room, dining room, living room, and kitchen.

A state description of a house, however, does not tell how it works as a process. To tell how the house works, one would need to devise a *process description* detailing how the electrical currents flow, how the water runs, how the air conditioning and heating systems operate by thermostatic control, how the water heater and doorbells work, and so on.

In order to express how communication works, various scholars have devised process descriptions, generally called *models,* of the communication act. A model of the communication process is usually a visual or a verbal diagram separating the communication act into its specific parts and indicating the "flow" of sense data through the various parts of the act. We have devised a model to explain the intrapersonal communication act (Figure 2–1) and then have expanded the model by adding another communicator (Figure 2–2).

Intrapersonal communication

Figure 2–1 represents stages in the process of "communicating with oneself," or *thinking.* Let us consider each stage individually so as better to understand and appreciate the complexity of this seemingly simple act. Begin to the left in Figure 2–1 and advance from left to right.

First, an *event* must occur somewhere. This event can be in the world around us, such as a passing car, a bolt of lightning, a bird chirping in a tree; or it can come from within your own body, such as heartburn, a headache, a memory.

In order for this event to trigger the process of self-communication, one must have *exposure* to it, and we know that people practice *selective exposure* in regard to many events: people intentionally and unintentionally expose themselves to some events and not to other events. For instance, you may deliberately and often place yourself in certain locations where you are likely to meet attractive members of the opposite sex, and you may deliberately avoid exposing yourself to the kind of events you fear may take place in some sections of our cities after dark. You may unintentionally avoid the

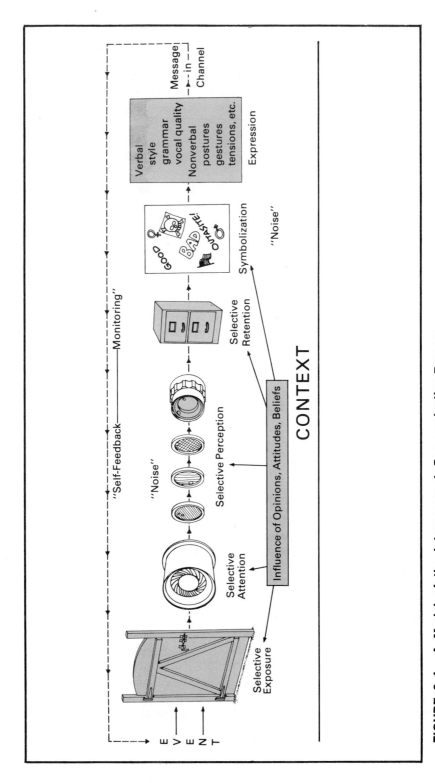

FIGURE 2–1. A Model of the Intrapersonal Communication Process

experience of meeting Europeans, Southerners, or New Englanders in their native surroundings because you have neither the time nor the money to travel to these places. And you probably become exposed unwillingly to a large number of commercial messages through the mass media and outdoor advertising.

Selective exposure, which we choose to represent in our model as a gate that can shut out facts or open to allow them in, will be discussed in Chapter 3.

Once you have exposure to an event, you must pay *attention* to it in order for it to "register." How often have you missed a point in a lecture, a feature of the scenery during an automobile trip, or a news item on TV because you were not paying attention? Actually, when we say someone was not paying attention, what we mean is that one's attention was being paid to something else. You might miss a point in a lecture because you were daydreaming; you might miss a feature of roadside scenery because you were searching the glove compartment for a road map; you might miss a broadcast news item because you were reading the newspaper. Attention is as selective as exposure is. Figure 2–1 represents the nature of *selective attention* as the shutter in a camera; in order to attend, the shutter must be *open* and *aimed* in the proper direction. Selective attention is covered in more detail in Chapter 3.

Perception is the "more complex process by which people select, organize, and interpret sensory stimulation into a meaningful and coherent picture of the world."[1] Perception is a highly personal process; it is what an event *means to the perceiver.* As Berelson and Steiner point out, "Which stimuli get selected depends upon three major factors: the nature of the stimuli involved; previous experience or learning as it affects the observer's expectations (what he is prepared or 'set' to see); and the motives in play at the time."[2] For instance, in an ordinary street scene in a downtown city a hungry person is likely to perceive only the restaurant sign, a young man only the attractive young lady waiting for a bus, someone needing to cash a check only the First National Bank sign ahead, a teenage boy only the sleek sports car at the curb. Thus, it can be seen that perception is also a highly selective process. Beauty (or ugliness) *is* in the eye of the beholder.

In our model we continue the camera analogy by representing *selective perception* as a lens accompanied by a series of photographic filters that screen out what is of little importance to the perceiver. The lens focuses on the aspects of the event that are vital to the perceiver. Chapter 3 takes up selective perception at greater length.

The next step in our model is *selective retention.* What we

remember affects how we choose to expose ourselves to, attend to,
and perceive the world. How and what we remember at any particular time depend upon our immediate perception and will largely
determine how we *symbolize* that perception to ourselves.

It is a well-known psychological fact that we tend to remember
some events and to forget others; generally, we tend to remember
the pleasant and forget the unpleasant (with some obvious exceptions). This process of selective retention, covered more thoroughly
in Chapter 3, is represented in Figure 2–1 as a filing cabinet filled
with bits and pieces of experiences we have filed away for future
reference—some of which we can find easily and some of which we
can find only with difficulty!

After you have perceived an event or experience—that is, when
you have decided what the event meant to you—you usually put this
meaning into symbols: words, numbers, pictures, emblems, or other
representations. In our model we call this *symbolization.*

There is some controversy over how the manipulating of symbols within the nervous system relates to the act of thinking, but
practically all scholars agree that the symbolization process is very
important to thinking. Chimpanzees can learn to use a long straw
to fetch tasty morsels from a termite mound, but only humans can
devise concepts, ideas, and organizations through the ability to use
symbols.

So, if you can conceive of thinking as selecting, arranging, and
manipulating symbols (mostly *words*) within the nervous system, you

will be able to see that thinking is the process of "talking to one-self." How you think—that is, what messages you send to yourself after filtering experiences through your perceptual apparatus—is a key component of your communicative behavior. We think that the process of symbolization, mostly the use of word symbols, is very important; thus we devote much of Chapter 4 to this concept.

The final step in our model of the intrapersonal communication act is *expression,* which results in the production of a message that goes out through some "channel." In the case of someone thinking silently, the message would proceed through the channel of electro-chemical apparatus we call the nervous system. This channel is rep-resented by the broken line going from "message in channel" back to "selective exposure." Here the message, or thought, becomes another event to be allowed into consciousness or not (selective exposure), to be attended to or not (selective attention), and so forth.

In addition to the chain of activity beginning with "event" and ending with "message in channel," three other concepts of the model must be explained: the influence of opinions, attitudes, and beliefs; the concept of "noise;" and the concept that communication always occurs within a context.

Psychologists do not easily agree on the distinctions to be made in defining *opinions, attitudes,* and *beliefs.* Some choose to make very fine distinctions; others, like Berelson and Steiner, lump the three together and simply refer to all opinions, attitudes, and beliefs as "OABs."[3] But whether one chooses to make fine distinctions or to generalize, there is no disagreement among communication scholars as to whether OABs affect how an individual will selectively expose himself to, attend to, perceive, and retain sense data: the effect of OABs is undeniable. In Chapter 3 we take up more thor-oughly the effect of opinions, attitudes, and beliefs on the selectivity of exposure, attention, perception, and retention.

Noise is defined as anything that interferes with or distorts the communicative process. Noise can be "actual" noise, such as static on a radio or a roaring motorcycle going past the classroom window. It can also be internal, such as inattention, anger, fear, distorted information, or a hearing defect of the listener.

Context, the foundation of the model in Figure 2–1, simply means that communication does not occur in a vacuum. Different communications take place in different and constantly changing cul-tural, social, economic, educational, and political milieus. Hera-clitus said, "You cannot step into the same river twice"; neither the river nor the wader will ever be the same again. From Chapter 7 through Chapter 11 we will see that the changing context of different types of communication will be significant in understanding different kinds of communication.

Interpersonal communication

Now that we have examined the process of *intra*personal (within the self) communication, let us consider the process of communication between two or more people, or *inter*personal communication. Figure 2–2 add a second person to the concepts and activities in Figure 2–1. This second person, represented in the bottom half of Figure 2–2, we call the listener, and the top half of Figure 2–2 we call the speaker.

The process for the speaker in Figure 2–2 is the same as in Figure 2–1, except that, in addition to creating a message that is transmitted back through the nervous system, the speaker now produces a message for a listener. This message can be oral (verbal) and can be transmitted "live" or electronically by sound waves to the listener. It can also be a visible message through facial signals and gestures carried by light waves to the listener. Much speaking is both oral *and* visible. As the speaker sends out this message, he or she also "listens in" on the message—the speaker *monitors* what is said to make sure it is what he or she intended to say.

This message now becomes the *event* for the listener. If the listener experiences *exposure* to the message, voluntarily or involuntarily, and selectively pays *attention* to it, the message has a chance of affecting him. The message will be processed through the listener's selective *perception/retention* apparatus; if the listener is then able to *symbolize* the same (or nearly the same) meanings for the message as symbolized by the speaker, communication has taken place. The listener responds to the speaker with a message the listener thinks appropriate. This response may take the form of an oral or a visible reply or both, or it may simply be a smile and nod of the head. This is *interpersonal feedback* to the speaker.

Inherent in any model of the communication process are the major *variables* of communication. A *variable* is simply a property or set of properties that will be likely to change from situation to situation. For example, the major variables of weather are air temperature, humidity, cloudiness, and wind intensity and direction. In this book we are concerned with four major communication variables: *speaker, audience, message,* and the *context* in which communication takes place.

Speakers vary along such dimensions as knowledge, attractiveness, age, credibility, and so on. *Audiences* vary on such dimensions as age, intelligence, education, and attitudes toward the

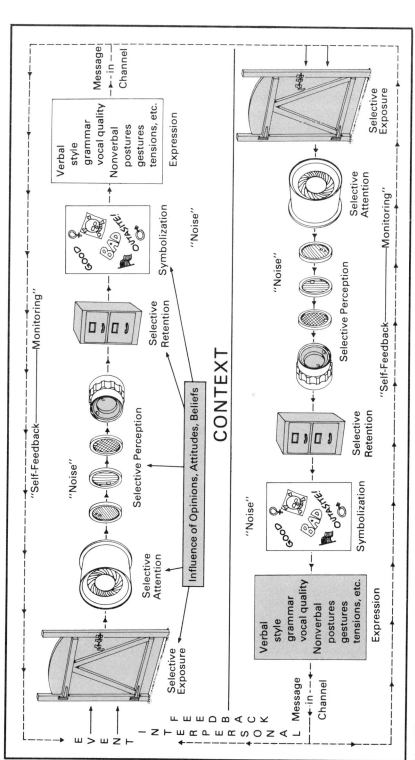

FIGURE 2-2. A Model of the Interpersonal Communication Process

speaker and toward the topic. *Messages* vary in such things as length, purpose, style of language, and in what channel they are transmitted. And communication *contexts* vary in such ways as formality, purpose or occasion, and physical arrangement of the location. How these major variables differ along various dimensions for different kinds of communication situations will be taken up later in this book.

The goal: Improved communicating

This book's purpose is to improve the communicative competence of its readers. Communication competence can be improved in two general ways: sensitizing the student to be a "better-tuned" communicator and providing the student with a larger repertoire of communication techniques.

Let us consider a person for a moment as a ham radio station, capable of sending and receiving messages. To increase the communicative ability of our station we could refine what capabilities it already has. For instance, we could install on our receiver a larger capacitor, capable of finer tuning, so that it could be tuned more precisely into an incoming signal. We could increase the power of the transmitter, thus improving the broadcasting range. By the same token, each person can improve as a communicator by increasing one's sensitivity to and awareness of the complexity of the communicative process, by becoming a better listener, by becoming more audience-centered, and by becoming more "open" as a speaker.

Activity

Think of the concepts, explained in this section, of both adding to your communicative repertoire and of more finely "tuning" your existing communication skills. The analogy used was a short-wave radio station. Try making your own analogies by comparing the two communication improvements to other concepts, such as photography, a printing press, magazine production, letter-writing; stage or film acting, cooking, wine production, and so on.

We could add to the communicative *repertoire* of our radio station. For instance, we could install new receivers that could receive

messages from different, formerly unavailable frequencies. We could replace our manual Morse code key with a high-speed key to accelerate the Morse code messages we send. We could add additional circuitry so that we could broadcast by voice as well as Morse.

The communicative competence of each individual can be increased by learning new techniques and skills, such as how to conduct interviews, present public speeches to inform and persuade, lead a problem-solving group discussion, and present oral reports. Although there is some overlapping among various chapters, those *primarily* aimed at more finely "tuning" people to become better communicators are Chapters 1 through 6 and 10; while Chapters 7, 8, 9, and 11 are primarily aimed at expanding people's communicative repertoires.

QUESTIONS FOR THOUGHT
AND DISCUSSION
CHAPTER 2

1. What is communication?
2. Of what significance is it to consider communication as a process?
3. What is intrapersonal communication?

4. Cite an example of selective exposure taking place at a local football or basketball game. What effects does this process have on the fans?

5. Assume for a moment you are in a store to purchase some records. How would the principle of selective exposure work on *you* while you are shopping? Be specific.

6. What influence would Young Democrats' perception have on their reactions to a speech by Senator Barry Goldwater?

7. What is interpersonal communication?

EXERCISES · ASSIGNMENTS | CHAPTER 2

1. Using an actual personal experience, sketch your own model of how communication works. Evaluate why communication in this instance was successful or unsuccessful.

2. Outline what kind of intrapersonal communication takes place when you go alone to the library to prepare an essay or a persuasive speech.

3. Observe a sermon, sales pitch, or political speech and describe how the principle of selective exposure influences what the speaker says and does and what members of the audience say and do.

4. Explain how the process of perception affects communication between young and old, between black and white, between city dweller and farmer.

ENDNOTES | Chapter 2

1. Bernard Berelson and Gary A. Steiner, *Human Behavior: An Inventory of Scientific Findings* (New York: Harcourt, Brace and World, 1964), p. 88.

2. *Ibid.*

3. *Ibid.,* pp. 557ff.

PSYCHOLOGICAL
SELECTIVITY
IN
SPEAKING
AND
LISTENING

Of paramount importance to individual liberty are the so-called Four Freedoms. The battle cries of various groups have appealed to the idealization of freedom: Freedom now! Free speech! Freedom of choice!

As has already been indicated, individuals exercise a great deal of personal freedom in their communication behavior. Much of it is conscious, but much of it is unconscious, too. In communication, the exercise of freedom has taken on the label of "psychological selectivity." This chapter expands on the concepts introduced in our models of the communicative process in Chapter 2: selective exposure, selective attention, selective perception, and selective retention. First, a general explanation and discussion of each concept is presented, then a brief application of these concepts to the role of the speaker is made, and last, listening is discussed, including how this important function may be affected by selectivity, for we probably practice selectivity more in listening than in speaking.

Selective exposure

You may have heard the old story about the heavy smoker who read so many scary newspaper and magazine articles linking cigarettes to lung cancer that he gave up reading! This encapsulates what psychologists have been gathering evidence for some time to prove: people tend to expose themselves to information and experiences that please them and tend to avoid information and experiences that make them uncomfortable.

Field tests have shown that it is primarily Democrats, not Republicans, who attend Democratic political rallies, and vice versa. Baptists, not Catholics, attend Baptist churches and meetings. People who have bought Chevrolets tend to read more Chevrolet ads than Ford or Chrysler ads. Those who read the *New Republic* are primarily political liberals, whereas readers of the *National Review* are predominantly conservative.

Years ago, Schramm suggested a rule of thumb to explain why people exposed themselves to different messages and situations and did not expose themselves to others. He called it the "fraction of selection":[1]

$$\frac{\text{expectation of reward.}}{\text{effort required}}$$

Such a fraction could easily explain such diverse observations as (1) a family sitting docilely before the television set while insulting and blaring commercials revile their senses and (2) a group of naturalists sweating and straining their way to the summit of Mount LeConte in the Great Smokies. In the first case, the subjects have little expectation of reward, but the effort required to avoid exposure is greater. The second requires great personal effort, but the rewards of self-mastery plus the gorgeous view are great enough to yield a large quotient when divided by the effort involved.

A review of studies of selective exposure conducted before 1965 or so, however, revealed that the "fraction of selection" was far from perfect. The reviewers concluded that, while field studies *do* point to a tendency for people to expose themselves to agreeable information and to avoid disagreeable information, there were interesting contradictions to the generalization.[2] Other reasons for exposure were finding information useful despite its discomfort and exposure due to "friendships, social roles and customs," and the like.

A study done later and with more methodological sophistication has found stronger support for the general self-exposure hypothesis.[3] This researcher, Wheeless, even investigated what factors in the situation affected whether people would accept or reject exposure to information. He found that the following factors cause people to expose themselves to messages: intensity of audience attitudes toward the content of the message; audience's degree of involvement with the content; audience's favorable perception of the message source's *competence, sociability, composure,* and *char-*

acter; and audience perception of the source's "homophily," or how much each audience member perceived the message source as being like himself. Of course, negative attitude intensity, involvement, and source perception led to rejection of exposure.

Even if Schramm's fraction cannot account for all self-exposure phenomena, each of us can be convinced by everyday observations that the general hypothesis is mostly true. Most people in the United States today prefer to watch "All in the Family" on television rather than read John Stuart Mill's *Essay on Liberty;* few of us prefer a trip to the dentist over one to Walt Disney World; and who amongst us would not rather lie on a Florida beach than work cutting sugar cane in Louisiana?

Even in communicating with oneself, a person practices selective exposure. At least this is the theory held strongly in such fields as Freudian psychoanalysis. This process is called *repression.* The basic idea is that through experience each individual has some internal psychological material he or she does not want to think about. So the individual merely excludes such material from consciousness. As English and English define it, *repression* is "the exclusion of specific psychological activities or contents from conscious awareness by a process of which the individual is not directly aware. Exclusion includes preventing entry into, forcing out of, or continuously preventing return to, consciousness."[4] This book does not argue for the viability of psychoanalytic theory, but some striking proofs of repression are evident in psychoanalytic literature.

A much milder and less unconscious form of repression, simple *selective retention,* is discussed later in this chapter.

Activity

Find five classmates who can remember the last magazine article or book he or she read (aside from assigned material). Ask each of these five what factors led to this choice of reading material. Do you think the reading material fits what you know of each classmate?

Selective attention

A person's interests, desires, knowledge and other predispositions greatly influence what stimuli that person will attend to. A mother and father with a sick child in the next bedroom may sleep through a thunderstorm but awake at a slight moan from their ailing off-spring. An audience may remain completely unaware of the miscue by an actor in a play, whereas that actor's rival, whom he had beaten out for the part, would find the error a glaring one. Most students remain unconscious of the fourteen steps to the front door of the classroom buildings, but the student on crutches for the freshly sprained ankle notices them acutely.

Other aspects of individuals affect their attending, primarily organic condition and social suggestion.[5]

Organic condition affects the selectivity of our attending. One who is fatigued is likely to pay little attention to any stimulus other than one that promises rest. A hungry person pays special attention to stimuli related to food. One who is restless will more quickly notice some avenue for physical activity.

Social suggestion plays a part in what we attend to. While walking along the sidewalk, have you ever noticed two or three people standing together and looking up? Did you look up to see what they were looking at? Did you ever stop where a crowd was assembled to see what was going on? Have you ever decided to read a book because it is a national bestseller, or go to a movie because you saw newspaper pictures of long lines outside the theaters showing it? If you have done any of these or similar things, you have directed your attention as a result of social suggestion.

When discussing attention, it is fashionable to discuss the so-called *factors of interest* with which a person can attract and maintain attention. Although these factors can be arranged in almost any set of classifications, we think that of Eisenson and his colleagues is as useful and common as any other. They classify the factors of interest as animation, vitalness, familiarity, novelty, conflict, suspense, concreteness, and humor.

Animation attracts and holds attention because movement is involved. Anyone who has been glued to the television by "Sesame Street" understands how it can be such a powerful tool for teaching small children, who have such short attention spans. The television commercial, which must capture your attention before you run for the refrigerator or the bathroom, often relies on dancing slices of bread, gyrating bottles of beer, zooming helicopters, and other fast-paced action leadoffs.

Vitalness refers to the vital interests of a person. A headline in the campus newspaper announcing a hike in tuition "jumps out" at a student. A car owner with worn tires more quickly notices ads for tire sales and more easily overhears casual remarks about tire discounts. A sick person who feels that medical care is not helping may pay more attention to ads for chiropractors, direct-mail nostrums, or faith healers. People worried over inflation and high prices often pay attention to politicians promising stable prices and full employment. Each person has strong concerns for Number One.

Familiarity reassures us. We easily spot a familiar face while visiting another city, state park, or vacation resort. When people tell us something we already know and believe, our egos are reinforced by shared knowledge and opinion. We even tend to attend to and accept that which is *similar to* what is familiar. For instance, on meeting someone and discovering that he or she lived in your home town, your interest in and attention to that person immediately rises.

Novelty, while seeming to conflict with familiarity as an attention device, nevertheless has powerful attention value. One of the most powerful (and over-used) words in advertising is *new!* If something becomes too familiar, boredom sets in, whether it is a brand name, an advertising campaign, or a geographical setting. Advertisers, who vie most competitively for the attention of the consuming public, constantly use novel techniques. Several years ago a well known antacid was not selling, so a novel and humorous ad campaign was tried (remember "I can't believe I ate the *whole* thing"?). Sales soared then leveled off, and finally began declining; then a new campaign seriously advocating the beneficial medical help the product could offer was launched. Sometimes a *mixture* of novelty and familiarity is a successful attention-grabber, such as a familiar concept worded in a new way. For instance, the old idea of loyal self-sacrifice has long been held to be a virtue, but John F. Kennedy made the old concept memorable: "Ask not what your country can do for you; rather, ask what you can do for your country."

Conflict appeals to each individual's competitive streak. We all compete for good grades, better jobs and salaries, attractive mates, status, wealth, and the like. We watch the close football game with bated breath and pounding heart but yawn during the 54–0 massacre. Literature and drama could not exist without conflict—conflict can be between two people, between people and nature, between a person and society, or within a single individual (as in *Hamlet*).

Suspense is vitally related to conflict. In Gestalt psychology this concept is called the "law of closure." Simply stated, once our attention is riveted on a conflict or some incompleted act or statement, we want to see "how it comes out." We are disappointed in movies or books that end without definite resolution of the conflict. Once involved in a jigsaw puzzle, we want to finish it; we feel a sense of frustration if we cannot and become downright angry if parts are found to be missing.

Concreteness, or what we might call definiteness of form, is usually more attention-holding than is abstractness, or *in*definiteness of form. A sharply focused closeup by the late photographer Margaret Bourke-White of the lined face of a Depression-era farm woman might stop a magazine browser from idly turning the page; that same browser might flip right past an abstract modern painting pictured in the same magazine (although an art connoisseur might attend more to the latter or equally to both). To refer to the late John Dilinger as a bank robber, murderer, and jail escapee will probably evoke a more concrete image than referring to him by saying, "Within the time-frame of his youth, it was his proclivity toward derring-do that led to further acts of doubtful legitimacy."

Humor can be an effective device to create and sustain attention. Civil rights activist Dick Gregory attracts young audiences through his reputation as a comedian. He holds attention by blending wit with straightforward attacks on racism and bigotry. Anyone who watches television has noticed that advertisers hold your attention through the use of humor as almost the sole means of attention-grabbing. Humor can apparently be used to sell just about anything except funerals. When Forest Lawn of Los Angeles tried to sell prepaid funerals through a humorous ad campaign, they infuriated customers who had already bought the service.[6] That humor can offend must be kept in mind. Also, if comedy is to be used successfully in advertising or any other communication, aptness, timeliness, and relevance must be considered. It seems that advertisers, in particular, recognize that humor in ads must be *quality* humor. Kalman Phillips has said so in his article, "When a Funny Commercial Is Good, It's Great!"[7] When *Television Age* recommended the use of humor in advertising, they warned in their title, "It Better Really Be Funny."[8]

A familiar tactic of public speakers is to use wit as an attention device. A growing body of experimental research indicates that the speech that already uses an optimal amount of attention-holding material other than humor will probably not enhance its interest-level by including humor. However, research also shows that if the speech is so lacking in attention devices as to be considered dull, humor *will* add to its interest value.[9]

Selective perception

The act of perceiving can be thought of as including both *becoming exposed* to a stimulus and *attending* to it. For this reason, much of what we have already said about selective exposure and selective attention is also true of selective perception. The three concepts have been treated separately here because exposure and attention are "simple" psychological acts, and perception is generally conceded to be more complex and to involve more psychological material. Of course, chronologically, one must become exposed to a stimulus before attention can be paid it, and "only after we attend can we perceive . . . [then] when we attend and perceive we respond and we manifest this response by some overt or covert muscular movement or glandular activity."[10]

Perhaps the complexity of the act of perception can be better appreciated by the fact that the *Comprehensive Dictionary of Psychological and Psychoanalytical Terms* devotes a whole page to definitions of perception and related terms.[11]

Perception is not only more complicated than either exposure or attention, it also involves both as prerequisites. For perception is usually thought of as an integrative psychological event involving (1) exposure to a stimulus, (2) sufficient attention to the stimulus to allow it to register on one's sense receptors, and (3) sufficient neural activity to relay electrochemical messages to the central nervous system, where (4) the stimulus is evaluated and understood in relation to one's frame of reference.

Frame of reference is used here to refer to what was once called one's "apperceptive mass," which is the sum total of all of a person's experiences, knowledge, attitudes, state of physical and emotional health, tendencies to action or inaction, and so forth that are relevant to the interpretation and response to a particular stimulus. Since the frame of reference of each individual differs from that of every other individual, it is easy to understand how any given event or statement could be perceived differently by different people. There is the old story of the group of people on a street corner who witnessed an automobile accident. The lawyer on the corner perceived it as a question of who was to blame and thus liable to be sued. The physician perceived it as possible injury to persons involved. The auto body repairer perceived it in terms of how many new parts and how much reshaping should be required to refurbish the automobiles. The woman on the corner perceived immediately the friction that would develop between the woman driver and her husband later that day. Each person saw the same event, but each perceived it differently.

A "Family Circus" cartoon exploited selective perception as a comic event. Billy asks his father a question indicating that he thinks his dad felt that being in the war was *fun.* The father responds that war is no fun, and asks Billy why he thought so. In the father's thought-balloon is a picture of himself, cold and miserable in a foxhole in the rain. Billy's thought-balloons are of opening his new "war game" for Christmas, playing soldier with his brother, shooting his toy cannon, watching a situation comedy set in an army camp, and the like.

Not too many years ago an entire series of cartoons, titled "It's Only Your Imagination," was based on selective perception. In one cartoon a man with a large bag of groceries is frantically trying to unlock his front door to get in to answer a ringing phone; his eyes are fixed at the door key in his hand. The key is pictured as being at least a foot long and weighing several pounds, far too large to fit the lock. Another shows a young man sitting on a crowded bus; he is sweating guiltily as he sits, the aisle crowded with standees—whom he perceives as cripples, blind war heroes, feeble old women and so on. A two-part cartoon in the same series first shows a man served "the pie you like." The triangle of dessert is so small that it is dwarfed by the plate. The second picture shows the same man served "the pie you don't like." The slice is huge.

If you are to become a better communicator, you must plan on a great deal of "tuning" to become more acutely aware of how differently your messages can be perceived by different people. Later chapters present advice on how to do this through audience analysis for different kinds of communicative situations. For the present discussion, however, let us merely stress the diversity of knowledge, experiences, and attitudes of various listeners.

For example, suppose you were to say, in the presence of several people, "The South is a great place to live." Most native Southerners and voluntarily transplanted Northerners might agree immediately, but they are likely to have much different perceptions of what is meant by "the South." To some it will be the states below the Mason-Dixon line. To others it will be specific places such as Shreveport, Louisiana, or Athens, Georgia. From "the South" some Southerners would exclude Florida and Texas, while others would include them. Some would specify the "true" *rural* South which has changed in the past century far less than have cities such as Atlanta and Birmingham.

Whether the South really *is* "a great place to live" would depend on likes and dislikes of geography, degree of urbanization, state and local government available, and other factors. Some favorable to the statement might agree it is fine to live in a rural area but would shun a large city, whereas a native Atlantan would abhor living in, say, Social Circle, Georgia. A native of the Appalachians might cringe at the prospect of moving to the Piedmont, and vice versa.

What about reactions to the person who made the statement about living in the South? Would it not depend upon the listeners' perceptions of the speaker? If you are perceived as a native Southerner who has lived nowhere else, a Northerner may think your statement reflects a lack of experience with other locales. If your listeners are Southerners and perceive you as inferior in status to themselves, they could infer that your remark is intended to ingratiate you into their circle and that you may have offered it with less than complete conviction. If you are a recently transplanted Northerner and have lived only a short time in an area that a listener does not regard as the "true" South, your remark may be passed off as uninformed ("He doesn't know what he's talking about").

Probably the single most important concept affecting selective perception, alluded to throughout this section, is one's motives. Motives are based on an individual's experiences, knowledge, activity level, and physical and psychological needs. A person's set of motives acts as a kind of filter that allows some perceptions to occur, others not to occur, and will distort other perceptions. So far we have mostly discussed those perceptions allowed to occur and those that have been distorted by the perceptual screening process. Events not allowed to enter consciousness were discussed briefly as a factor of selective exposure and attention, but let us look now at perceptions that can be screened from consciousness because of motives.

In the 1940s some researchers were working on the problem of how to liberalize the racial and ethnic attitudes of people. It was known that prejudiced people, through the selective exposure process, managed to avoid ordinary messages aimed at refuting prejudice and bigotry. A series of experiments was conducted to see whether bigots could be persuaded by anti-prejudice messages cloaked in the outward appearance of entertainment, to which prejudiced people would be likely to voluntarily expose themselves for their entertainment value.[12]

What the researchers found, generally, was that prejudiced people erect a battery of psychological defense mechanisms to keep themselves from perceiving the anti-prejudice thesis of the entertaining messages.

For instance, prejudiced people were exposed to a series of cartoons featuring a highly prejudiced, unsympathetic character named Mr. Biggott. The cartoons ridiculed Mr. Biggott for his prejudice. For instance, one cartoon had Mr. Biggott in a hospital about to receive a blood transfusion; he tells the attendants that he wants only "sixth-generation American blood." The anti-bigotry message was highly distorted by prejudiced viewers. For instance, one prejudiced subject pooh-poohed Mr. Biggott for being so uppity about being a sixth-generation American; the prejudiced person, himself, declared that *he* was an *eighth*-generation American! Other responses included: "You mean it is possible to go to a hospital and be given the blood of just *anyone?*" As the researchers put it,[13]

What they [prejudiced people] do is to evade the issue psychologically by simply not understanding the message . . . .

This technique was used in a broadcast dramatization, "The Belgian Village," presented on the CBS series, "We the People." In the story, a Jewish couple in an occupied Belgian village are saved by the loyal support of the villagers who hide them from the Gestapo. The dramatization was followed by a direct appeal, spoken by Kate Smith, for sympathy and tolerance toward the Jews. Considerably more of the apparently prejudiced respondents than of the others in the test audience refused to admit the applicability of this dramatic story to other situations. They called it an "adventure story," a "war story," they discussed the dramatic highlights with great interest, but treated the explicit appeal attached to the incident either as if it had not occurred or as an unjustified artificial addition.

And so it goes. Can it be any wonder that communication is such a difficult accomplishment in light of selective exposure, attention, and perception? Berelson and Steiner point out:[14]

People tend to misperceive and misinterpret persuasive communications in accordance with their own predispositions, by evading the message or by distorting it in a favorable direction.

For example, anti-Semites tend to misread the tolerance propaganda put out by Jewish groups; political partisans misinterpret the position of their candidate to bring it more nearly into line with their own position on the issues; partisans on both sides tend to judge neutral speeches as favoring their own point of view; partisans are more likely than others to accept as "fact" those news reports supporting their own position. . . . Accidental exposure, apparently, is apt to lead to misperception of the message.

Activity

Select a sample of people of various ages. Take a youngster about 10; two or three of your classmates; a teacher; one or both of your parents; and a grandparent or older aunt or uncle. Ask each one, separately, to answer these questions, then compare the answers.

1. Mr. A makes a "comfortable living." This means he makes at least _____ dollars a year.
2. Mr. B is "wealthy." This means he is worth at least $_____.
3. Miss C is a "tall girl," so she must be at least _____ tall.
4. Mrs. D is "middle aged," and so is between age _____ and age _____.
5. Mr. E buys "expensive" suits; each costs at least $_____.

Selective retention

As with exposure, attention, and perception, what information we *retain* after we have learned it is also determined selectively, primarily by our motivations. We tend to remember pleasant experiences, requests, and ideas and to forget unpleasant experiences. There is probably not a parent in the world who has not marvelled at the way children "forget" they have been told to pick up their rooms or do other chores yet remember with crystal clarity when the parent made some foolish mistake long ago.

The term *repression* was used earlier as a factor in selective exposure; it also operates in selective retention of information. Ernest Hilgard once reviewed all the clinical and experimental evidence available on repression and selective retention and concluded:[15]

> There is abundant clinical evidence for repression as a mechanism of defense. . . . Despite the crudity of the experiments, nearly all of them have shown that pleasant items or experiences are more readily recalled than unpleasant ones, and that memories that reduce self-esteem are recalled with greater difficulties than those that enhance self-esteem.

Coping with selectivity as a speaker

At this point you may be likely to throw up your hands in despair, believing communication to be impossible. You have something to say, but people you wish to talk to may choose to avoid your message. Confronted with the message directly, they may pay no attention to it. If unable to avoid it because of its intensity or many repetitions, they may consciously or unconsciously distort your message. If they do "get the message," they will probably forget it rather quickly if it disagrees with their previous ideas.

This chapter has overemphasized communication difficulties resulting from selectivity so as to make readers all the more conscious of and sensitive to selectivity. One can cope with anything better by simply becoming more aware of it. A speaker who is urgently aware of how selectivity operates in the communication process will take greater care that his messages are heard, then correctly attended to, perceived, and remembered. Aware of selective exposure, the speaker sees the necessity of taking a message to wherever the audience is, perhaps using a variety of media. Aware of selective attention, the speaker will strive to use the factors of attention mentioned earlier. Aware of selective perception, the speaker will labor to make the language and intent clear and unmistakable. And aware of selective retention, the speaker will try to phrase propositions in memorable, vivid prose. Much of the remainder of this book is designed to help the speaker cope with audience selectivity.

Chapter 4 is designed to improve the clarity, appropriateness, and vividness of your language. Chapter 5 can help you enhance the vocal and bodily expression of your messages. Chapter 6 should be an aid to finding and using effective content for your communications. Chapter 10 is designed to help you understand the operations and use of information from the mass media. And the remaining chapters should help you improve your effectiveness in communicating different kinds of messages in different kinds of settings.

While these chapters, plus some directed practice of the principles described in them, are designed to improve your ability to cope with audience selectivity as a *speaker,* there is one other important aspect of becoming a better communicator: one should become a better *listener* also. For as Wilson Mizner has reminded us, "A good listener is not only popular everywhere, but after a while he knows something."[16]

As a listener, you are as subject to the pitfalls of psychological selectivity as is your audience when you speak. The remainder of this chapter recounts what research tells us about the listening process and attempts to indicate how you can overcome selectivity to become a better listener.

Listening

To begin with, recall that listening is represented in our model (Figure 2–2) in Chapter 2. The dynamics of listening are further interwoven with the principles of selective exposure, attention, perception, and retention in this chapter. The phenomenon of listening was first noted in the 1928 and 1930 reports of Rankin, who stressed that, of the time 68 adults spent in communication, they spent 42 percent listening, on the average, 32 percent speaking, 15 percent reading, and 11 percent writing.[17] The most recent study that confirms the order of time spent in communication activities was done in 1969.[18] These findings, from a sample of 173 adults, were: listening 37.3 percent, speaking 27.3 percent, reading, 11.1 percent (they were not concerned with writing).

Ralph Nichols's pioneer work in 1948 describing factors of effective listening made listening a field of its own in speech communication.[19] Since then, many studies have been published. Few aspects of communication have been probed as much and concluded with so little consistency in their findings as those on listening. Yet we do listen daily, we encounter continual problems, and we need help increasing the efficiency of how we listen.

Definition

Perhaps the major obstacle to any set of rules of listening is deciding on a definition. Listening is a complex process consisting partly of hearing, partly of perception, partly of reflection, and partly of memory. Listening is the reception, recognition, understanding, interpretation, and evaluation of aural stimuli. *Receiving* occurs when your nervous system changes in reaction to sound. *Recognizing* occurs when individual sounds can be separated and related to previously-heard sounds, as in some hearing tests which require the person tested to repeat words presented aurally. *Understanding* must be added in order to react meaningfully to words and sentences, such as in following oral directions to get to the Post Office. If some sounds are unclear initially, *interpreting* must come into play (as, when a Britisher refers to a car's *hood* as its "bonnet"). *Evaluating* by the hearer determines whether a statement (radio/TV commercial, observation on the weather, etc.) should be acted upon, taken seriously, dismissed as inconsequential, etc.

Goals

As you participate in public and interpersonal communication, effective listening should help you achieve at least four goals:

1. *You should increase your knowledge.* Discriminative listening will help you gain the most in lectures and is therefore an aid in taking examinations. After you leave school, the habits learned now will assure better retention in innumerable speaking occasions.
2. *You should be better able to evaluate messages.* As an active listener using aids in this chapter and in Chapter 6, you will be able to sift the wheat from the chaff among the myriad communications bombarding you.
3. *You should develop keener social sensitivity.* In interpersonal relations you can begin to remember names better and to be a partner in a helping relationship as you realize that some people need to talk out their problems.
4. *You should expand your appreciation of entertainment.* This may be a byproduct as you develop the active listening habits suggested.

What affects listening

Since we process a staggering amount of data daily through listening, obviously many factors influence how well we listen. From the considerable research done in this area, the following conclusions seem warranted:[20]

1. *Sex.* Though most investigators report that males comprehend slightly more from lectures than females do, the differences are probably caused by the testing situation rather than by inherent sex differences.
2. *Personality.* In general, experimenters have found no definite relationships between the ability to comprehend aurally and personality characteristics.
3. *Intelligence.* Certainly intelligence is an influential element of aural comprehension, but we cannot really predict listening ability from this alone.

4. *Scholastic achievement.* There are positive but moderate correlations between cumulative grade-point averages and listening ability which seem to indicate that those who learn to listen get higher grades. And since listening and reading have about the same correlation with grade-point average, some researchers suggest that scholastic achievement depends as much on aural comprehension as on reading skill.

5. *Verbal ability and vocabulary.* Like intelligence, the verbal component in listening is important. Children with higher listening than reading scores do have higher "nonlanguage" than "language" IQ scores, which suggests there are other abilities that aid our listening.

6. *Note-taking.* Note-taking does not have a significant effect on listening comprehension and retention— probably because most listeners take poor notes. However, if you take good class lecture notes and study them thoroughly, you will probably do better on examinations.

7. *Motivation.* Perhaps one of the most important factors in listening lies in three subdivisions of motivation: interest, emotional appeals and attitudes, and set. If a listener has an *interest* in the topic before the speech, if interest is created during the speech, or if the listener will be tested after the speech, comprehension improves. Second, the intensity of the listener's *emotional* reaction tends to affect comprehension. Third, various methods of producing an anticipatory *set* increase listeners' understanding. For instance, introduce your speech with a statement that your speech is going to be *critical* of censorship, and your audience is likely to better remember your *criticisms.* You have created an audience "set" to anticipate *criticisms.*

8. *Organizational ability.* The better the structure of the message and the better the listener's ability to organize, the higher the comprehension.

9. *Environment.* In general, good listeners remove distracting elements such as poor ventilation or extraneous noises. Research shows distracting environmental factors hinder good comprehension. Distance from the speaker may also affect communication. In one persuasion experiment involving single listeners, the speaker fourteen to fifteen feet away was more persuasive than one five or six feet or one to two feet from the listener.[21]

We would like to be able to give more definite conclusions about listening from research studies, but listening ability seems to combine a constellation of factors. The important factor for our consideration is that, given stable personality and average IQ, there is no particular personality trait or intelligence level that types us or "locks us out" of being a good listener. Listening is a skill and we can learn to become better listeners and to become better at teaching listening skills.

Guides to good listening

Attitude adjustment. Why are you "turned on" by one speaker and "turned off" by another? Many reasons come to mind, but most likely your attitude or frame of reference will greatly determine how you perceive the speaker, whether you will pay attention, and how much you will retain after exposure. Let us illustrate how your attitudes toward the speaker, the message, the medium being used, and toward yourself can affect your listening and suggest ways to improve.

If a *speaker* impresses you as being arrogant and condescending, chances are you will tune him out. You may do the same to a person who is unkempt or slovenly, one who clears his throat every few seconds, or clogs his speech with "and-ah's." You *can* overcome the negative attitude and determine to concentrate on the message. Some years ago one of the authors attended a banquet at a debate tournament. The banquet speaker was an expert on the debate topic and had been quoted all year by debaters. His speech was filled with "er's" and "and-ah's." One debater, asked to evaluate the speaker, replied, "Terrible; I counted 420 vocalized pauses." A debater from a different school was asked, and she said, "He sure knows his economics; I finally understand the free trade concept." The questioner asked further, "Were you bothered by the speaker's delivery?" She replied, "I guess he did hesitate some and had a few 'ah's,' but I was so interested in the topic that it didn't bother me." She had concentrated on what was important at the time.

To illustrate further, can you imagine newscasters concentrating on Henry Kissinger's German accent during a briefing? Of course, all these communications would have had a much higher chance for overall success if the speakers had been ideal communicators. However, since we live in an imperfect world, the listener must often compensate for speaker shortcomings.

The listener's attitude must often be adjusted to the speaker's *message.* The topic may strike you as Sahara-dry or may tread upon your tenderest prejudice. If you have no interest in the topic, you may first have to resort to a purely selfish, what's-in-it-for-me attitude. With a school subject, you may decide that if you listen carefully you won't have to study so much outside class, freeing yourself for more pleasant pursuits. In the process you may discover some topics are really fascinating once you learn the fundamentals, and you could remind yourself of G. K. Chesterton's observation, "There are no uninteresting topics, only uninterested people." With a nonschool situation, you may have to generate a fresh curiosity by asking questions such as: Why does the speaker take this approach? How else could this material be organized? How will the topic be discussed afterwards?

Messages with high emotional content that prick your prejudices present a different problem. Instead of the apathy that accompanies the dry topic, now an overcharged emotional circuit threatens to block a fair hearing. It may be a red-flag word that raises your ire. When we are overstimulated we lose our critical faculties and cease to be good listeners. A speaker need but mention Democrats or Republicans, hippies or hard hats, socialized medicine or the AMA, and the emotions can turn cartwheels. If the speaker seems to favor a pet hate, the listener begins planning a rebuttal or plotting an embarrassing question, or perhaps the listener's thoughts just meander while missing subsequent qualifying remarks that would have justified a fair hearing.

Whether it is a word or an argument that provokes us, we need first to hear out the speaker. Complete understanding of the point may nullify our disagreement. To prevent "knee-jerk reactions" from recurring, we need to analyze what caused our reaction and then set about to gain new information and insights that will let us approach future confrontations with a more dispassionate attitude. When we discover, for example, that all government health programs aren't "socialized medicine," or that all doctors aren't "money motivated conservatives," we will be better listeners when government financing of medical care is the topic.

At times you need to adjust your attitude toward the kind of communication *medium* or *channel* used. Let's face it. Nobody likes listening to boring, long-winded speeches, and we have a negative attitude toward attending committee meetings. One antidote is to shift your perspective. If you expect something to be boring, it probably will be. Raise the level of anticipation, follow the suggestions above for listening to both speaker and message, and you may have a profitable and pleasant experience.

Another warning is in order here. People lend more credibility to television than any other mass medium. Because of constant exposure, a newscaster is assumed an expert on events reported.

Though Walter Cronkite has been cited as the most credible public figure in the United States, he is the first to declare that he is first a news reporter. Remember the nature of television reporting and guard against being overawed at the medium. Chapter 10 contains a more thorough treatment of mass communication.

One's preoccupation with oneself can prevent good listening. This attitude can take at least two forms. One form is simply concern with one's own problems—an upcoming test, an important appointment, a letter that needs writing—while the speaker is explaining how the negative income tax would work. The other form is self criticism. This attitude may take the form of, "Why didn't I read the assignment so I could follow better," or, "I wish I had a better vocabulary so he wouldn't lose me so often."

To avoid preoccupation with self, deposit your troubles and daydreams outside before coming in to listen. Taking notes to keep your mind on the track can be an additional help. For the person who feels guilty about poor preparation, notes can help, along with jotting down unfamiliar words, looking them up later, and then using them before "losing" them.

Environmental control. Poor listening is sometimes caused by distractions in the listening environment, such as too much noise, bad acoustics, a faulty public address system, a stuffy room, or hard seats. To be sure, once there, it may be too late to change some of these conditions, but the efficient listener will try to improve the scene. At a large state university commencement exercise, held in a coliseum, the featured speaker was suddenly cut off because the microphone went dead. After a minute a faculty member rose to his feet and shouted, "Mr. President, we can't hear." The poor listener might have welcomed the silence in order to daydream or sleep. The good listener tried to alert those responsible that the public address system needed to be fixed.

Physical fitness. Listening is an active, not a passive, process. When you work at it, your heart beats faster, the blood circulates faster, and the body temperature even increases slightly. If this process takes more energy than just sitting relaxed, it is no wonder college students tend to come to class tired and begin listening too late, missing much that would aid comprehension of the entire lecture. Research reports are clear: be well rested, assume a comfortably erect posture, and begin listening early.

Determine your purpose in listening. Unless you decide early what you want out of the listening experience, it may be almost a total loss. Just as the speaker must decide on a purpose, the listener must determine if the message is for recall on a test, for advice to be followed when making your next presentation, or for pure relaxation—seeing how the drama is resolved or how the story unfolds.

Many times your purposes will overlap. You will want to enjoy a joke as pure entertainment, but you may also wish to repeat it later. This requires different concentration on the joke and follow-up repetition. The same holds true for remembering names. When introduced, it is a new interpersonal encounter, a new audience to adjust to, and the goal is usually just to be as pleasant and agreeable as possible. This is hardly a time for a pop quiz on who the two people are you just met. Yet you also want to remember their names. In this situation the minds receptive function is often insufficient to retain the name. Firm intent to remember, relating the name to something familiar or bizarre, and use of the name soon after first hearing it are commonly recommended aids for remembering names.

Determining your purpose in listening, then, is related to both thinking and feeling. *Thinking* helps you organize *how* you will listen, but your attitude or feeling may determine *whether* to listen.

Anticipating the speaker's intent. What you want to gain from a presentation and what the speaker intends you to gain may differ. If the speaker purports only to inform but ends up trying to sell you something, you become wary. Since you may need information to make a decision on buying, you may make the best of it—but you downgrade the speaker's credibility.

The listener may need to analyze language and delivery early to determine whether the speaker is serious or satiric.

In public and in interpersonal communication, be wary of jumping to conclusions about the speaker's motives or about what stand the speaker may take. Suppose you learn a certain congresswoman is considered quite conservative; you may then suppose that she strongly favors the congressional seniority system, since it is part of the *status quo.* But if she is also quite *young* (a fact you did not learn or you have ignored), she may favor changing the seniority system. Your selective exposure might thus distort your image of the person.

Rate of speech versus rate of thought. If you are physically and mentally ready to listen, you may be so alert that someone who speaks at about 140 words per minute will leave your rapid-thinking brain with time to spare. These are the times daydreams intervene and mental meandering begins to take over. It has been found that listeners can comprehend up to 275 words per minute without appreciable loss. Speed can serve several purposes: you can anticipate the organizational pattern of the communication; you can decide what information category you are going to "plug" this new information into, thus decide how to remember it; you can review your own experience with the topic and relate it wherever possible; and you can evaluate the speaker's points objectively, trying first to make sure you understand them from the speaker's point of view and then assessing the points according to evidence and reasoning.

With the burgeoning output of information today, more is going to have to be transmitted in less time. A new method called "mnemonic speech" has been developed which compresses recording without deletion and, for example, can compress a 57-second commercial into 37 seconds. One way to build up to these methods is to become more efficient in ordinary listening situations.

Seeking ideas, not just facts. Well-intentioned listeners continually deceive themselves by trying "to get all the facts." In both school and nonschool studies, however, it is not unusual to find a mere 25 percent efficiency in understanding what message was intended. But we persist in trying to absorb all the facts when the communicator is most likely trying to get across a central idea with two or three main points. Francis E. Drake reported a U.S. Air Force study in which a speaker in a brilliantly organized speech was developing the concept that we need to see the other person's point of view in world affairs. The speaker pointed out that we must understand Asian countries in terms of their history. As an example, he mentioned that parts of China had been carpetbagged by Western nations for decades. In developing the failure of Americans to recognize the Asian's attitude toward us, he noted that nationalistic pride dislikes charity. A few students, when asked, came up with the intended generalization, but far too many put down miscellaneous points such as: "China has been carpetbagged," and "Asians are proud."[22]

Of course, concentration on specific facts will sometimes take priority over concentration on generalizations, but even then facts will probably be remembered longer within the context of the main ideas. Seek first the central idea, and facts will more likely be added unto you.

Use of notes. The most time-honored method of retaining what the speaker has said is note-taking. There is no one magic method. The major finding to come out of studies on the subject is the usefulness of a reflection period some time after hearing the speaker. If you have followed the other listening suggestions, such as recognizing a pattern of organization and seeking the central idea, much of note-taking will take care of itself. If you have been used to an

outline format, continue to use and adapt it; if you have used another method, do the same. Follow any method with a review on the same day of the talk.

Activity

1. Observe a class you are taking and prepare a written or oral analysis of how well students listened to the instructor and how well the instructor listened to students. What were the causes of poor listening experiences in the communication process? How could the situation have been improved?

2. Prepare a three- to five-minute written or oral report of an experiment on listening published in a book or journal (see *Communication Monographs* or the *Journal of Communication*).

3. After looking for articles listed in the *Business Periodical Index,* read articles on what is being done in business to improve listening habits.

Practice listening to difficult material. The on-deck batter in baseball swings two or three bats before stepping up to hit. Before a fight, a boxer flails away at a punching bag bulkier and less resilient than his next opponent. The listener who wants to increase in skill should listen to more challenging material.

Nichols found that one reason for the difference between the best and worst listeners was the habits of the best listeners included listening to such programs as "Meet the Press," while the worst listeners were content with Bob Hope and "The Lone Ranger."

Listen for total meaning. In public communication and especially interpersonal communication, the receiver should always try to listen for total meaning. The words of the message taken in a straightforward manner may not be what the speaker intends. We need to discover early if the speaker is fond of irony, for instance. Nonverbal communication also plays an important role here. Some speakers deliver the funniest lines with a straight face and their most cutting remarks with uproarious laughter. When a student hands in a term paper and says, "Here's the paper," the words may say one thing, but the halting approach to the desk and crestfallen look may communicate much more to the instructor. It is to feelings that one must respond and not merely to words if we are successfully to complete the communication cycle.

QUESTIONS FOR THOUGHT
AND DISCUSSION
CHAPTER 3

1. What factors in life cause a person to expose himself or herself to messages?
2. What factors of interest are operating when a child attends an animal movie produced by Walt Disney?
3. What factors of interest might one find (or not find) in a history lecture?
4. In what way do knowledge, experience, and attitude affect human perception?
5. How can a better understanding of how people perceive messages improve your communication?
6. In what way do motives influence what an observer perceives?
7. What is taking place when one person listens carefully to another? Explain the dynamics of such an event.
8. What specific factors affect listening?

EXERCISES · ASSIGNMENTS | CHAPTER 3

1. Think back on events you have observed within the past week. What about those events caused you to focus your attention on those events instead of on other experiences you had?

2. Study one ad in a magazine and one commercial on television and see if you can determine what strategy the creators of those ads used to win their audiences' attention. What kinds of persons probably read that magazine? And what kinds probably watched the television program? Were the ads created for persons with special attitudes, experiences, and interests?

3. Analyze a political campaign speech to determine what the speaker did to capture the attention of a particular audience. See if you can find evidence that the campaigner changed his or her speech when talking to different audiences. Explain such changes.

4. Why are you more interested in one major field of study than another?

5. What would a teacher have to do to make the classroom as exciting for students as planning for a beach party in Florida. Or must a classroom of necessity be boring?

6. Explain why you find yourself listening more attentively to one teacher than another. What could you do to improve your listening in these situations?

ENDNOTES | Chapter 3

1. Wilbur Schramm, "Channels and Audiences," in *Handbook of Communication,* edited by Ithiel de Sola Pool, Wilbur Schramm, et al. (Chicago: Rand McNally, 1973), p. 120.

2. J. L. Freedman and D. O. Sears, "Selective Exposure," in *Advances in Experimental Social Psychology,* vol. 2, edited by Leonard Berkowitz (New York: Academic Press, 1965).

3. Lawrence R. Wheeless, "The Effects of Attitude, Credibility, and Homophily on Selective Exposure to Information," *Speech Monographs,* 41 (November 1974): 329–338.

4. Horace B. English and Ava C. English, *A Comprehensive Dictionary of Psychological and Psychoanalytical Terms* (New York: Longmans, Green, 1958), p. 458.

5. Jon Eisenson, J. Jeffery Auer, and John V. Irwin, *The Psychology of Communication* (New York: Appleton-Century-Crofts, 1963), p. 240.

6. "Mortuary Humor Gets Cold Reception," *Business Week,* April 20, 1974: 42–43.

Psychological selectivity in speaking and listening

7. Kalman Phillips, "When a Funny Commercial Is Good, It's Great!" *Broadcasting*, May 13, 1968: 26.
8. *Television Age*, June 5, 1967: 28.
9. See Charles R. Gruner, "The Effect on Speaker Ethos and Audience Information Gain of Humor in Dull and Interesting Speeches," *Central States Speech Journal*, 21 (Fall 1970): 160–166.
10. Eisenson et al., *op. cit.*, p. 237.
11. English and English, *op. cit.*, pp. 378–379.
12. Eunice Cooper and Marie Jahoda, "The Evasion of Propaganda: How Prejudiced People Respond to Anti-Prejudice Propaganda," *Journal of Psychology*, 23 (1947): 15–25.
13. *Ibid.*
14. Bernard Berelson and Gary A. Steiner, *Human Behavior: An Inventory of Scientific Findings* (New York: Harcourt, Brace and World, 1964), pp. 536–537.
15. Ernest R. Hilgard, "Experimental Approaches to Psychoanalysis," in *Psychoanalysis as Science*, edited by E. Pumpian-Mindlin (Stanford: Stanford University Press, 1952), pp. 7–8.
16. Wilson Mizner, as quoted in Lewis Henry, *Best Quotations for All Occasions* (New York: Fawcett Publications, Inc., 1955), p. 135.
17. Paul T. Rankin, *The Measurement of the Ability to Understand Spoken Language.* (Ann Arbor: University of Michigan, unpublished Ph.D. dissertation, 1926).
18. Larry A. Samovar, Robert D. Brooks, and Richard E. Porter, "A Survey of Adult Communication Activities," *Journal of Communication*, 19 (December 1969): 301–307.
19. Ralph G. Nichols, *Factors Accounting for Differences in Comprehension of Materials Presented Orally in the Classroom* (Iowa City: State University of Iowa, unpublished Ph.D. dissertation, 1948).
20. Charles R. Petrie, Jr., "Informative Speaking: A Summary and Bibliography of Related Research," *Speech Monographs*, 30 (1963): 79–91. *See also* Sam Duker, *Listening Bibliography*, 2nd ed. (Metuchen, N.J.: Scarecrow Press, 1968); Sam Duker, *Listening Readings*, vols. 1 and 2 (Metuchen, N.J.: Scarecrow Press, 1966; 1971); Larry Barker, *Listening Behavior* (Englewood Cliffs, N.J.: Prentice-Hall, 1971); Carl Weaver, *Human Listening* (Indianapolis: Bobbs-Merrill Company, 1972).
21. Stuart Albert and James M. Dabbs, Jr., "Physical Distance and Persuasion," *Journal of Personality and Social Psychology*, 15 (July 1970): 265–270.
22. Francis E. Drake, "How Do You Teach Listening?" *Southern Speech Journal*, 16 (May 1951): 270.

4

SYMBOLIZATION

Humans are the only creatures on earth that practice symbolization to any appreciable extent. *Symbolization* means transforming sense data into words and other symbols; these symbols then represent the sense data. Put more simply, we use symbols to "stand for" things.

Our most prolific set of symbols is the language we speak and write; it is composed of hundreds of thousands of symbols called words. We do create and react to other symbols, of course. We salute the flag because it represents our country; we react to certain gestures, modes of dress, postures, and facial expressions since we have learned that these may represent certain attitudes and other attributes of people. But it is our use of language that makes us so different from other animals:[1]

> Animals live without knowing how they live, and they communicate without knowing how they communicate. By and large, so do we. Unlike animals, however, we speculate about how we live and how we communicate. Our better brains and our unique means of communication—language —make such speculation possible.

We recognize that a map represents territory and the Stars and Stripes stand for the United States. But what do words stand for? Words are used to stand for anything that human beings can observe or conceptualize.

In general, *referent* is used to denote what a particular symbol stands for. The referent for a noun is usually an object: *apple* stands for edible fleshy fruits that grow on trees of the family Malaciae.

Symbolization

Other nouns refer to abstractions: *love* stands for a complicated state of psychophysical symptoms and attitudes one person has toward another person. The usual referent for a verb is an action or state of being: *to fly* refers to the action of moving through the air without support. The referent of *is* (a form of *to be*) is usually some state of existence ("is fat," "is alive"). Adjectives and adverbs usually have as referents some abstract and relative, usually descriptive quality: *fast* means a speed of movement that exceeds other speeds of movement.

Words, like any symbol, must represent mutually agreed upon referents to be effective. Suppose I say, "Fine day, isn't it?" You reflect briefly on my words, quickly check the meteorological situation, agree that the temperature, humidity, wind speed, and absence of clouds meet your concept of a "fine day," and respond, "Yes, sure is."

Like maps, words must closely reflect the "territory" they represent. If you should habitually and incorrectly use the word *mushrooms* when the referent is actually what we call *toadstools,* someone is apt to be poisoned. To label as a "dishonest act" what your friend considers one of his "unfortunate mistakes" may ruin your friendship.

Words may symbolize different things to different people, so care must be taken in choosing words. To a poverty-stricken unemployed person living in an urban slum, the Stars and Stripes may symbolize all that is ugly in life. To a "middle American" who has been successful in education and in business, the flag may stand for all the good things in life. By the same token, *home* probably means, to your instructor, where he or she goes to dinner at the end of the day; to the college student *home* may mean some distant town or city where one does not go until college recesses for vacations.

Principles to remember

Now consider several ideas about choosing words that can be inferred from what has been said about the nature of words. Though considered separately, these principles are interdependent.

1. *Meanings are in people, not in words.* The word *apple* means nothing to someone who has never experienced one. We can describe that an apple is a round, sweet, red edible fruit that grows on trees. Our apple-illiterate may then conceive *some* meaning, depending upon past experience and knowledge of those qualities. But this person's understanding of *"apple"* will be far different from that of people who have actually eaten apples.

2. *Words do not transmit meaning; they merely "stir up" meanings already present in people.* If people you are speaking to have little or no understanding of words you use, or, because of their different backgrounds, experiences, perceptions, and motives they have *different* understandings of your words, communication between you will be difficult (see Chapters 2 and 3). In the heyday of radio a police drama called "Gangbusters" opened with a loud "signature" that included sirens, screeching tires, and the rattle of machinegun fire. From this developed the expression, "he comes on like Gangbusters!" meaning "he comes on strong." The expression would have little or no meaning for today's college students, but it would have instant and fairly standardized meaning for those middle-aged and older.

3. *The speaker must choose words the listeners will understand.* The speaker should abandon plans to use pet phrases, favorite words, or erudite-sounding words that may dazzle but will not enlighten the audience.

The discriminating communicator will try to ensure that his or her use of language will demonstrate three attributes: *clarity, appropriateness,* and *vividness.*

Clarity

To be clear, we must be simple, precise, and concrete. Napoleon is reported to have had a particularly dull sergeant read all his orders before issuing them. If they were simple enough for the sergeant to understand, Napoleon issued the orders, figuring everybody could understand them. Though we may not have to resort to that kind of simplicity, we should not choose a long, hard word where a shorter, better known word will do. Franklin D. Roosevelt's Secretary of Labor Frances Perkins relates how the president gained clarity through simple language:[2]

> In one campaign he asked me to write a speech in which he wanted to stress what had been done in social security and why, and to sketch the future of this program. I summed up one section by saying, "We are trying to construct a more inclusive society." I heard that speech over the radio some weeks later, and this is how he, with his instinct for simplicity, wound up that section: "We are going to make a country in which no one is left out."

Simplicity is promoted by saying the most in the fewest words. Read the paragraphs below and note the second paragraph takes less than half the words of the first:

I haven't checked the figures, but eighty-seven years ago, I think it was, a number of individuals organized a governmental set-up here in this country. I believe it covered certain eastern areas, with this idea they were following up based on a sort of national independence arrangement and the program that every individual is just as good as every other individual.

Fourscore and seven years ago our fathers brought forth on this continent a new nation, conceived in liberty, and dedicated to the proposition that all men are created equal. (From *Lincoln's Gettysburg Address*.)

Clarity can be achieved through precision. Instead of saying, "Postal workers start out at a low salary and have a low ceiling after years of experience," say, "Postal workers begin with subsistence pay of $10,898 and even after twelve years can earn only $13,483."

If you strive for accuracy, you will avoid the dangers of verbal overkill. Movies, for example, are not just entertaining, good, or even excellent. They are supercolossal, involve ecstasies undreamed of, and so on. It may be a compulsion of advertisers to distort language. You can help give language its full value and meaning by speaking precisely and accurately.

Avoid vague wording that forces your listener to fill in the gaps: "There's lots of crime in Capital City." Also avoid jargon that obscures instead of specifies. Imagine trying to follow this sentence, excerpted from an actual speech: "It is hypothesized that such premature consolidation of these reaction patterns [of children] tend to preclude modification for later experience." What the speaker meant was, "If children have to act like adults too soon, they can't change." Jargon is often misused by those attempting to sound intellectual or knowledgeable.

Be exact. Mark Twain observed that "the difference between the right word and the almost right word is the difference between lightning and the lightning bug." For example, using *satisfied* when you mean *convinced* may result in an absurdity: "The man's family is satisfied that he was murdered." Know the difference between *disinterested* and *uninterested.* These two words have been used imprecisely so much that "by now a 'disinterested judge' is one that goes to sleep on the bench."[3]

Activity

Try your hand at improving the clarity of language on the samples of "bureaucratese" below. Then check the rewrites we give (upside-down below).

1. "Upon departure from the premises, ensure that the interior illumination is terminated."
2. "In potential problem analysis, 20/20 hindsight in reverse is applied to identify future problems that may keep the plan from being successful."
3. "The occupational incidence of the demand change is unlikely to coincide with the occupational profile of those registered at the employment office." (From a U.S. Department of Labor publication.)
4. "(Employee failed) to accurately estimate drawer closure speed for timely removal of digit." (Supervisor's account of an office accident involving an employee's thumb and a filing cabinet.)

4. He closed the file drawer on his thumb.
3. The jobs may not fit the people.
2. 20/20 hindsight in reverse means good foresight.
1. When you leave, turn out the lights.

Appropriateness

A sense of fitness dictates most human encounters. Some of our behavior is regulated by law; for example, we don't park the car on the sidewalk. Other behavior is influenced by good manners which reflect social mores and customs: we don't eat peas with a spoon. Manners in a society dictate preferred behavior, including speech. As anthropologist Margaret Mead says, "I have a respect for manners as such; they are a way of dealing with people you don't agree with or like, a way of getting through the day with them, or the evening or dinner or whatever. Otherwise, all you can do is throw rocks."[4]

Appropriateness in language depends on a speaker's adaptation to the subject, audience, and occasion. Interpersonal speech communication continually demands adjusting to changing circumstances. A private foundation director interested in a migrant project was in the field with a summer volunteer. A truck full of cucumbers pulled up, the Mexican worker got out, and the director asked him,

"Is that produce in the rear of the truck the result of a single laborer?" The worker looked to the volunteer for help. "Didja pick all that yourself?" he translated.

In public communication, the choice of words and the speaker's demeanor in a dramatic address to Congress will differ markedly from a classroom speech supporting a proposition of fact. Of course, the style will be appropriate to the speaker and adapted to the audience in any case. To illustrate, here is the introduction of General Douglas MacArthur's address before Congress on April 19, 1951, after he had been relieved of command in Korea by President Truman:[5]

> Mr. President, Mr. Speaker, and Distinguished Members of the Congress. I stand on this rostrum with a sense of deep humility and great pride—humility in the wake of those great American architects of our history who have stood here before me, pride in the reflection that this forum of legislative debate represents human hopes and aspirations and faith of the entire human race.
>
> I do not stand here as advocate for any partisan cause, for the issues are fundamental and reach quite beyond the realm of partisan consideration. They must be resolved on the highest plane of national interest if our course is to prove sound and our future protected. I trust, therefore, that you will do me the justice of receiving that which I have to say as solely expressing the considered viewpoint of a fellow American. I address you, with neither rancor nor bitterness in the fading twilight of life, with but one purpose in mind: To serve my country.

The classroom situation is illustrated by the introduction to a speech by Carolyn Kay Geiman, a sophomore at the University of Kansas, who maintained in her speech that culturally deprived children are teachable. This topic, too, is serious, but the speaker skillfully uses a familiar cartoon character, identification with grades, and three short rhetorical questions to get attention and define her purpose:[6]

> In Charles Schultz's popular cartoon depiction of happiness, one of his definitions has special significance for the American school system. The drawing shows Linus, with his eyes closed in a state of supreme bliss, a broad smile across two-thirds of the face and holding a report card upon which is a big, bold "A." The caption reads: "Happiness is finding out you're not so dumb after all." For once, happiness is not defined as a function of material possessions, yet even this happiness is practically unattainable for

the "unteachables" of the city slums. Are these children intellectually inferior? Are they unable to learn? Are they not worth the time and the effort to teach? Unfortunately, too many people have answered "yes" to these questions and promptly dismissed the issue.

Nowadays we are urged to "tell it like it is." It is now more acceptable to use slang than it was a decade ago. Slang is often vivid and colorful and can be used when it communicates and does not offend. For example, don't say "act on an individual basis" to a young audience when "do your own thing" will communicate better. But, since slang depends on novelty for its effect, the phrase may be out of vogue next year. What's "cool" today may be "hot" tomorrow. Of course, formal speech avoids slang as a general rule. As you become more informal and know the audience better, more slang is generally acceptable. But since much slang becomes trite, outdated, or a substitute for concrete expressions, be careful not to overuse it.

Vividness

A speaker can be clear and appropriate and still be boring. The listener needs to be involved. Invoke as many of the senses as possible with vivid words or, as an Arabian proverb says, "He is the best orator who can turn men's ears into eyes."

Newsweek once recruited vacationing college students for on-the-job training that could lead to a permanent position. Note how *Newsweek*'s description of some ideal qualities it sought in candidates appeal to several senses: "a scholar's penchant for accuracy, a Dickensian eye for mood and color, a cynic's ear for baloney, a sport writer's blunt lyricism, a gentleman's literacy, a lawyer's tenacity, a philosopher's compulsion for truth, a retired colonel's need to spin a yarn, and a boulevardier's flare for ironic wit." These qualities would also become any speaker!

Other methods that can help language be more vivid are figurative language, overstatement and understatement, rhetorical questions, and parallel structure.

Figurative language

Calling an object by its correct name helps make an identification clear; pointing to an object makes it even clearer. But objective naming and pointing can get boring for fertile minds. Thus, good conversations sparkle with figures of speech that add color and force.

The most common figures of speech are similes and metaphors. The *simile* uses *like* or *as* to make comparisons. Perhaps our similes won't be quite as memorable as Ring Lardner's comment that in high society, he "attracted about as much attention as a dirty fingernail in the third grade" or Josh Billings's "most men are like eggs—too full of themselves to hold anything else." A Vietnamese official explained that conventional warfare tactics against the shadowy Viet Cong were "like playing soccer with a tennis racquet."

James Kilpatrick almost poetically compared the U.S. Constitution to a beautiful woman: "The Constitution has all the charms of a lovely woman: It is at once strong and yielding, open and mysterious, constant and changing; it both restrains and frees; it leaves interesting possibilities to the imagination."[7]

The *metaphor* also compares things or ideas but does so in a more direct manner without using *like* or *as*. To use a simile to explain, the metaphor is more like a magnifying glass than a telescope; the metaphor amplifies a concept to make it more vivid or to point out some distinguishing detail. It may link up the familiar with the unfamiliar. Francis Bacon highlighted the difference between health and sickness: "A healthy body is a guest-chamber for the soul; a sick body is a prison." John Milton raised books above the mundane: "A good book is the precious life-blood of a master-spirit, embalmed and treasured up on purpose to a life beyond life."

Good speakers have long appreciated the invigorating effect of metaphor to make a point. One speaker, instead of citing statistics to show how human reproduction has exceeded the capacity to feed the world, assessed the crisis: "The Stork has won out over the Plow." A speaker trying to urge audience members to become active participants in society instead of being victims of its changes implored, "What we need in this country are fewer *thermometer* people and more *thermostat* people."

Personification attributes human traits to inanimate objects or abstract ideas. A student speaker began his speech, "A sudden spasm of hate ripped through the south central district of Los Angeles, now familiar to us all as Watts." In pleading for support for the League of Nations, President Wilson said, "This is a covenant of compulsory arbitration or discussion, and just as soon as you discuss matters, my fellow citizens, peace looks in at the window." If not overdone, personification can lift the tone of a speech from the ordinary to the memorable.

Principles to remember   **61**

Overstatement and understatement

To achieve the desired effect, such as humor or dramatic impact, speakers—especially some comedians—may use exaggeration or understatement. Adlai Stevenson's opening words to the tenth anniversary convocation of the Center for the Study of Democratic Institutions build one on another: "When Bob Hutchins lured me here to speak at this meeting, he said, with customary modesty, that it would surpass in importance the Constitutional Convention. I thought he might be exaggerating a bit, but, looking around this room, I'm not so sure."

Understatement is the reverse of exaggeration but can be just as effective. It lets the listener fill in the intended meaning. When the Londoner reported on radio during the middle of the worst World War II bombing that "we are having a bit of a problem here," he was exemplifying the famous British penchant for understatement.

Rhetorical questions

When a speaker addresses a rhetorical question to the audience, no answer is expected. Rhetorical questions help the listener follow a line of reasoning and make it easier to prepare a response to the speaker's appeal. A rhetorical question sharpens a point. In explaining the relation between national and state government, Alexander Hamilton used the rhetorical question effectively:

> The Union is dependent on the will of the State government for its Chief Magistrate and for its Senate. The blow aimed at the members must give a fatal wound to the head, and the destruction of the States must be at once a political suicide. Can the national government be guilty of this madness? What inducements, what temptations, can they have? Will they attach new honors to their station? Will they increase the national strength? Will they multiply the national resources? Will they make themselves more respectable in the view of foreign nations or of their fellow-citizens by robbing the States of their constitutional privileges?

Parallel structure

You can make ideas stand out by repeating certain parts of a sentence in succeeding phrases or sentences. One of the most famous

Symbolization

examples comes from Winston Churchill's speech to the House of Commons on June 4, 1940:

> We shall not flag or fail. We shall fight in France, we shall fight on the seas and oceans, we shall fight with growing confidence and growing strength in the air, we shall defend our island, whatever the cost may be, we shall fight on the beaches, we shall fight on the landing grounds, we shall fight in the fields and in the streets, we shall fight in the hills; we shall never surrender.

Activity

Over the years, speakers and writers have written or uttered remarks so vivid as to render them classics. Below are some famous sayings paraphrased, perhaps as a beginning speech student might say them. Try to figure out the original vivid form of each:

1. Well, you know, people goof up all the time, and that's normal, you know. Everybody does it. But to say to someone that's goofed in such a way as to bug you or put you out, "That's OK, forget it," now that, you know, is really extra, maybe superhuman.

2. I don't want to tell you to take it easy and cool throughout life; I do want to urge you to rise off your duff, to be active and to do things.

3. If you do a lot of listening, you maybe will learn a lot; if you do a lot of talking, you may say a lot of things you will regret later.

4. People, when they fall in love, well, they tend to take leave of their senses and do a lot of crazy things.

1. To err is human, to forgive, divine. (Pope, *Essay on Criticism*.)
2. I wish to preach not the doctrine of ignoble ease, but the doctrine of the strenuous life. (Theodore Roosevelt.)
3. From listening comes wisdom, and from speaking repentance. (Italian proverb.)
4. The first sign of love is the last of wisdom. (Antoine Bret.)

Oral versus written style

This is primarily a book about *speech* communication, as contrasted to written or other forms of communication. Therefore, in addition to stressing that the communicator's language should be clear, appropriate, and vivid, one other topic with regard to language must be made here: the differences between oral and written language style.

We speak differently than we write. If you don't think so, read aloud your last English paper. Though we have sensed this for over two thousand years, only recently have scholars begun to quantify this concept and to characterize oral style.[8] A composite of these studies shows speech communication language or style to have:

1. Shorter sentences
2. Fewer different words
3. Words with fewer syllables
4. More contractions and interjections
5. More colloquial and nonstandard words
6. More self-reference words
7. More qualifying statements, such as *if, however, but, except*
8. More extreme or superlative words, such as *none, all, every, always, never*
9. More repetition of words and syllables
10. More qualifying terms such as *apparently, to me, it seems, it appears*
11. Fewer quantifying terms or precise numerical words

Of course, all oral communication would not necessarily include all the characteristics listed. In fact, one study casts doubt on the idea that there exists a single oral style.[9] It is agreed that speeches with few words per sentence and with few syllables per word are easier to understand, so speakers having difficulty making a point or sustaining attention should doublecheck their speech against the list.

Something happens to a speaker in the interaction of face-to-face communication. A speaker wants to be direct and to be understood. Almost as if anticipating feedback, the speaker builds in qualifying restrictions on his or her claims. If the message were written, say, in a newspaper, the chances would be few for a letter-to-the-editor reply. To make sure your speeches have this oral quality, do not write out entire speeches verbatim. Work on word choice, yes, but not at the expense of "marrying a phrase" so it cannot be changed as the occasion demands.

Activity

Use a small cassette tape recorder to record, secretly, a conversation between you and a friend (make it a friend who would not mind your recording). Make sure you think the conversation is understandable and easy to follow. Later, transcribe two or three minutes of the conversation into writing. Does it read well? Does it resemble oral style as defined in the list of its characteristics?

Summary

The uniquely human aspects of communication is the exchange of symbols called words. Words communicate well when they stir up in the listener's or reader's mind the meanings those words hold for the speaker or writer. To serve this purpose, the language used ought to be clear *and* appropriate *and* vivid.

Clarity is achieved by simplicity, precision, and concreteness. As a professional writer and speaker has said, "Skilled speakers go easy on abstractions and heavy on specific example."[10] Appropriateness is achieved through a speaker's adaptation to a particular audience and subject; in addition, the speaker must adapt to the particular speaking occasion, as some occasions may be more formal than others. Vividness results from uncommon, striking use of language. Some figures of speech that help make language vivid are simile, metaphor, personification, overstatement and understatement, rhetorical questions, and parallel structure.

The effective speaker uses a clear oral style, not by writing out his speech word for word but by outlining thoughts carefully and knowing the material well without becoming wedded to exact wording. More instructions for preparing a speech for extemporaneous oral presentation are in the next chapter.

QUESTIONS FOR THOUGHT AND DISCUSSION
CHAPTER 4

1. What is the referent for the word *freedom?*
2. What is meant by the statement, "Meanings are in people, not in words"?
3. If you are attempting to explain a topic clearly to your listeners, what guidelines should you follow in selecting words?
4. What makes one's choice of words clear?
5. What questions can you ask to decide whether your wording is appropriate?
6. What is the difference between *metaphor* and *simile?* How are they alike?
7. What distinguishes oral from written language?

EXERCISES · ASSIGNMENTS | CHAPTER 4

1. Locate a recording of an original speech and compare its wording with the version printed in an anthology or other written source. What differences do you find? Why are these differences present?
2. Analyze the words used by a politician in a speech. Do you find the language to be clear? Why or why not?
3. What characteristics would make a fifty-year-old person's words inappropriate for an eighteen-year-old?

4. Study a discourse in *Vital Speeches of the Day,* list the figures of speech you find, and explain what contribution those figures of speech make to the communication.

5. Read an essay in a highly technical science journal and list words you don't understand. Why did the author select such language?

ENDNOTES | *Chapter 4*

1. John R. Pierce, "Communication," in *Communication* (San Francisco: W. H. Freeman, 1972), p. 3.

2. Cited by Ernest Brandenberg and Waldo Braden in *History and Criticism of American Public Address,* vol 3, edited by Marie Hochmuth (New York: Longmans, Green, 1955), p. 505.

3. Charles W. Ferguson, *Say It with Words* (New York: Alfred A. Knopf, 1959), p. 191.

4. "A Conversation with Margaret Mead and T. George Harris on the Anthropological Age," *Psychology Today,* 4 (July 1970): 59.

5. *Congressional Record,* 82nd Congress, 1st session, 1951, 97, pt. 3: 4123.

6. Carolyn Kay Geiman, "Are They Really 'Unteachable'?" in *Contemporary American Speeches,* 2nd ed., edited by Wil A. Linkugel, R. R. Allen, and Richard L. Johannesen (Belmont, Calif.: Wadsworth, 1969), p. 95.

7. James Kilpatrick, "The Enduring Constitution," *Athens* (Ga.) *Daily News,* September 27, 1973, p. 6.

8. G. L. Borchers, "An Approach to the Problem of Oral Style," *Quarterly Journal of Speech,* 22 (1936): 114–117; G. L. Thomas, "Effect of Oral Style on Intelligibility of Speech," *Speech Monographs,* 23 (1956): 46–54; J. A. DeVito, "Psychogrammatical Factors in Oral and Written Discourse by Skilled Communicators," *Speech Monographs,* 33 (1966): 73–76; and J. W. Gibson et al., "A Quantitative Examination of Differences and Similarities in Written and Spoken Messages," *Speech Monographs,* 33 (1966): 444–451.

9. Fred B. Goodwin, "A Study of the Relationship between Certain Codings Environments and Selected Aspects of Speech Style," *Speech Monographs,* 36 (1969): 218.

10. Jenkin Lloyd Jones, "Short Course in Public Speaking," *Greenville* (N.C.) *News,* November 28, 1970.

5 ⌐⌐

EXPRESSION
IN
COMMUNICATION

5 ₪

Our response to any speech . . . is controlled by more than its paraphrasable sense. The speaker's particular diction and syntax, his emphases, pauses, and repetitions (and, when he is speaking aloud to us, the modulations of his voice, his facial expressions and other gestures) all become incorporated in our perception of his meanings and motives. We respond not only to what he is saying but to how he is saying it and, thereby, to what is making him say it: his emotions, his intentions, and all those most subtle and delicate qualifications of paraphrasable sense which the total act of speech may reveal.[1]

The last chapter discussed symbolization, and we now consider how symbols are expressed and how we respond to them. We respond to the total act of speech, and that act reflects our intrapersonal and nonverbal communication and the overall delivery of speech. These are the major topics of this chapter.

Intrapersonal communication

We first express ourselves to ourselves. Whether we call it thinking, reverie, reflection, meditation, or intrapersonal communication, the mind is constantly processing sensory or abstract data. These data form the basis for the day-to-day activities of life. We progress from sensory observations of a round ball and a square block to deciding which candidate for office to vote for or whether a person has a right

Expression in communication

to choose to die. Since experience has taught us that order is preferable to disorder, the mind organizes these data in categories, and among other logical processes, we learn to discriminate causes and effects. Efficiency results from predictable procedure being carried out with minimum wasted time and effort.

Much of this ordering is unconscious and built into the way we have learned to say and think in words lined up into sentences. More talented speakers practice word organization more consciously. As one of the greatest preachers of this century said, "I would never think of speaking without, in some way, ordering my thoughts."[2]

So intrapersonal communication in some form, whether it be going over the speech in your mind, talking to yourself, or saying a prayer, takes place as we prepare to communicate with others.

Nonverbal communication

How you dress, stand, move about, and act will probably affect the way your audience perceives you and your message. One usually thinks of fluency, for example, in relation to verbal communication; yet one study concluded that "as of now it would seem justified to say that fluency may have more visual phenomenal attributes than voice and diction attributes."[3] Your appearance may influence more than your voice.

Indeed, "interaction exists, as it exists in all life—between the body of the language and the body of the speaker, there is interchange; there is always *tensiveness.* It is in the give and take, the stretch and relaxation, the ebb and flow that life lives."[4]

To break down nonverbal communication into categories might be useful in examining this important dimension of human interchange. We will base this examination on Knapp's breakdown that includes body movement, physical characteristics, touching behavior, paralanguage, proxemics, artifacts, and environmental factors.[5]

Body movement

The study of body language has been labeled *kinesics* and has been investigated by R. L. Birdwhistell and A. E. Scheflen, among others. Researchers tell of the importance of body communication but warn that "we must not try to tie up specific posture changes to specific vocal statements. We should beware of deciding that one postural shift always means this, another always that. 'The meaning or function of an event,' Scheflen explains, 'is not contained in itself, but in its relation to its context.' A shift in posture means that something is happening. It does not always tell us what is happening. We must study the shift in relation to the entire incident to find that out."[6]

In both public communication and interpersonal encounters, four expressions of body movement are important: gestures, posture and torso movement, facial expression, and eye contact.

Gestures. Just as you should be mentally alert when running the high hurdles, you should be physically alert when speaking. Gesturing is an important part of your delivery. Some speakers like to gesture more than others, but all should understand and practice certain important principles. Hand, head, shoulder, and body movements should be coordinated with your ideas. At the same time, they should appear spontaneous and natural.

What is habitual to some people, of course, is not good communication. By *natural* we mean that which is truly expressing one's nature, not something that is superficial. Do not attempt to memorize each gesture or plan exactly where each will be used. At first you may have to practice controlling some gestures, but with experience you will want to use bodily movements extemporaneously. Strive for physical activity that is comfortable for you, well coordinated, spontaneous, and appropriate for the particular speaking situation.

Gestures serve several purposes. They convey thought and feeling: a shrug of the shoulder can reveal contempt. Hand and arm movements can express determination and concern—for example, a speaker driving a point home with a clenched fist. Through gestures you can demonstrate the size of a computer used in a space capsule or how to kick a soccer ball.

Posture and torso movement. Again, we must be careful not to conclude too much from postural shifts, but we do know from Mehrabian's studies that a person's body orientation, which is the degree to which the speaker's shoulders and legs are turned toward the listener, does suggest a measure of how much the speaker likes or dislikes the listener. He found no difference in body orientation when standing speakers were addressing those they extremely like or extremely dislike. However, when speakers were seated, there were sex differences. Male speakers offered a less direct body posture toward those they liked very much. Female body orientation was the opposite and was more varied. A female's orientation was least direct when talking to someone she disliked, relatively direct when speaking to someone she liked, and was most direct when speaking with a person for whom she had no strong feelings. Whether the body is tense or relaxed also reflects how a person feels toward another, according to Mehrabian.[7]

Posture and torso movement also affect whether our listeners see us as confident, indifferent, or anxious. If you approach your speaking position alertly with an erect yet comfortable posture, you tend to *feel* confident because you walk and stand confidently. If you drag up to the speaker's stand and slouch over it, the audience quickly gets the message that you do not care very deeply about your subject. Again, if you proceed reluctantly or too quickly, giving furtive glances or with head down, you probably communicate a degree of anxiety.

Facial expression. It is no accident that "wanted" posters in post offices feature a picture of the wanted person's face. It is the focal point of identification for most people. In greeting friends, you assess by their facial expression whether they had a good day. In asking for a raise or a loan at the bank, you "read" your respondent as to your chances of success. When explaining a complex subject to a beginning speech class, the teacher monitors the students' faces for feedback. Getting through? Fuzzy point? Unfamiliar word? The pleasant expression with a hint of a nod gives you the green light to proceed. The furrowed brow may shout "Hold on! Back up."

The complexity of the face, the number of personality factors that may influence facial expression, and the various contexts in which expressions take place combine to make facial expression very difficult for researchers to analyze. The fact that people can show more than one emotion at a time complicates interpretation even further. Research at this point cannot provide conclusions from which you could accurately predict the exact emotion being expressed by a person you are talking to.[8] You will have to rely on experience most of the time.

Eye contact. The poet has long exalted the eye in human relationships. Whether it be "a still soliciting eye" of Shakespeare's King Lear or "an eye full of gentle salutations—and soft responses" in *Tristram Shandy,* the eye is believed to control important components of communication.

In the face-to-face relationship, eye contact becomes an important guide for each successive rhetorical transaction. The speaker may look at the audience to convey a friendly, confident attitude and at the same time to check for feedback (as in facial expression, above) on the reception he or she is getting. To look at a person in the audience is to say you care about that person.

Obviously, the larger the audience, the fewer individuals you will be able to look at. But audiences understand this problem, so you need only look in the direction of each portion of the audience to maintain "contact."

If you are in a group, you become alert to eye behavior that signals your contribution to the conversation—that channels are open and your contribution is welcome. You quickly assess that the furtive glance labels a shy and reluctant member and the icy stare issues a warning and challenge. You will return to the person who responds positively. Efran and Broughton, in an experiment, found male subjects engaged in more visual interaction with a person whom they had had a friendly conversation with just before the experiment and who nodded during the subject's presentation.[9]

Physical characteristics

If you have noticed an increase in the number of health spas and weight-watcher clubs over the past few years, you are aware of the premium our society places on a person's appearance. Physical attractiveness is important to the way we see ourselves and others. Most movie and television heroes are attractive; many of the people we laugh at, like Phyllis Diller, are not. Advertisements reinforce these impressions by associating the good things of life with "beautiful people." Several factors, such as body shape, height, color, and hair, combine to affect people's perception of our bodies.

Body shape can even suggest a person's personality and temperament. In the classic study in this area, Sheldon placed body shapes into three types: the round, soft, fat body of the *endomorph*; the muscular, athletic, bony body of the *mesomorph*; and the thin, tall, frail body of the *ectomorph*.[10] Wells and Siegel showed drawings of these three basic body types to a group of adults and found the following personality traits associated with each: (1) the endomorph was rated fatter, less good looking, more old fashioned, more good natured and agreeable, and more trusting of others; (2) the mesomorph was rated stronger, better looking, more adventurous, younger, and more self-reliant; (3) the ectomorph was rated thinner, more ambitious, more suspicious of others, more pessimistic, and quieter.[11] Experience tells us there are many exceptions to such categories, but if people's preconceptions of one another are affected, these factors will affect communication.

The *height* of a person affects our response. We tend to associate tallness in males with leadership. Short leaders, such

Expression in communication

as Napoleon and Hitler, are exceptions that weaken the generalization, however. We expect females to be shorter than males.

Minority membership has been a pervasive factor in our society in determining our response to fellow citizens. Such responses have led to federal laws which prohibit discrimination by race, sex, age, religion, creed or national origin. The black minority has experienced such prejudice most acutely, though Indian, Mexican, Puerto Rican, Japanese-American, and other groups have felt the results of minority status.

Body hair in the last decade has become more important as a cue in influencing our responses in interpersonal and public communication. Views of college-age people toward long hair and beards differ from the views of employers. In a 1969 study with undergraduates, the researcher thought women were picturing an idealized husband when they described bearded men as masculine, mature, and sophisticated.[12] In a 1974 comprehensive survey of employers' attitudes by the Western College Placement Association, company personnel officers rated twelve male faces for effect on the decision to hire a particular applicant (see Figure 5-1). The only face rated strongly positive by a majority was face 9. The only face rated as having a strong negative effect was face 6. Considered mildly negative were faces 1, 3, 4, and 12. Faces 2, 8, 10, and 11 were rated neutral or having no effect, and face 7 was mildly positive.[13]

Touching behavior

Some years ago a soap advertiser's popular slogan was "the skin you love to touch," yet we in the United States are not particularly a "touching society." Jourard's study[14] of the number of times per hour people in cafes in different cities touched each other underscores this: San Juan, Puerto Rico, 180; Paris, 110; Gainesville, Florida, 2; London, 0. We are familiar with the German's handshake, with the Frenchman's custom of greeting a friend by a kiss on both cheeks, with Greek men who folk dance together. But American society, which sees itself as generous in sharing material things, is apparently more restrained in sharing affection by touching.

We have become aware of the importance of early tactile experiences for mental and emotional maturity. Children need the feeling of being loved that comes from being touched and handled. The growth in the last decade of "body awareness" and other encounter group workshops suggests adults also feel the need for the confirming communication by touch.

1 = Strong positive influence.
2 = Mild positive influence.
3 = Minor or no influence on decision.
4 = Mild negative influence.
5 = Strong negative influence.
N = Never considered — irrelevant.

FIGURE 5–1.   Faces rated by respondents

Activity

1. Seat yourself unobtrusively in a coffee shop, snack bar, or other place where fellow students hang out. Count the total number of times you see individuals touch one another for, say a period of thirty minutes. Do Americans your age seem to engage in much touching behavior?
2. If you are adventuresome, engage in conversation with someone you don't know very well. Get very close, physically, to that person as you talk. Initiate touching behavior, such as putting your hand on the arm or shoulder of the conversational partner. Observe his or her reactions.

Paralanguage

Paralanguage refers to the nonverbal aspects of conversation. Words comprise *what* we say; paralanguage is *how* we say it. Paralanguage is also known as *vocalic communication.*

Though columnist Sydney Harris does not use the word, he graphically describes paralanguage in his essay "On 'Communication' ":[15]

> We hear a great deal about "communication" these days —about our need to listen more carefully, to read more skillfully, to grasp the essence of what another person is trying to say. But it seems to me that communication, even more than charity, begins at home. The most important person to listen to is oneself, and our most important task is to develop an ear that can really hear what we are saying.
>
> Anyone who has ever listened to a playback of a hidden tape recorder will know what I mean. It seems impossible that these are our voices—these babbling, incoherent sounds, more like monkeys than human beings. Is that raucous tone our own? How did self-pity sneak into that sentence? And listen to that phrase, unctuous with hypocrisy, or vibrating with false heartiness.
>
> Without refraction, the voice cannot hear itself, any more than the eye can see itself. The whining wife does not know she whines, the bellowing husband is unaware of his bellow, the self-satisfied prig cannot detect the smugness dripping from his lips.
>
> Just as we do not know what we sound like in timbre

and cadence of voice, so we do not hear the unconscious attitudes that are revealed to others by our speech—the hostility thinly masquerading as humor, the fear hiding behind cool precision, the pomposity or envy or greed or any other unlovely trait we desperately try to conceal from others and from ourselves.

To communicate well and meaningfully it is not enough to make one's meaning plain to a listener. It is, first of all, to make one's meaning plain to oneself, to understand the real motives for our attitudes, to hear the half-tones and flats and sharps of our own prejudices, and to separate (however imperfectly) the voice of reason from the voice of childishness.

This is the hardest job of all, and this is where all genuine communication must begin. For people do not so much listen to what we say as to how we say it; the expression of a statement carries a stronger charge than its content; two men can make the same observation, and one will be accepted, the other met with suspicion or disbelief.

The world listens to the secret language of our emotions, and not to the bald denotations of the words themselves. And mastering that secret language calls for a true ear as much as for a true heart.

Verbal communication

The characteristics that convey these subconscious and hidden meanings come from the products of the speech process: pitch, quality, volume, and rate of our speech and from our pronunciation and articulation. Let us first describe the process, then consider the other aspects.

The process

Speech is an overlaid process. This means that organs such as the lungs, necessary to the production of speech, were originally intended to serve some other biological function. Humans through continuing adaptations developed the ability to communicate by using the lungs, larynx, mouth, tongue, lips, and teeth. The human voice can be compared to a musical wind instrument in which forced air vibrates a reed (the vocal folds in the larynx) and the resulting sound is amplified in the tubes and bell. There are four parts to this act of speech production: respiration, phonation, resonation, and articulation.

Respiration. The energy of the speech process is supplied by the expelled breath from the *respiration cycle.* Used in respiration are the lungs, bronchi, trachea or windpipe, and diaphragm.

The lung, with its branches of spongy tissue (the bronchi), is really a passive organ receiving oxygen and expelling carbon dioxide when acted upon by the diaphragm and other muscles. Though the lungs interchange about five hundred cubic centimeters of air in each respiratory cycle, the body uses only ten to twenty percent of the total amount of air the lungs are capable of holding. The diaphragm, a tendonous sheath separating the heart and lungs from the digestive organs, only contracts in inhalation, allowing the lungs to expand and oxygen to rush in to equalize the pressure. In the exhalation stroke of the cycle, the weight of the rib cage and the abdominal muscles help the lungs expel the used air through the windpipe. This expelled air becomes the energy of speech.

Phonation. *Phonation,* the second step in the speech process, is the vibration of the vocal folds as the expelled air passes over them. These highly sensitive muscles are housed in the *larynx* (the Adam's apple), which consists of muscles and cartilage. The larynx allows air, not food, into the lungs and allows the vocal folds to open and close (see Figure 5-2). These vocal folds or bands (not the vocal cords) open when we breathe silently and come together when we want to speak. The opening for air is called the *glottis.* The appendage above the glottis that prevents foreign matter from entering the larynx and windpipe is called the *epiglottis.*

Resonation. Since one could barely hear the vibrations alone, resonation is necessary. *Resonation* in its simplest form means amplification. This process takes place in three areas: the pharyngeal cavity, the nasal cavity, and the oral cavity. After the vibrations pass through the glottis, sympathetic vibrations are set up in these three areas, and, as molecules bump one another much like freight cars bumping one another, the energy is passed along. Each cavity has a natural vibration rate, and when vibrating air with the proper frequency enters, the original vibrations are strengthened or amplified.

Articulation. A final step, *articulation,* is needed to produce the variety of sounds we call speech. Without this step we have amplified something like the "ah" the doctor asks for, but little else. The organs of articulation are the lips, teeth, tongue, jaw, and soft palate. Their function is to modify the airstream in order to produce speech sounds. You know, for example, when you make a sound with the

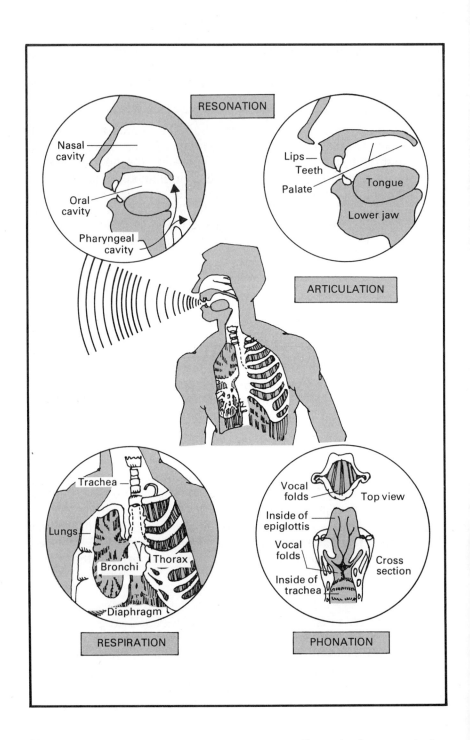

Expression in communication

lips, it can be a *p, b,* or an *m.* In the case of *p* and *b,* you have blocked the expelled air behind the lips and suddenly released it. The twenty-three consonants of the English language all result from having the airstream modified in some way. How precisely the articulators are used determines whether your speech is careless and pedantic or precise and clear.

The elements of voice

Sounds produced by the speech process can be described through four basic elements: pitch, quality, loudness, and rate.

Pitch. Pitch is our subjective reaction to changes in frequency of vibrations of the vocal bands. We hear a high or a low tone depending on the frequency. Tension, mass, and length of the vocal bands affect frequency directly. The more the tension and the shorter the band's length, the higher the pitch. Conversely, the less the tension and the longer the bands, the lower the pitch. Thus, male voices, because of males' longer and thicker vocal bands, are usually pitched lower than female voices. The average vocal frequency for males is 128 cycles per second; it is 256 cycles per second (middle C on the piano) for females.

By *inflection*—pitch changes for particular words in a sentence —we can determine the meaning of that sentence (see exercises at the end of the chapter). We convey excitement and joy with high pitch and seriousness or sadness with low pitch. Pitch can even suggest personality characteristics. One of the most thorough studies in this difficult area was carried out by Addington, who concluded that males using increased pitch variety tended to be perceived as more dynamic, feminine, and aesthetically inclined and that the increased pitch variety in females resulted in their person-alities being perceived as more dynamic and extroverted.[16]

Quality. This characteristic may also be called *tone* or *tone quality.* Quality tells you the difference between a trumpet and trombone (both brass wind instruments), or between a violin and a cello (both stringed instruments). The pitch, loudness, and rate of a sound from these instruments may be identical—yet you can detect a difference. That difference is tone quality.

◀ **FIGURE 5–2. Steps in speech process.** © **1960 by Harcourt Brace Jovanovich, Inc. Reproduced from** *Improving Your Speech,* **by John A. Grasham and Glenn G. Gooder, by permission of the publishers.**

Verbal communication   **81**

In the human voice, quality is differentiated by terms such as nasal, hoarse, strident, or guttural. These terms generally refer to the main location from which a sound is projected or resonated. For example, the nasal tone has excess nasal resonance—it sounds like you're talking through your nose. A guttural quality sounds as if it came from deep in the throat. A normal, full, or *orotund* quality results from a balance of proper resonation from all resonating chambers. Taking two of these qualities from the Addington study, we note that "increased simulation of nasality by both sexes provoked such a wide array of socially undesirable characteristics as to make the isolation of any clear cut images difficult if not impossible."[17] On the other hand, the orotund quality in males appeared to be more energetic, healthy, artistic, sophisticated, proud, interesting, and enthusiastic. Orotund quality in females led to perceptions of increased liveliness, gregariousness, and aesthetic sensitivity; however, these females were also felt to be proud and humorless.[18]

Volume. A third element of vocal sound is loudness or volume. Pitch is a result of frequency of vibration of the vocal folds, whereas volume is initially a result of the amplitude or swing of the vocal folds. As described earlier, resonation adds to volume.

To speak louder, you need to increase the energy with which the exhaled air passes over the vocal folds, done by squeezing the air through a smaller opening. This increases the volume so the listener can hear you more easily.

The paralanguage your listener hears when you raise your volume is that you are more emphatic, angry, or excited. Have you ever heard a person say, "Well, that's just dandy!" and convey great anger? If you speak softly you may "telegraph" secrecy, intimacy, or reassurance.

Rate. The rate represents the time element in the speech process. How quickly or slowly you speak determines whether your speech is intelligible, interesting, and emphatic.

This time element of speech can be broken down into *duration,* when sounds are being emitted and *pause,* which indicates absence of sound. Though research results on rate vary, the following conclusions may be made.

College students reading aloud vary considerably in rate, with the middle two-thirds ranging between about 155 and 185 words per minute. These limits come close to limits judged most effective, though a rate as low as 140 is acceptable for speaking to some listeners.

Speaking rate is slower than reading rate and has a wider range

Expression in communication

for the middle two-thirds of the college population. You're in this group if you speak extemporaneously at some rate between 135 and 183 words per minute. Longer and more variable pauses and phonations of greater variability in duration distinguish trained from untrained speakers.

Syllable duration is significantly correlated with intelligibility of spoken communications; that is, the longer your syllables, the more intelligible you are. Longer syllable duration distinguishes good from poor communication. However, if rapid speech becomes necessary in some circumstances, context clues may compensate for mis-articulated and mis-heard message elements.

Increased duration is one of the most common techniques to achieve vocal emphasis. Time factors also help to distinguish different emotions.[19] In addition, it helps to pause before presenting a statement in an extemporaneous informative speech.[20] While the speaker shouldn't overdo it, research indicates that listeners remember more when the speaker has paused than when there was no pause in the statement.

In the Addington study, as male and female speakers increased their rates of speaking, they were perceived as more animated and extroverted.[21]

Pronunciation and articulation

When words are spoken, we hear them as articulated distinctly or carelessly or pronounced correctly, incorrectly, or with a dialect. Many people use the terms articulation and pronunciation interchangeably, but *articulation* refers to modifications in the airstream enabling you to produce a *k* or a *b* sound, while *pronunciation* refers to the correctness of speech and is concerned with accent on syllables (*a'–dult* or *a–dult'*), omission of sounds (*chilren* for *children*), addition of sounds (*grievious* for *grievous*), and substitution of sounds (*beaudiful* for *beautiful*).

Combined, these processes comprise American speech. To many, our speech, in its many varieties, leaves much to be desired. One critic has written, "Americans—perhaps because they have become deranged by the babble of so many parochial tongues—have always been the most lingually sloppy and tone deaf peoples on earth. Listening to them talk, particularly after one has been away from the country long enough to have stopped taking the sound for granted, is like listening to parrots just coming out of ether."[22] Harsh words, perhaps, but the United States has not been known for emphasizing aesthetics; ours has been an industrial society concerned with conquering frontiers, and our speech is utilitarian and has paid minimal attention to standards of sound production.

Pronunciation. Standards of correctness in pronunciation are found in current unabridged dictionaries and are usually descriptive of the speaking habits of the educated people of one's own region. There are three major dialect regions in the United States: eastern New England, Southern, and general American. Of course, several sub-areas, such as New York City, have unique dialects.

Since the spelling of English words has not kept pace with changes in their pronunciation, many unphonetic results occur in the written language. George Bernard Shaw demonstrated this by spelling "fish" *ghoti.* The *gh* he took from *enough,* the *o* from *women,* and the *ti* from *nation.*

Since English has seventeen vowel sounds but only six vowel letters, much confusion arises for a person learning to speak the language from written symbols. The same sound or same symbol can represent many different pronunciations. The vowel sound of *e* in *see,* for example, can appear as m*ea*t, f*ee*t, pol*i*ce, C*ae*sar, p*eo*ple, conc*ei*t, and f*ie*ld. The letter *i* sounds differently in: s*i*t, c*i*te, and pol*i*ce. The same inconsistencies appear in consonants; although there are symbols for most of the twenty-four consonants, some stand for more than one sound, as *c*ar, *c*ity; *g*ive, *g*entle; beg*s*, pa*s*t.

Many meanings may be conveyed by regional pronunciations. When one hundred Georgians went to New Hampshire for a door-to-door canvass for Jimmy Carter's presidential primary campaign, one campaigner reported, "At the first house I visited, the gentleman opened the door and seemed startled to hear someone with a Southern accent question him."[23] Comedian Lenny Bruce used to say he could never associate a nuclear scientist with a Southern accent; now here is a Southerner who is a former engineer from a nuclear submarine, and he is running for president! The 1960 Democratic ticket featured two distinct regional accents: Americans heard about "Cuber" from New Englander President Kennedy and "Amurrican" from Texan Vice President Johnson. A study to determine which dialect is preferred showed general American speech to be first choice. The same study found that, though there is a tendency for subjects to prefer their local pronunciation, the opposite was true of New York City subjects.[24]

In summary of this important dimension of paralanguage, how we express ourselves by pitch, quality, volume, rate, and pronunciation creates the climate for our communication and may very well determine the meaning interpreted by the listener.

Activity

1. Tune in a TV soap opera, such as "All My Children." Keep the volume turned all the way down to nothing. How well do the actors communicate nonverbally?
2. Now turn the volume up and listen, but close your eyes. Do the verbal and vocalic communications of these actors reveal how they look and are behaving, physically? Open your eyes and peek occasionally to check your perceptions.

Proxemics

Proxemics refers to the perception and use of space in communication. When someone tells you to "keep your distance," that person is in no mood to deal with problems. But when one cups a hand to an ear, he or she is prepared for an intimate thought to be shared. If a small crowd shows up for a public evening lecture, the speaker may well invite the audience to come down front or gather in chairs in a circle.

Spatial communication meanings seem to be culturally determined. Americans tend to protect their "personal territory" differently than do people in other cultures. We have become familiar with Archie Bunker's chair which he guards like a goalie in front of a hockey net. Lot lines and even state lines become focal points of human dispute.

Anthropologist E. T. Hall categorized the informal space of middle-class Americans into four subgroups with appropriate distances for each: *intimate* distance ranges from physical contact to eighteen inches; *casual personal* distance begins at eighteen inches and goes to four feet; the *social-consultative* distance extends from four to twelve feet; and *public distance* covers the range from twelve feet to the limits of seeing and hearing.[25] Further research continues on how various factors affect our spatial communication.

Artifacts

Artifacts "include the manipulation of objects in contact with the interacting persons which may act as nonverbal stimuli."[26] They include clothes, eyeglasses, make-up, jewelry, perfume, and the like.

Little research has been done in this area. One study reported that people who wore eyeglasses were rated higher in intelligence and industriousness by college students.[27] This result suggests that what is communicated may not necessarily be logical but does indicate what relationship people *think* exists.

Environmental factors

If objects on one's person—like diamond rings—communicate as artifacts, objects not directly related to the communicators, such as furniture, lighting, and temperature, can also "speak" to those present. These are labeled *environmental factors.* If you went to high school in an "open classroom," that atmosphere created a certain climate for learning. Or, what effect does that first warm, sunny spring day have on the classroom? If you visit a home where there are no ashtrays, what does it tell you? Architects and contractors are still concerned with bricks and mortar, but they are ever more aware of living centers at home, "quads" on campuses to encourage student interaction, shopping malls to make congregating easier, and the like.

Public speaking: "enlarged conversation"

Chapter 4 ended with the admonition that you should not write out your public speech word for word and then memorize and recite it; instead you were urged to learn to give speeches extemporaneously. Let us now consider that concept.

First, think back to some speeches or lectures you have heard that were read from a script. What did the speaker communicate to you by keeping his nose in and his eyes on a sheaf of papers? What did the speaker communicate to you by the monotonous, singsong rendition of the printed page? What did the speaker's lack of physical alertness and animation tell you? How often did you yawn? How many times did you wish you were elsewhere?

People like to be *talked to,* not *read at.* As newscaster Harry Reasoner once pointed out, people like to think that Bob Hope is ad-libbing all the one-liners in his monologues.[28] They like to think that politicians are so sure and sincere in their beliefs that they can talk without reference even to notes.

Speakers should try to make their public speaking conversational; in fact, public speaking should be thought of as simply *enlarged* conversation. After all, any aspect of good conversation is also an aspect of good public speaking, and any aspect of poor conversation is also an aspect of poor public speaking. In each we like interesting content, clear and easy-to-follow organization, direct and alert delivery, and so on. How do you prepare a speech to be conversational? We recommend seven distinct steps.

1. *Pick a topic.* The topic should be one you are already familiar with and one you can find more on. It should be one that can be useful and interesting to your audience.

2. *Narrow the topic to manageable proportions.* The speech should fit the time limits and intellectual capacity of your proposed audience. You cannot cover photography in a five-minute speech, but you can explain how 35 mm black and white film is developed.

3. *Decide on a specific purpose in terms of audience response.* Do you want audience members to be able to develop film after your speech? Do you simply want them to see how simple it is? Do you want them to better appreciate the work of those who develop film?

Your specific purpose is highly important. It tells you which direction to go in and how to know when you have reached your destination. The speaker with the hazy, ill-defined purpose wanders, lost in the topic, like the Sunday driver whose only purpose is to "go for a ride." The speaker with a clear specific purpose is like a careful traveler with a destination in mind, one who has checked the routes on current road maps, computed estimated travel time and where to stop for lunch, and so on.

4. *Decide what main ideas you must explain or prove.* A clear purpose makes this step easy. You wish to show the audience how to operate the Polaroid camera? Then you must teach them:

    a. How to load the camera.
    b. How to take the picture.
    c. How to develop the picture and treat it for permanence.

You wish to prove that a new law or policy should be instituted? Then you must prove:

    a. At present we have a serious problem.
    b. My solution will solve the problem.
    c. My solution is the most practical of any.

5. *Gather the materials you need.* You will need to prepare how to explain or prove each main idea. We suggest doing it in two stages.

First, write down all you know that you can say in your speech, with questions about any material you do not know and still need to find. Next, take your list to the library or other research source and answer the questions on your list (see Chapter 6).

6. *Organize the materials into an outline.* The outline should have a purpose-sentence, introduction, body, and conclusion. (See Chapter 8 for specific ways to organize speeches to inform, and see Chapter 9 for specific ways to organize speeches to persuade.)

7. *Rehearse from the outline.* Rehearse until you have gone through the speech enough to feel confident with the materials. Rehearse aloud, on your feet, in a room like the one where you will speak. Secure an audience of one or two people—your spouse, roommate, friend, parents. Get feedback from this audience. Did they understand? How did you look and sound to them?

When you now give the speech, you know what you are talking about. You can use a few notes on a card to remind you of the order of your ideas. Unfettered by a manuscript, you can speak directly to the audience; you can look them in the eye, demonstrate alert posture, gesture naturally and meaningfully. You can communicate to your audience that you are poised, confident, alert, and mindful of their needs and desires.

QUESTIONS FOR THOUGHT
AND DISCUSSION
CHAPTER 5

1. In what way is nonverbal communication related to fluency of expression?
2. How does context influence one's perception of nonverbal communication?
3. What can you communicate with body movements?
4. What meanings do you associate with tallness in males?
5. What is *paralanguage?*
6. Why is speech called "an overlaid process"?
7. What takes place during the following four steps of speech production: respiration, phonation, resonation, and articulation?
8. Describe what is meant by "pitch variety."
9. What determines the *quality* of one's voice?
10. Define *pronunciation* and *articulation* and distinguish between them.
11. How does *proxemics* relate to human communication?
12. What is the conversational mode of expression?
13. What specific steps can you take to make your speaking delivery more conversational?
14. Compare and contrast the expression of one's thoughts during interpersonal communication with the expression of one's thoughts during public speaking. How do these two differ? How are they similar?

EXERCISES · ASSIGNMENTS | CHAPTER 5

1. Tape a conversation with a friend and, using the principles discussed in this chapter, evaluate what you do well and what you should improve.
2. Tape a four-minute speech and, using the principles discussed in this chapter, evaluate what you do well and what you should improve.
3. If possible, videotape a four-minute speech. Turn the sound off and observe what you communicated nonverbally. Then observe what you communicated both verbally and nonverbally. Using the principles discussed in this chapter, evaluate what you do well and what you should improve.
4. Using a tape recorder, practice developing a conversational mode of delivery. Give special attention to varying your pitch, rate, and volume.
5. Find a place in your community or on your campus and observe how people communicate with their body movements. Using principles

discussed in this chapter, attempt to classify certain kinds of gestures, movements, and looks. Can you tell what they mean?

ENDNOTES | Chapter 5

1. Barbara Hernnstein Smith, *Poetic Closure* (Chicago: University of Chicago Press, 1968), pp. 17–18.
2. Harry Emerson Fosdick, as quoted in William N. Brigance, *Speech Composition* (New York: Appleton-Century-Crofts, 1937), p. 40.
3. Milton Horowitz, "Fluency: An Appraisal and a Research Approach," *Journal of Communication,* 15 (March 1965): 112.
4. Wallace Bacon, "Alone on the Moon: Our Stammering Society," *Western Speech Communication,* 39 (Fall 1975): 226.
5. Mark L. Knapp, *Nonverbal Communication in Human Interaction* (New York: Holt, Rinehart and Winston, 1972), pp. 5–8.
6. Quoted in Julius Fast, *Body Language* (New York: M. Evans, 1970), p. 128.
7. Albert Mehrabian, "Significance of Posture and Position in the Communication of Attitude and Status Relationships," *Psychological Bulletin,* 71 (1969): 359–372.
8. Paul Ekman, Wallace V. Friesen, and S. S. Tomkins, "Facial Affect Scoring Technique: A First Validity Study," *Semiotica,* 3 (1971): 53.
9. J. Efran and A. Broughton, "Effect of Expectancies for Social Approval on Visual Behavior," *Journal of Personality and Social Psychology,* 4 (1966): 103–107.
10. W. H. Sheldon, *Atlas of Man: A Guide for Somatyping the Adult Male at All Ages* (New York: Harper and Row, 1954).
11. William D. Wells and Bertram Siegel, "Stereotyped Somatypes," *Psychological Reports,* 8 (1961): 77–78.
12. D. G. Freedman, "The Survival Value of the Beard," *Psychology Today,* 3 (1969): 36–39.
13. Jane L. Anton and Michael L. Russell, *Employer Attitudes and Opinions Regarding Potential College Graduate Employees* (Hayward: California State University, 1974), p. 8. Used by permission of the authors and the Western College Placement Association Research Committee.
14. S. M. Jourard, "An Exploratory Study of Body Accessibility," *British Journal of Social and Clinical Psychology,* 5 (1966): 221–231.
15. Sydney Harris, "On 'Communication,' " *The Daily News* (Athens, Georgia), September 24, 1975, p. 6. Used with permission of Mr. Harris and Field Newspaper Syndicate.
16. David W. Addington, "The Relationship of Selected Vocal Characteristics to Personality Perception," *Speech Monographs,* 35 (November 1968): 502.

17. *Ibid.*
18. *Ibid.*
19. Theodore D. Hanley and Wayne L. Thurman, *Developing Vocal Skills,* 2nd ed. (New York: Holt, Rinehart and Winston 1970), pp. 149–150.
20. Ray Ehrensberger, "An Experimental Study of the Relative Effectiveness of Certain Forms of Emphasis in Public Speaking," *Speech Monographs,* 12 (1947): 94–111.
21. Addington, *op. cit.,* p. 502.
22. John W. Aldridge, "In the Country of the Young, Part II," *Harper's* (November 1969): 103.
23. Jill Read, "Report from the Campaign Trail," *The Athens (Georgia) Observer,* January 15, 1976, p. 8.
24. W. Wilke and J. Snyder, "American Speech Preferences," *Speech Monographs,* 9 (1942): 91–110.
25. E. T. Hall, *The Hidden Dimension* (Garden City, N.Y.: Doubleday, 1966), pp. 113–129.
26. Knapp, *op. cit.,* p. 8.
27. G. Thornton, "The Effect of Wearing Glasses upon Judgments of Personality Traits of Persons Seen Briefly," *Journal of Applied Psychology,* 28 (1944): 203–207.
28. Harry Reasoner, "The Strange Case of the English Language; CBS television production (1968).

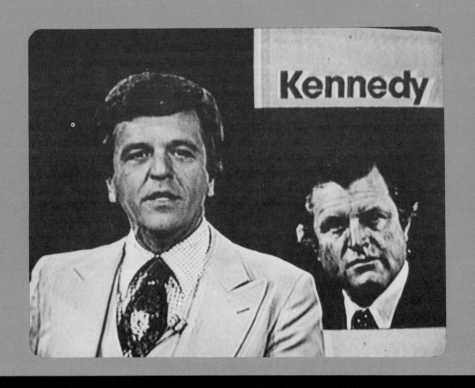

COMMUNICATION CONTENT: THE MESSAGE

The message—*what* is communicated—is a vital part of the communication process. Periodically, for example, the Congress and the people of the United States hear the president's State of the Union message. A friend who missed class probably asks you, "What did the teacher talk about today?" The substance of what is communicated deserves our careful attention. To ensure that you will have a worthwhile and effective message to share, you must know how to find information and know how to use that information in communicating with others.

Finding supporting materials

When you communicate, whether in an interview, small group, or public speaking situation, your listeners attempt to determine whether you are well informed and whether you understand the topic you are discussing. Do you have a message worth hearing? How confident you feel in speaking will depend in part upon your knowledge of the subject. The first task, then, is to find information.

You may use a variety of sources: personal experiences, newspapers, pictures, records, letters, diaries, speeches, books. The personal interview, for example, is an excellent way to gather current information from a qualified source. You can talk with a government official, forest ranger, store owner, or clergyman. Successful interviewing is discussed in detail in Chapter 7.

Regardless of the subject, always make a thorough library

search. The key to using a library is knowing how to use research tools that can aid you in finding books, periodicals, newspapers, and other library resources.

Finding books

The *card catalog* is the key to the library. You can find books by looking up the author, the title, or the general subject. If you know the name of a book's author, look under the author's last name. If you know the title of a book, check alphabetically under the title. (Some libraries separate the author catalog from the title catalog.) Often, however, you can't recall authors or titles; you only know you want to find books on a general topic such as "humor." This is when you would look under the subject (or, in some libraries, in the separate subject catalog). Remember to check related subjects too; in this case, "laughter" or "satire" may list more books relating to humor.

Finding periodicals and reference books

When studying a topic, always investigate to see what journal articles have been written in that area, as these may be the source of the most current information. The term *periodical* includes magazines and journals that appear in continuing series. For example, the *Reader's Digest* and *Time* are periodicals of a general nature, while the *Harvard Business Review* and *Quarterly Journal of Speech* publish specialized essays. When making a library search, go to journals that specialize in covering your topic.

How do you locate articles in journals? By using the appropriate *index.* The Yellow Pages of the phone book is an index. There is an index to almost any subject you want to study. For example, suppose you want to find articles in a wide variety of specialized journals on the topic, "business communication." Find the index of journals on business communication, and turn to "business communication" or "communication, business." Here you will find information necessary to locate the articles: title of article, author, magazine title, volume, date, and page.

Once you locate the proper index or *bibliography,* using it is easy. The difficulty may be in finding the right index. Most persons have heard of the *Readers' Guide to Periodical Literature,* but they don't realize that index only covers journals of a general nature. To use only the *Readers' Guide* when studying business communication, teaching social studies in elementary schools, or raising corn would be a critical mistake. So how do you find more specialized indexes? Two sources will help you find indexes on most subjects. The first is *Ulrich's International Periodical Directory*, where approximately 55,000 periodicals are classified by subject. This book also indicates where the periodicals are indexed. Second is the *Guide to Reference Books,* 8th ed., by Constance M. Winchell, with three supplements (1968, 1970, and 1972). This guide lists basic research reference books. For example, if you were researching the topic, "guidance," you would find "guidance" to be a subheading in the table of contents under "education."

You might also check the card catalog for indexes listed under the subject.

Here are samples of indexes available in a wide variety of subject areas: *Biological and Agricultural Index, Art Index, Business Periodicals Index, Writings on American History, Education Index, Applied Science and Technology Index, Social Sciences and Humanities Index, New York Times Index, Public Affairs Information Service (PAIS), Cumulative Book Index, Sociological Abstracts, Abstracts for Social Workers, MLA International Bibliography of Books and Articles on the Modern Languages and Literatures, Engineering Index, Biography Index, Index to Legal Periodicals, Industrial Arts Index, Occupational Index,* and *Granger's Index to Poetry.*

The source for locating government publications is the *Monthly Catalog of United States Government Publications.* Many of the publications published by the government can be ordered from Superintendent of Documents, Government Printing Office, Washington, D.C.

Activity

To find speech materials, you should be able to do each task below. If you cannot, you should practice each at least once in the library.
1. Locate the *Readers' Guide to Periodical Literature.* In the front of one volume find the list of publications indexed and look them over.
2. Find *A World Bibliography of Bibliographies.* How many volumes are in it?
3. Find the *New York Times Index* and look through it until you learn how to use it. Your library probably has the *New York Times* on microfilm (as well as some other publications). Check out the reel that contains the *Times*

issue published on your birth date. Put it in a microfilm reader and look over that issue to see what other important events occurred on that date.

4. Find the *Education Index* and learn how to use it. Find three articles on the use of television in teaching.

5. Find where the *Monthly Catalog of United States Government Publications* is kept. Who issues this catalog?

6. Find *Standard and Poor's Register of Directors and Executives.* Who is the president of Bethlehem Steel?

7. Find the bound volumes of the *Quarterly Journal of Speech.* Check the index at the end of the bound (four-issue) volume. What kind of topics do the titles of the articles suggest are important to the field of speech communication?

8. Find where your library keeps its collection of telephone directories. Find the address and telephone number of the Statler Hilton Hotel in New York City.

Using message materials

After collecting raw information from your own experiences, interviews, specialized articles, and books, you need to assemble those materials in a coherent and interesting way in order to inform or to persuade. Historically, this process of gathering materials and working them into meaningful messages has been called *invention* to emphasize that one's communication should be an original product based on the best available information. We discuss this invention process in more detail in Chapters 7 and 8; this chapter explains three categories of communication content you can use to develop a meaningful message: supporting material, reasoning, and visual aids.

Supporting material

Supporting material is information used by a speaker either to clarify or to persuade. For example, in an informative speech on "littering the United States," you could compare findings from a reliable poll to show what Americans *say* are their attitudes toward littering with reliable figures that indicate how much we actually *do* litter and what it costs to clean up the mess. In an informative communication, the speaker makes statements and uses appropriate supporting materials to explain and support the statements. The goal is increased understanding. Figure 6–1 is an illustration of communication designed to explain a statement by means of two supporting *examples.* As we will see, there are several kinds of supporting materials that could be used to help clarify or explain a statement.

Supporting materials are also used to support an argument. In persuasive communication you go beyond explanation to advocacy —you attempt to convince listeners that a position or belief should be accepted or that some action should be taken. Instead of just explaining the critical problem of "litter in the United States," you persuade your audience to *stop littering!*

Persuaders use arguments. An argument can consist of three parts: (1) a conclusion, (2) a reason for reaching that conclusion, and (3) materials, when available, to support the reason or conclusion. We can illustrate how supporting materials work in persuasive communication in Figure 6–1.

Supporting materials, then, can support a conclusion or argument and can be useful in explaining an idea or issue to an audience. Supporting content can also make your message more persuasive. In summarizing research on the effects of evidence on audiences, McCroskey concluded that when the speaker is considered by the audience to be highly credible, the addition of "good evidence" to the communication seems to add little to the speaker's persuasive

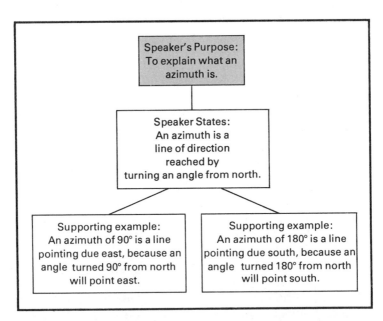

FIGURE 6–1. Supporting a statement with examples

effectiveness.[1]   In other words, if listeners will believe a statement just because the speaker says so, the addition of evidence usually does not make the speech more persuasive.   When your family physician tells you to lose weight, you may accept the prescription on the basis of the doctor's good reputation and without supporting evidence.

McCroskey also found, however, that if the audience does *not* consider the speaker to be highly credible, the persuasive appeal *is* significantly improved by use of good evidence.   When you speak to a speech communication class or some other audience, will you be considered highly believable by your audience because of your reputation?   Will your audience judge you to be an expert on the subject?   Will they believe as you advocate or act as you recommend on the basis of their perception of you?   Most of us need more than just reputation; we need good evidence.   The kinds of materials you may find to support informative and persuasive communication are factual information, examples, comparison and contrast, testimony, restatement and repetition, definition, description, and humor.

Factual information

The late industrialist Owen D. Young once remarked that "Facts are our scarcest raw material."   Perhaps so, but his remark can be taken at least two ways.   He may have meant that we have little factual information about the ocean bottom, Mars, or how the stock market will react next month.   But he may have meant that people do not bother to find and use facts that are available.   Digging out facts is more difficult than is stating personal assertions.   Factual information to support your ideas exists if you search carefully by using appropriate research tools.

To be effective and to be interesting enough to hold your audience's attention, your information must be clear and specific.   In a speech on air pollution you might assert that, "Our rising population in urban centers is causing more people to die there from air pollution."   But such a broad and general statement is likely to draw a yawn and a "ho-hum, seems I've heard that before."   Contrast this generalization to the way championship college speaker Charles Schalliol specified the problem:[2]

> The increasing size of the metropolitan areas is compounding the problems local authorities must face.   Since 1940, our population has grown by 50,000,000, the use of energy has quadrupled, disposable income has increased 60 per-

cent—yet our air supply remains the same. In such a setting air pollution is a murderer. According to Edward Parkhurst, a noted health authority, death rates are "consistently higher in the central cities of 50,000 and over than in places under 10,000 and in rural areas in non-metropolitan districts." The Census Bureau further establishes that life expectancy is three years greater in rural states than in the urban areas.

Doesn't Schalliol's technique make the problem of air pollution sound more concrete and serious than does a vague generalization?

While campaigning for the presidency in 1960, John F. Kennedy could have claimed, "Lots of people in the United States are without adequate diet." Instead, he used specific factual information: "In this country 17,000,000 Americans go to bed hungry every night."

A speaker can be too specific, especially when large numbers are used. To say in a speech, "And the total cost of the program to date has been $4,757,643.72" may confuse the audience, causing them to remember only the seventy-two cents at the end. You can round off figures like this to make them simple for the audience. "Just under five million dollars" would be more easily understood and retained.

McCroskey's summary of studies on the use of evidence suggests another important factor we should require in the evidence we use. In one of the studies, two speeches on different topics were used, each employing "good" evidence. One speech changed attitudes, but the other did not. The researchers conducted post-experimental interviews with those who listened to the two speeches to determine why only one was effective. Those hearing the ineffective speech generally commented on the fact that the evidence presented in the speech was trite and "old hat"; they had heard it before. Conversely, they reported the evidence in the effective speech was *new;* in fact, people often referred to the "shocking facts" contained in the effective speech. McCroskey's conclusion: evidence, to be persuasive, must be previously unknown to the audience; it must be new evidence to be effective.[3] This conclusion makes sense. If you already knew the evidence and were still unpersuaded, how could you be persuaded by a repetition of it? Perhaps this is one reason why so few smokers are persuaded to quit smoking by the argument that cigarettes cause cancer—they *already know* they cause cancer, but they continue to smoke.

Communication content: the message

Examples

Two types of examples can be used to inform or persuade. The *illustration* is a story, a somewhat lengthy narration of events exemplifying a generalization or conclusion. The other type, the *specific instance,* is relatively brief, and is either self-explanatory or instantly recognizable.

There are two types of *illustrations:* the literal (factual) and the hypothetical. Many speech scholars, including the late William Norwood Brigance, have considered illustration to be the most powerful form of support when speaking to general audiences. The illustration can make an abstraction concrete and vivid by applying that generalization specifically and understandably to the experiences of the audience. In addition, many people just like to be told a story! Often an audience winces visibly from the strains on attention span and reasoning ability as the speaker toils to make clear to them some abstract point—then the audience sits back with a relaxed smile as the speaker illustrates with, "The principle operates like this: Suppose you buy a new house. . . ." How painlessly the speaker can make a point if the illustration is representative and concrete.

Eric Johnston, former motion picture industry magnate, often used illustrations in his speeches. When he wanted to make vivid and memorable the fact that our motion pictures exported overseas do more than just entertain people, he used the following two illustrations:[4]

> I went to a screening in Warsaw given by the Communist minister of labor for Stakhanovite workers, the elite of the Communist labor force. An American film was shown, a rather innocuous romance, and it went over big. What most moved the audience was a scene in which the heroine met her fiance at a factory where he worked. Outside the factory were thousands of American workers' cars.
>
> The minister of labor was deeply disturbed. "Why do you try to fool us?" he asked me. "What do you mean, fool you?" I said. "Oh, now, you know your exploited workers don't have cars like that!" he said. "That's just propaganda!" But he didn't really believe it was propaganda, nor did the Stakhanovites. I still remember them as the party broke up, talking eagerly about American workers and their cars.
>
> I remember another evening on a mountain-top near Djakarta, Indonesia, where our motion-picture representative lives. Each Saturday night he puts up a bedsheet on

his front lawn as a movie screen and invites the whole countryside to attend an American film. I watched the audience arrive at sundown, women walking up the mountainside with their babies on their shoulders, workers from the local tea estates, soldiers from the nearby garrison. I was told that even the guerrilla fighters turned up for these shows, parking their guns outside along with the police. . . .

The movie that night was a rather antique but complicated Western without subtitles. I doubted that the audience could make head or tail of it. But they cheered and responded in the right places, and afterward a native priest came up to me. "Americans believe as we do," he told me through an interpreter. "How do you mean?" I asked. "Well," he said, "our religion tells us that good men prosper and evil men don't. From your fine movie, we see that you Americans believe this too!"

Because they make a topic concrete, vivid, and therefore interesting for an audience, illustrations are ideal for speech introductions. Consider the following, with which Charles Schalliol opened his prize-winning oration:[5]

The stranger struck in Donora, Pennsylvania, in October of 1948. A thick fog billowed through the streets enveloping everything in thick sheets of dirty moisture and a greasy black coating. As Tuesday faded into Saturday, the fumes from the big steel mills shrouded the outlines of the landscape. One could barely see across the narrow streets. Traffic stopped. Men lost their way returning from the mills. Walking through the streets, even for a few moments, caused eyes to water and burn. The thick fumes grabbed at the throat and created a choking sensation. The air acquired a sickening bitter-sweet smell, nearly a taste. Death was in the air.

Before the clouds of fog lifted from Donora, twenty had died, and 600, or half the population, were bedridden. Donora was the site of America's first major air pollution disaster.

Thus far we have considered only literal illustrations. But hypothetical illustrations, or stories of "what might happen if," can be useful, too. A student at St. Lawrence University gave a speech several years ago in which she opposed a law then before the New York legislature that would legalize the practice of wiretapping. Her hypothetical illustration went something like this:

And what would passage of this bill mean to you, personally? It would mean that someday your local sheriff or chief of police might decide to see what it is you talk about on your phone. So he clips an inexpensive device onto your telephone line, without so much as a word to you, and he listens. He listens to your intimate conversations with your girl or boy friend. He listens to your complaints to your neighbor about the poor garbage service and the tedious delay in fixing the chuck hole in front of your house. He listens as you tell your best friend how you voted in the last election. And, as he listens, he might decide to tape record a few juicy bits for the amusement of his close friends. You will never know when Big Brother is on the other end of the line.

Or take Ben Franklin's classic argument against the requirement of ownership of property as a condition for voting: "To require property of voters leads us up to this dilemma: I own a jackass, I can vote. The jackass dies, I cannot vote. Therefore, the vote represents not me, but the jackass."

The type of example we call *specific instances* forms succinct examples which, together, tend to support a particular conclusion. They need no extended explanation. For instance, President Franklin D. Roosevelt, in asking Congress to declare war on Japan, December 8, 1941, used six specific instances, leading inductively to his conclusion:

Yesterday, the Japanese government also launched an attack against Malaysia.
Last night the Japanese forces attacked Hong Kong.
Last night Japanese forces attacked Guam.
Last night Japanese forces attacked the Philippine Islands.
This morning the Japanese attacked Wake Island.
Japan has, therefore, undertaken a surprise offensive extending through the Pacific area.

In a state speaking contest, contestants were to address the question, "Is a college education a necessity today?" The young man who won argued that a college education is *not* a necessity. His main body of supporting materials was the naming of twenty different individuals who, despite leaving school at an early age, had achieved great distinction in business, in the arts, and in politics.

The main thing to remember about specific instances is to use them in groups. One or two may not suffice. And they should be either instantly recognizable or self-explanatory. For if they are neither instantly recognizable nor self-explanatory, they do not serve the function of *support.* For instance, suppose you were to hear in a speech the following generalization followed by four specific instances:

1. Popularity and large circulation are no guarantee to a magazine that it will continue to exist.
   a. For instance, think about what happened to the *Literary Digest.*
   b. Ponder, also, the fate of *Liberty* magazine.
   c. And you all remember, I am sure, the demise of *Collier*'s.
   d. Recently we have seen the *Saturday Evening Post* and *Look* fade from the scene.

Perhaps you remember the *Saturday Evening Post,* which lasted until 1969; but how about *Literary Digest, Liberty, Look,* and *Collier*'s? To make these examples understandable and useful as support, they would have to be expanded through narration; that is, they would have to be converted into illustrations.

Comparison and contrast

Comparisons are used to show similarities between things, whereas *contrasts* are designed to emphasize differences. Comparisons, sometimes called *analogies,* are generally used for one of three reasons: to compare something meaningless with something meaningful, to compare something known with something unknown, or to compare something new and unacceptable with something old and acceptable.

Some concepts we discuss are actually meaningless to us, even though we think we know the meaning behind the words. For instance, take the idea of a billion dollars. We can say the words, "one billion dollars." We know this figure is twice as much as five hundred million dollars and half as much as two billion dollars. But do we comprehend what a billion dollars really is, what it will buy, how long it would take to earn it? Those of us used to spending money a dollar or two at a time have difficulty imagining this amount. Perhaps this is why an employee of the Defense Department once remarked, "It's awfully difficult to spend a billion dollars and get your money's worth." We need some sort of *comparison* to make this figure more meaningful. We might put it on a scale; for instance, suppose you were to spend a hundred dollars per minute, sixty minutes per hour, twenty-four hours per day (without stopping to eat or sleep). How long would it take you to spend a billion dollars? A little over nineteen years!

Or, take the amount of time humans have lived on earth in comparison to the whole of geological time. In terms of years it might not be meaningful. So use the scale of one year, as *Quote* magazine did:[6]

> Take one year, and let it represent the whole of time since the beginning of the world. How long—on the scale of one year—has the human race lived? The earliest prehistoric man arrived about 14 hours ago. The first pyramids were built 93 seconds ago. Christ was born 21 seconds ago. And the American Revolution was fought two seconds ago. Man is a newcomer to this planet which he now claims to dominate.

Suppose you want to explain to members of your audience something almost totally unknown to them? Compare it to something known. A student in one of the author's speech classes gave a speech on the automatic transmission so popular in American automobiles. But some people in the class were not familiar with transmissions. How could he get across to them the idea of a torque converter? He used a comparison. He set up on a table at the front of the room two electric fans facing one another, about six inches apart. He plugged in one and turned it on. The air blowing from that fan caused the blades of the second fan to spin. "This," he explained, "is how your torque converter in your automatic transmission works. Except that one fan blows a stream of oil, not air, against the other one, and they are both encased in a steel tube instead of just sitting on a table." A speaker once also explained the function of a resistor in an electrical circuit by comparing it to placing a garden hose atop a stone and then stepping lightly on it to slow down the flow of water.

People may mistrust any new idea, any new strategy for solving problems. Conservatism in this regard comes naturally for some people. That is why, when you are urging some plan of action that might be considered new, you may need to show that it is very much like some older, accepted idea. Proponents of Medicare pointed to the conclusion that their plan was not new in principle: Do we not pool our money through the government for protection from foreign enemies? Do we not pool our money through the government to protect ourselves from natural disasters? From the criminal element? From destitution in our old age, through Social Security? Then why not protection from economic ruination by medical bills?

Be certain the things you compare are really comparable. That is, the things you compare should be in the same class of things or must be truly comparable *in principle*. For instance, Medicare is in the same class of things as Social Security (social legislation); constricting the flow of water through a garden hose with one's foot and a stone is similar in principle to a resistor in an electrical circuit. But a comparison of things not really comparable proves or explains little, and such a comparison is usually called a *figurative analogy.* For instance, to say, "Criminals should never be paroled; after all, leopards cannot change their spots," is to compare factors that are not in the same category. Certainly leopards cannot change their spots, but this fact has nothing in common with human rehabilitation. Several years ago when Great Britain was fighting the people of Cyprus who were rebelling against England's colonial rule, and France was fighting to prevent Algeria from becoming independent, American newspapers and magazines editorialized against such bloody repression in maintaining colonial rule. One Briton, irked over the stand of the American press, railed in a letter to the editors, "So you Americans are opposed to colonialization, are you? Well, then, I suggest you give Louisiana back to France, Florida back to Spain, and Alaska back to Russia." His letter would have been a sound argument from analogy had the United States won and kept these territories as colonies (not as states) through military force, instead of having purchased them.

Contrast can be a powerful method of support because it can show in stark detail the differences you want to emphasize. Juxtaposing differences exposes them harshly and clearly. In order to make her point that women in the United States suffer from acute discrimination, Edith G. Painter, dean of women at Youngstown State University, contrasted then and now and men versus women to show women's relative place:[7]

> . . . in 1930 women made up 30 percent of college faculties; today 22 percent. Twenty years ago nearly all elementary school principals were women; today only 37 percent. In 1930 women earned 40 percent of master's degrees; currently, 34 percent. Women's doctorates are down from 14 percent in 1930 to 12. In the professions, 25 years has seen women decline from 45 percent to 37. Turning to politics, the 87th Congress included 19 women; the 92nd had 11 women. Latest median pay figures for all full-time workers show men, $8945; women, $5826.

Testimony

The testimony of experts can substantiate your arguments, especially if the audience is not likely to take your word as authoritative. You can use this technique in speeches or in term papers, as in the following example:

Communication content: the message

1. People seem to start their adult lives as liberals and romantics, but later, when older, become conservatives and realists.

    a. Clarence Darrow, that giant of American lawyers, put it this way: "At twenty a man is full of fight and hope. He wants to reform the world. When he's seventy he still wants to reform the world, but he knows he can't."

    b. Ralph Waldo Emerson expressed the idea more poetically: "We are reformers in spring and summer; in autumn and winter we stand by the old; reformers in the morning, conservers at night."

    c. A statement attributed to Disraeli supposedly explains the reason: "Any man of twenty who is not a liberal has no heart; any man of forty who is not a conservative has no head."

There are at least two other ways to use testimony in a speech. First, you can use the testimony of experts to condense arguments and save valuable time. For instance, several years ago college debaters were debating whether nuclear testing in the atmosphere should be stopped. Those arguing it should be stopped were faced with the task of proving that nuclear testing in the atmosphere produces dangerous radioactivity. One way to prove such a point is to define radiation, explain how it is measured, and where it occurs, and to tell what norms have been established for "mild," "serious," and "lethal" amounts. This complicated technical argument could consume much time (and possibly bore the audience). So the debaters simply quoted well-known nuclear scientists on the developing danger levels of radioactivity.

Second, you can use quotations as spice in your speaking, to add flair and interest. You can check to see if anyone has said what you want to say in such an artistic way that it makes the point better than you could in your own words. A student once made a plea for the United States to liberalize its immigration and naturalization laws. She concluded:

Let us go back to that shining philosophy of Emma Lazarus that is chiseled into the base of the Statue of Liberty:

Give me your tired, your poor,
Your huddled masses, yearning to breathe free,
The wretched refuse of your teeming shore.
Send these, the homeless, tempest tossed to me.
I lift my lamp beside the golden door.

Finding imaginative literary quotations for your speech will not be difficult if you will keep handy while working on your speeches some reference work such as *Best Quotations for All Occasions,* an inexpensive paperback.[8] This work arranges quotations by subject matter and in alphabetical order. Suppose your speech is on communism, and you want to define the term for your audience. You look up communism in the reference book and find that G. W. Gough has said that, "The Communist is a Socialist in a violent hurry." You also discover an amusing bit of doggerel by Englishman Ebenezer Elliott which comically defines the Communist:

> What is a Communist? One who hath yearnings
> For equal division of unequal earnings.
> Idler or bungler, or both, he is willing
> To fork out his copper and pocket your shilling.

Perhaps you want to give a speech on the thesis, "Honesty is the best policy." You look up honesty, but find nothing you wish to use. So, look up its *opposite,* falsehood. Daniel Webster stated: "Falsehoods not only disagree with truths, but usually quarrel among themselves."

Restatement and repetition

Repetition and restatement are forms of support. They explain and amplify. Repeating something over and over again, or restating it by changing its wording, actually does work the same way as *evidence* to influence beliefs or actions. Certainly professional persuaders such as advertising agencies think so. We are inundated daily by advertisers' repeated messages: "Things go better with Coke." "Pepsi beats the others cold." "You're in good hands with Allstate." "When you're out of Schlitz, you're out of beer."

Does such repetition and restatement work in public speeches? Winston Churchill, one of the twentieth century's greatest speakers, used repetition and restatement:

> We shall defend our island, whatever the cost may be. We shall fight on the beaches. We shall fight on the landing grounds. We shall fight in the fields and in the streets, and we shall fight in the hills. We shall never surrender.

Consider the continuing restatement in a prize-winning speech by Ralph Zimmerman, as he asked for help for victims of hemophilia, a disease which prevents blood from clotting.[9]

You might ask—but what can I do? What do you expect of me? The answer lies in the title of this oration: mingled blood. For all that boy needs is blood, blood, and more blood. Blood for transfusions, blood for fresh frozen plasma, blood for serum fractions. Not Red Cross Bank blood, for stored blood loses its clot-producing factors. But fresh blood directly from you to him in a matter of hours. Your blood, dark and thick, rich with all the complex protein fractions that make for coagulation—mingled with the thin, weak, and deficient liquid that flows in his veins. Blood directly from you to the medical researcher for transformation into fresh frozen plasma or antihemophilic globulin. During those [early] years, his very life is flowing in your veins. No synthetic substitute has been found—only fresh blood and its derivatives.

Definition

Depending upon the point in question, you may find definition to be a useful way to develop an idea. For instance, for over twenty years the basic argument of the United States against the admission of the People's Republic of China to the United Nations was one of definition: the United States claimed that Mainland China, by definition, did not meet the United Nations charter's requirement for admission: that of a peaceable, peace-loving nation.

Notice how John C. Stephens, Jr. used a quotation defining two terms to strengthen his point that *leadership* in education should not be supplanted by *management* skills:[10]

> But in these times of stress for . . . higher education, management skills—important as they are—are not enough. And so I turn to a quotation from George B. Weathersby, who says:
> "We often confuse management with leadership, to the detriment of both. Leadership is knowing where to go; management is knowing how to get there. Leadership is setting desirable objectives; management is discovering efficient methods of achieving these objectives. Leadership is charismatic, qualitative, idealistic; management is analytical, quantitative, pragmatic. Managerial tools are reproducible, exportable, and politically demonstrable; while leadership is unique, innate, and amorphous. . . . Today the operational constraint on an improved academic, social and per-

sonal environment within our colleges and universities is leadership, not management."*

Yes, good management is important in higher education. But, ladies and gentlemen, let us not manage ourselves into educational, scholarly, and intellectual receivership.

Description

For some issues, description may be the most appropriate kind of support. Occasions may arise in which vivid, sustained, imaginative description will succeed where statistics and examples will not. Consider the problem of highway safety. Almost every driver has heard the slogans: "Slow down and live," or "The life you save may be your own." But we go busily on our speeding way, slaughtering over 50,000 other Americans each year and hospitalizing many more. A *Reader's Digest* article, first published in 1935, republished in 1940 and again in 1966, so vividly described the results of speed and poor driving that over five million reprints of it have been distributed by law enforcement and safety experts. It relies almost totally upon description for its impact. It says that highway posters should depict:[11]

> the flopping, pointless efforts of the injured to stand; the queer grunting noises; the steady, panting groaning of a human being with pain creeping up on him as the shock wears off. It should portray the slack expression on the face of a man, drugged with shock, staring at the Z-twist in his broken leg, the insane crumpled effect of a child's body after its bones are crushed inward, a realistic portrait of a hysterical woman with her screaming mouth opening a hole in the bloody drip that fills her eyes and runs off her chin. Minor details would include the raw ends of bones protruding through flesh in compound fractures, and the dark-red oozing surfaces where clothes and skin were flayed off at once.

Such description cuts through the dryness of accident statistics and the blandness of safety slogans and will perhaps slow down at least those drivers inclined to faintness of heart. A second quotation from this article concerning accidents further dramatized the effectiveness of a vivid description:[12]

---

* "PPBS: Purpose, Persuasion, Backbone, and Spunk," *Liberal Education,* 57 (May, 1971): 211–212.

A trooper described . . . an accident—five cars in one mess, seven killed on the spot, two dead on the way to the hospital, two more dead in the long run. He remembered it far more vividly than he wanted to—the quick way the doctor turned away from a dead man to check up on a woman with a broken back; the three bodies out of one car so soaked with oil from the crankcase that they looked like wet brown cigars and not human at all; a man, walking around and babbling to himself, oblivious of the dead and dying, even oblivious of the daggerlike sliver of steel that stuck out of his streaming wrist; a pretty girl with her forehead laid open, trying hopelessly to crawl out of a ditch in spite of her smashed hip.

Wit and humor

Most writers believe that *humor* adds interest to a speech. "There can be no doubt that humor is one of the valuable sources of interest in examples."[13] Wilson and Arnold list humor as a "factor of attention."[14]

The results of two studies, however, indicate that humor can add interest to a dull speech but it does not add interest to an already highly interesting speech.[15] Just as you cannot get any more water into a jar already filled to the brim, so you cannot create an appreciable amount of interest through the addition of humor to a speech already full of rich but simple language, vivid, concrete examples, and many other interest-evoking features. Also, whether interest is added or not, the addition of humor to speeches does not seem to cause people to remember information from the speeches.[16]

Why use humor in speeches to inform? For one reason, audiences usually appreciate some humor in such speeches, as long as it is appropriate to the occasion and relevant to the subject. Also, the two studies by Gruner indicate that one aspect of source credibility, *character,* is rated more highly in the speaker using humor. In other words, audiences seem to *like* the speaker using humor more than they do the speaker not using humor.

Humorous stimuli are generally divided into relatively harmless humor which has no serious purpose and more biting wit, such as satire, which generally is considered entertainment but, through the addition of irony or satire, has a more important, serious point to make. For instance, Highet has claimed that the purpose of satire is "to cure folly and to punish evil . . . to expose evil to bitter contempt."[17] The creations of the late editorial cartoonist Edmund Duffy, who insisted that "the best cartoons are *against* something," have been described as "more effective than well-aimed brickbats."[18]

Would either harmless humor or satire serve as support for *persuasive* speeches? Several studies have explored this question but have found no evidence that humorous material enhances the persuasiveness of otherwise straightforward speeches.[19] Other studies using oral messages containing *only* satire as support have failed to substantiate satire's effectiveness as a persuasive agent.[20] A study by Berlo and Kumata[21] and one by Gruner[22] found evidence of persuasiveness resulting from satire, but the former used a professionally produced radio program and the latter used printed satires by columnist Art Buchwald. It is difficult to generalize from these to face-to-face speaking situations.

One reason why satire may not be persuasive is that many people fail to perceive the serious persuasive message imbedded in the humorous message.[23] A second reason is that, in order to appreciate satire, one must already be familiar with the facts of the matter. For instance, if you did not already feel that the House Un-American Acivities Committee (HUAC) had committed questionable acts, you could hardly appreciate the Mort Sahl remark: "Every time the Russians throw an American into jail, HUAC retaliates; *they* throw an American into jail!" A third reason is that there is some evidence that people distort and deprecate satire that advocates a position different from their own.[24] Satire and humor are indirect in that double meanings are often involved, and some people miss the intended meaning. Satire is usually sarcastic in that it says one thing but means the opposite. So it is easy not only to be *not* understood, but to be *mis*understood. A beginning speaker is therefore advised to present his message in a straightforward rather than a satiric style.

Activity

Pick a single proposition you strongly believe, one that you would perhaps like to use as a thesis or as a point in a speech to your class (such as "The right to die should not become legal," or "A life insurance program should be begun as soon as possible"). Try to find one example of each of the kinds of supporting material for your proposition: one set of facts and figures, one illustration or set of specific instances, one comparison or contrast, one case of testimony, one definition, and one description (repetition may figure in the totality of assembled materials).

Reasoning

An argument reaches a conclusion and must include a reason for that conclusion. Conclusions may be used to support other conclusions in a chain-like sequence. Eventually, conclusions are going to have to be supported with some form of supporting material, as defined earlier. We now take up the ways of linking conclusions and their supporting materials in order to make whole arguments. These ways of connecting conclusions and their support we call *reasoning*.

Probability in argument

Before detailing the various patterns of reasoning, a brief point on the nature and use of probability in argument is in order. When we give speeches to persuade, we are for the most part talking about probabilities, not certainties. It is useless to argue about verifiable facts. If you and I disagree, for instance, on what Pete Rose's batting average was in 1976, we could simply look it up in the almanac rather than waste time and energy arguing over it. But suppose you and I disagree over whether Lee Harvey Oswald alone assassinated President Kennedy or did it with the help of conspirators? A considerable amount of investigation has been done on just how this event, witnessed by hundreds of people, actually occurred. Even today substantial numbers of people are not satisfied with the conclusions of the Warren Commission. We can only argue that, based on the evidence we do have, it is more or less probable that Oswald alone killed President Kennedy.

We can argue that the Safeguard antiballistic missile system will probably work, but we cannot tell for certain unless we have World War III. We can argue that a negative income tax will more equitably and inexpensively meet the needs of the poor, but the only way we can know for certain is to adopt it and find out.

Here is where communication plays a vital role. We can talk about what probably are the best programs and actions. We must gather evidence and employ our reasoning abilities to demonstrate that these policies and actions will *probably* work or not work. Let us now consider several kinds of reasoning used in human communication.

Generalizing through induction and deduction

Writers dealing with the reasoning process generally differentiate between induction and deduction, though reasoning is a continuous process that involves both.

Induction is the process of reaching a general conclusion or generalization from several examples or cases. This is arguing from the specific to the general. Much of our learning is done inductively. A child touches a hot stove and it hurts, strikes a match and is burned, reaches out to grab the gas heater and is told "No! Hot!" Thus, by specific experiences with hot stimuli, the child learns a generalization: "Things that are hot will hurt you."

By the time we get in high school or college we have inductively developed generalizations about numerous factors. What conclusions come to your mind when you hear the following words: person with long hair, college professor, person over thirty, big business, Republicans, or America? There are many ways you may have developed generalizations about these and other subjects—by listening to one you consider an authority or by scientific investigation, for instance. But you have probably learned inductively. For example, if a person who fishes regularly goes to a lake she has never been to before, where will she fish? There is a good chance her fishing behavior will reflect generalizations formed inductively from long years of fishing at other lakes. These generalizations might include: "Persons who fish near the bank where there are dead trees and stumps will catch fish." This generalization may have been learned from the specific experiences in Figure 6–2. Of course, there are variables other than the locale and conditions of the place where you fish: proper fishing equipment, method of using the equipment, time of day, temperature of the water, and so forth; and the fisherman could have generalizations about all of these factors, too.

Deduction is reasoning from a generalization to the specific instance. You apply your general conclusion concerning a category or family of items to a specific case within that group. For example, you may believe that Frankenstein monster movies are great. This is a generalization concerning a category of movies—those that have Frankenstein in them. Now when you find that a new Frankenstein monster movie is coming to town, you *deduce:* "This particular Frankenstein movie will be great." When we diagram how deductive reasoning works, it looks like Figure 6–3.

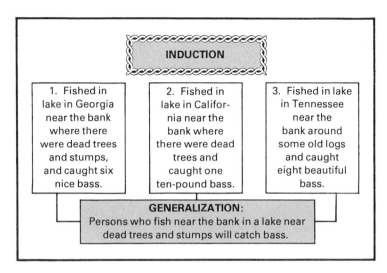

FIGURE 6–2. Inductive reasoning process

Deduction begins where induction leaves off. How did the moviegoer arrive at the generalization concerning Frankenstein movies? Early in life he saw a movie about Frankenstein and enjoyed it. Later he saw a second and considered it great entertain-

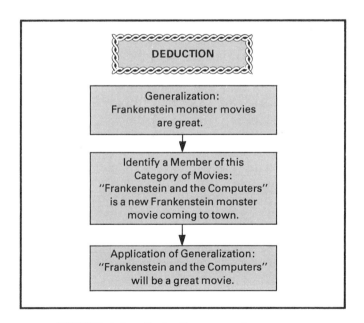

FIGURE 6–3. Deductive reasoning process

ment. Later he attended a third and a fourth. Each experience was fun. So, inductively (through specific experiences) this person *induced* a conclusion about this category of movies. He would not recall every event in every movie; what he remembers is what he generalized about each movie: "I enjoyed it!" Now he has stored in himself this generalization, and when he reads in the newspaper that a new movie, "Frankenstein and the Computers," is coming, he applies that stored conclusion about all Frankenstein shows to this coming attraction. We diagram the entire inductive/deductive process in Figure 6–4. Note how the generalization is both the end of inductive reasoning and the beginning of deductive reasoning. Thus, the generalization is part of both kinds of reasoning.

In speaking, you will use a combination of induction and deduction to argue from what we call "argument from generalization." Chapter 8 on persuasive communication explains how the speaker and listener reason *together* deductively—when a speaker makes a statement about a topic, the listener supplies deductively to himself a conclusion or generalization that will influence his attitude toward the topic.

Argument from causal reasoning

"Accidents do not happen; they are *caused*," reads a safety slogan. Its purpose was to remind people that accidents have definite causes, causes that can be removed or circumvented; they do not just happen due to uncontrollable fate.

Scientists take the view that phenomena are caused. They do not accept the explanation that a particular event simply "happened." It is their task to discover causes and effects, categorize and test them, then publish and teach about them. In the task of isolating causes, the physical scientist has an advantage over the social scientist. The chemist can predict that when hydrogen and oxygen are mixed in certain amounts, their reaction will form water. But an economist can recommend a ten percent income tax surcharge to cause the economy to cool down without knowing what effect the surcharge will actually have because it will be impossible to isolate the effects of the surcharge from other things happening at the same time. A psychologist studying learning theory can explain the results of learning as caused by a reward; a Gestalt psychologist might claim that the learning was caused by sudden insight. Each may have a difficult time *proving* the cause to the other.

You will use argument from causation in your speeches, if only

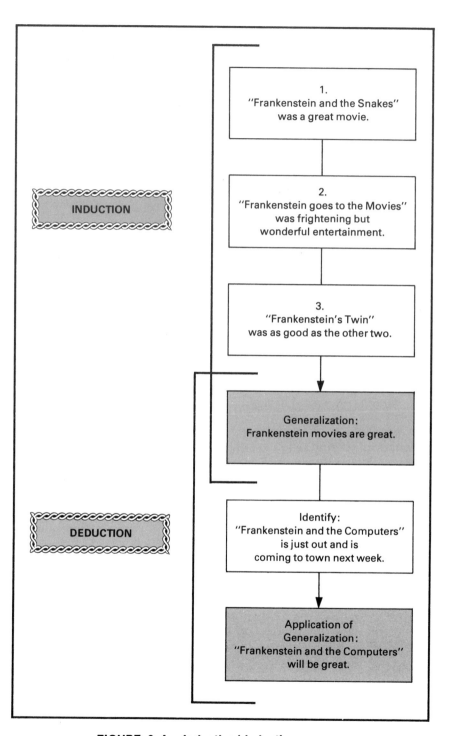

INDUCTION

1.
"Frankenstein and the Snakes"
was a great movie.

2.
"Frankenstein goes to the Movies"
was frightening but
wonderful entertainment.

3.
"Frankenstein's Twin"
was as good as the other two.

Generalization:
Frankenstein movies are great.

DEDUCTION

Identify:
"Frankenstein and the Computers"
is just out and is
coming to town next week.

Application of
Generalization:
"Frankenstein and the Computers"
will be great.

FIGURE 6–4. Inductive/deductive process

because we tend to think in terms of causes and effects. If you speak to solve a problem, you need to show what caused the problem and how removing the causes can remedy the difficulty. There are three general patterns of argument from cause: (1) arguing from causes to effect, (2) arguing from effect to causes, and (3) arguing from effect to effect.

The argument for stricter censorship of books, magazines, television, and movies is often one of *causes to effect*. Proponents of stricter censorship point primarily to the "causes": the large number of violent incidents in television programs; pornographic books on the newsstands; the nudity and immorality of a motion picture. They then argue that these "causes" must have brought about some dangerous *effects* on our young or on the nation as a whole. They may quote the rising crime rate as proof of the "effects."

The *effect to causes* pattern is the reverse of the above. The effect (problem) is explained, and proof or explanation follows. This pattern was used to explain the fall of Rome:[25]

> Alaric's Goths finally poured over the walls of Rome. [Effect.] But it was not that the walls were low. It was that Rome, itself, was low. The sensual life of Pompeii, the orgies on Lake Trasimene, the gradually weakened fibre of a once-disciplined people that reduced them at last to seeking safety in mercenaries and the payment of tribute— all these [causes] brought Rome down.

Let us look at an example of *effect to effect* reasoning. Some teachers of foreign languages argue that students who take foreign languages also do well in English courses. Therefore, they reason, taking a foreign language causes success in English. Opponents argue that one is not a cause of the other, but a common cause is responsible for both. People with high ability and interest in language do well in English and elect to take a foreign language. Thus, students get good grades in English (effect) because of high ability and interest in language (causes), and they enroll in foreign language courses, in which they do well (effect). Such reasoning is actually *effect to cause to effect*.

The idea of causation is, of course, inferential. No one has ever seen "a cause." It is possible to infer that a particular event, or several specific events, caused another event, but the idea remains an inference. The inferential nature of causation renders it more of a verbal or mental abstraction than actual entity. In making these inferences, there are several pitfalls to avoid.

For instance, avoid the fallacy of *post hoc ergo propter hoc* (after this, therefore, because of this). The *post hoc* fallacy assumes that because *A* happens before *B*, *A* must cause *B*. For instance,

Chanticleer the rooster noticed that shortly after his early-morning crowing the sun would rise; he therefore assumed his crowing caused the sun to rise. Since Herbert Hoover was elected president in 1928 and the entire world plunged into a disastrous depression in 1929, President Hoover accumulated most of the blame for the depression. "Night air" was once believed a cause of yellow fever in the tropics, because it was frequently noted that persons coming down with the disease had earlier taken a walk at night (in the mosquito-laden night air).

Avoid the fallacy of attributing a single cause to a single effect, for few effects can be attributed to a single cause, especially in the realm of human actions. Keep in mind the idea of *multiple* causation, emphasized in this chapter by the frequent use of the word "causes." For example, in 1948 the polls predicted the election of Thomas Dewey as president over incumbent Harry Truman. Newspaper headlines of Dewey's victory were prematurely printed. But Truman won and stayed in the White House. What was *the* cause of the unexpected victory? Some people would say the 1948 polls were not scientific. Pollster George Gallup said they stopped polling too soon. Democrats might say that people came to their senses at the last minute. Republicans might say that they were overly optimistic and thus did not work hard enough to get out the vote. Some claim that Truman's last week or two of persuasive personal speaking won enough converts to push him into the victory column. Astrologers could claim that positions of stars and planets prevented a Dewey victory. One columnist thought Dewey's being likened in appearance to "the bridegroom on the wedding cake" caused his defeat. What was *the* cause? Probably several of the above factors, plus others, *combined* to produce the Democratic victory.

Visual aids

Several years ago a group of young Air Force enlisted men were undergoing a five-week training course at Keesler Air Force Base. The course was designed to teach them to become Air Force instructors in their specialties. One day their instructor asked a student to go to the front of the room and describe a circular staircase to the class members, assuming they had never seen one. The student was allowed only to talk; he could not use his hands for gesturing. Predictably he was unable to give a satisfactory description.

A second student was told he could talk and use his hands to describe a circular stairway. He did a better job of describing it, but still fell short. A third student was asked to perform the same task, with the additional advantage that he could use the blackboard. Through talk, gestures, and a crude blackboard drawing, the third student did the best job thus far of describing a circular staircase. A fourth student was told he could use voice, gestures, the blackboard, or anything he found around or under the lectern. Under the lectern he found a ten-inch scale model of a circular staircase (hidden by the instructor) and held it up. Of course, he did the best job of all at "describing" a circular staircase.

Often a visual aid enhances communication. Pictorial material can make ideas vivid and understandable. Some of the most successful speakers have bolstered their ideas with photographs, slides, graphs, charts, models, mockups, and so forth. When the United States learned in 1962 that the Soviet Union was building offensive missile launch sites in Cuba, our ambassador to the United Nations, Adlai E. Stevenson, made a dramatic speech before the Security Council in which he confronted the Russians with this subterfuge. Stevenson's most effective evidence was a set of giant enlargements of aerial photographs showing the missile sites before and after construction had begun.

Visual aids, then, are helpful in developing your ideas, whether your speech is to inform or to persuade. Also, using visual aids gives you "something to do with your hands," a great help if you are nervous!

There has been little scientific research on the effectiveness of using visual aids in speeches to inform. But studies that have been done tend to agree that the use of visual aids in speeches to inform results in higher *retention* of information than speeches without such visual aids.[26] Whether visual aids can enhance the effect of a persuasive speech has yet to be studied directly through experimentation, although professional persuaders have long believed in the effectiveness of visual aids whenever their use seems reasonable.

Visual aids are anything an audience can see and which will help the audience understand or believe the points you want to make. If you have the resources, you can use slides and a slide projector; pictures from books, magazines, or newspapers; or an opaque projector. Even the blackboard, skillfully used, can extend verbal ideas. You will have to plan and practice, however, if you hope to use the blackboard effectively.

Hints in using visual aids

Although the use of visual aids can help you evoke greater interest and understanding, quite the opposite effect is possible. Primarily through lack of advance preparation, many speakers bore and confuse audiences by ineptly handling visual materials. The following

Communication content: the message

suggestions are offered for using visual aids for most effective communication.

1. *Make sure your materials are large enough to be seen.* It is beyond belief how many student speakers expect classmates in the back row to see their 3 x 5 snapshot, their miniature hand-held model, their pencil-drawn chart, and the like. With charts, graphs, and other drawings make your lines dark enough to be seen easily. The only way to determine whether your materials are large enough and distinct enough is to test them. Stand them up from yourself as far away as the farthest audience member will be sitting and see if *you* can see them clearly.

2. *Keep your visuals simple.* Do not crowd many details into any one visual. Focus attention on one point at a time so the audience can follow your argument in an orderly manner. With too many items on a chart this is difficult to achieve.

Simplicity is probably the most persistent and consistent requirement when using audiovisual materials. A recent summary of research in this area reports several studies recommending simplicity of presentation in the use of visuals.[27] For instance, the study states when presenting material graphically that "in all cases, it was noted that the simpler the presentation, the more likely it was to be readily understood and remembered."

Simplicity is apparently even more important than realism. A study of the use of visuals in teaching knot-tying found that "the presence of hands is not important for demonstrating knot-tying but may interfere with learning. The findings suggest that demonstrations should include only the basic elements of what is to be demonstrated."[28] The authors of this monograph point to the reason why simplicity is probably so important:[29]

> the rate of assimilation of material is an important factor to take into account. . . . The data suggest that the information processing system of the human learner is a limited capacity. . . . It may well be that simplicity of presentation is necessary for effective learning because the learner has a limited capacity to utilize information. A source of information has generally a vastly greater capacity for transmitting information that the human learner has for receiving.

3. *Talk to the audience, not the visual aid.* With your chart set up or demonstration material in your hands, you may yield to the temptation to look at the visual aid instead of at the audience. We have all

seen speakers (and professors!) who look at everything but the audience. The tendency to avoid contact with the audience is an adaptation of the urge to escape the source of discomfort. If you must point to a visual aid, look at it and fix your finger or pointer there, then turn and speak directly to the audience.

4. *Don't play with your visual aid.* In your early speeches you will naturally be a bit nervous, but don't do too much with your hands! Speakers who slice the air and jab in concert with each word spoken may lose the audience's attention. The speaker who nervously plays catch with a piece of chalk will probably induce the audience either to count consecutive catches or to wonder when the speaker will miss the chalk. Your audience will reflect as much nervousness as you demonstrate through the process of empathy, so keep your audience comfortable with a minimum of fidgeting.

5. *Show your visual aid only when you are using it.* Bring the aid out only when you are ready for the audience to see it. Then remove it from sight when you are through with it. Don't let an unused visual aid, such as a chart or an intriguing piece of exotic equipment, distract from your point. Keep small objects in a sack or box. Have a blank piece of poster board to place over charts when not using them, or turn them to the wall. Keep large objects covered with a sheet or blanket until time to use them, then cover them again. If people are trying to figure out a chart or odd gadget over in the corner, they won't be paying much attention to what you are saying.

6. *Rehearse realistically with your visuals.* Practice under conditions as close as possible to those under which you will give the actual speech. The history of student speakers giving "visual aids speeches" is rife with failures to communicate because this suggestion was not followed. Charts that were beautifully clear in a dormitory room have turned up hopelessly small for the large classroom where the speech is delivered. Embarrassed speakers have searched endlessly for a place to stand a poster. Speakers who borrow projectors may realize too late that they do not know how to operate the equipment. A small projector may cast pictures too faint to be seen in a room with deficient shades. Students have been amazed and confused when heavy posterboard charts could not be firmly stuck to a dusty blackboard by means of two miniscule scraps of cellophane tape. Many of the same desperate students have then experienced further humiliation (and wasted more time) by trying to stand their drooping charts on the chalk tray. Vacuum-cleaner demonstrations have failed because ancient classroom building wiring delivered less than full voltage.

Another thing to remember is that visuals take time. Student

speakers are often surprised that their five-minute speech takes eight minutes when they add visual aids. Your only protection against these catastrophes is planning and practice.

7. *Remember, projectors present extra hazards.* Most projectors have a motor-driven fan to cool the projection bulb. It makes a steady noise, so remember to speak a little louder. Know how to operate the projector or arrange to have someone else run it. What would happen if your projection bulb burned out in mid-demonstration? Would you have a spare? What about an electrical outlet and extension cord? Have an alternative plan in case the equipment simply will not work.

Is the seating arrangement conducive to projection, or will heads be in the beam? Can the seating arrangement be changed easily, or can you use a projection table that beams above the heads of the audience? A little planning can save trouble and embarrassment.

8. *Do not have the audience pass objects around.* Remember, the strategy of public speaking is to focus everyone's attention on the same point at the same time. To have the audience pass items around is to compete with your own visual aids!

Several years ago a student gave a classroom speech on the Hawaiian Islands, which she had recently visited. She wanted to impress the audience with the beauty of the islands, so she handed a stack of snapshots to the left and another stack to the right. All during her speech people were looking at different pictures, some oohing and ahing over the hula girls, others buzzing, turning, squeaking their chairs, dropping pictures and picking them up. The speaker's flustered expression showed she realized how little attention she was getting from the audience.

It is all right to use handouts when each person receives a copy. Students have duplicated and handed out small copies of their charts instead of showing one large one. An additional advantage from this practice is that the audience can carry away the information for future reference.

Although misused visual aids can create unexpected problems, properly used aids can improve communication tremendously. Consider the following summary statement by a trio of audiovisual experts:[30]

> Graphics continue to occupy an increasingly important place in your world today. They provide assistance in building more effective communication, particularly when masses of otherwise complicated statistical data or relationships are involved.
> Both teachers and students need to be familiar with the principal characteristics and unique advantages of using cartoons, posters, graphs, charts, and diagrams. . . . Very often . . . students increase their own ability to communicate effectively and economically—helping others to "see what they mean."

Summary

William Shakespeare wrote that "The play's the thing." In speaking, the content of the speech is the thing. The unskilled speaker belabors the audience with assertions and generalizations of his own. The skilled speaker certainly presents his or her own original assertions, generalizations, ideas, and observations. The audience expects that. But the skilled speaker will back up these ideas with the kind of material detailed in this chapter: facts, statistics, and examples. This speaker will make his or her points come alive with illustrations, description, apt visual aids, and perhaps some humor.

QUESTIONS FOR THOUGHT
AND DISCUSSION
CHAPTER 6

1. In what ways are books indexed in most libraries?
2. If you wanted to find all books on crime in your school library, where would you look first?

3. What information do you get from a periodical index?
4. What index covers government publications?
5. What purposes do supporting materials achieve in your communication?
6. In what way can repetition be both a supporting material and an important dimension of effective word choice?
7. What is inductive reasoning? Give an example.
8. What form does deductive reasoning often take in a speech?
9. How can a visual aid be used effectively?
10. Explain how causal reasoning is used in a speech you find in *Vital Speeches of the Day.*

EXERCISES · ASSIGNMENTS | CHAPTER 6

1. Go to the magazine *Vital Speeches of the Day* or to *Representative American Speeches* and find examples of the following kinds of supporting materials in several recent speeches: factual information, examples, comparison, testimony, restatement, definition, description, and humor.
2. Using a topic of your own choosing, demonstrate how you could use each of the supporting materials listed above to explain or prove your ideas.
3. Find one example in a book or magazine of a good visual aid. Find an example of a poorly designed visual aid. Be prepared to explain to the class the strength and weakness of each.
4. Using microfilm in your library, look through the *New York Times* and the local newspaper for the day you were born. Note the prices, fashions, news items, and so on.
5. Which indexes cover journals in your major field of study?
6. Find the main national and regional organizations in your major field of study. What journals do these organizations sponsor and publish?
7. Identify four indexes that cover subjects of interest to you.
8. Investigate recent speeches made by the president of the United States by looking them up in the *New York Times Index.*

ENDNOTES | Chapter 6

1. James C. McCroskey, "A Summary of Experimental Research on the Effects of Evidence in Persuasive Communication," *Quarterly Journal of Speech,* 55 (April 1969): 169–176.
2. Charles Schalliol, "The Strangler," *Winning Orations* (Detroit: Interstate Oratorical Association, 1967), p. 55. Reprinted by permission of the Interstate Oratorical Association.
3. McCroskey, *op. cit.,* p. 175.

4. Eric Johnston, "Hollywood: America's Travelling Salesman," *Vital Speeches,* 23, no. 18 (June 1, 1957): 573–574.

5. Schalliol, *op. cit.,* p. 54.

6. *Quote,* 32 (June 16, 1957): 2.

7. Edith G. Painter, quoted in *Parade* (June 15, 1969): 6.

8. Lewis C. Henry, ed., *Best Quotations for All Occasions* (New York: Fawcett, 1955).

9. Ralph Zimmerman, "Mingled Blood," *Winning Orations* (Evanston, Ill.: Interstate Oratorical Association, 1956). Reprinted by permission of the Interstate Oratorical Association.

10. Untitled report to the faculty of the Franklin College of Arts and Sciences at Athens, Georgia, May 19, 1976.

11. J. R. Furnas, "—And Sudden Death," *Reader's Digest,* October 1966: 154. Printed by permission of *Reader's Digest.*

12. *Ibid.,* p. 156.

13. Donald C. Bryant and Karl R. Wallace, *Fundamentals of Public Speaking,* 3rd ed. (New York: Appleton-Century-Crofts, 1960), p. 110.

14. John F. Wilson and Carroll C. Arnold, *Public Speaking as a Liberal Art,* 2nd ed. (Boston: Allyn and Bacon, 1968), p. 100.

15. Charles R. Gruner, "Effects of Humor on Speaker Ethos and Audience Information Gain," *Journal of Communication,* 17 (September 1967): 228–233; Charles R. Gruner, "The Effect of Humor in Dull and Interesting Informative Speeches," *Central States Speech Journal,* 21 (Fall 1970): 160–166.

16. Charles R. Gruner, "Effects of Humor on Speaker Ethos," *op. cit;* "The Effect of Humor in Dull and Interesting Informative Speeches," *op. cit.;* also Donald E. Kilpela, "An Experimental Study of Effects of Humor on Persuasion," (Detroit: Wayne State University, unpublished M. A. thesis, 1962); Pat M. Taylor, "Research Report No. 51: The Effectiveness of Humor in Informative Speaking," *Central States Speech Journal,* 15 (November 1964): 295–296; and Allan J. Kennedy, "An Experimental Study of the Effect of Humorous Message Content upon Ethos and Persuasiveness," paper read at Speech Communication Association Convention, New Orleans, December 28, 1970. A study by John D. Gibb, "An Experimental Comparison of the Humorous Lecture and the Nonhumorous Lecture in Informative Speaking," (Salt Lake City: University of Utah, unpublished M. A. thesis, 1964) *did* find a significant difference in retention favoring the inclusion of humor in informative material, but used a speech prepared upon a standardized test as its basis (instead of vice versa) and also may have been contaminated by differences in time of day that subjects were exposed to his experimental messages.

17. Gilbert Highet, *The Anatomy of Satire* (Princeton: Princeton University Press, 1962), p. 156.

18. "Milestones," *Time,* 80 (September 21, 1962): 65.

19. P. E. Lull, "The Effects of Humor in Persuasive Speech," *Speech Monographs,* 7 (1940): 287–298; Gary F. Pokorny and Charles R. Gruner, "An Experimental Study of Satire Used as Support in a Persuasive Speech," *Western Speech,* 33 (Summer 1969): 204–211; Paul D. Brandes, "The Persuasiveness of Varying Types of Humor," paper read at the Speech Communication Association Convention, New Orleans, December 28, 1970; Kilpela, *op. cit.;* and Kennedy, *op. cit.*

20. Charles R. Gruner, "An Experimental Study of Satire as Persuasion," *Speech Monographs,* 32 (June, 1965): 140–154; "A Further Study of Satire as Persuasion," *Speech Monographs,* 33 (June 1966): 184–185.

21. David K. Berlo and Kideya Kumata, "The Investigator: The Impact of a Satirical Radio Drama," *Journalism Quarterly,* 44 (1956): 287–298.

22. Charles R. Gruner, "An Experimental Study of Editorial Satire as Persuasion," *Journalism Quarterly,* 44 (Winter 1967): 727–730.

23. *Ibid.;* Gruner, "An Experimental Study . . .", *op. cit.*

24. E. Cooper and M. Jahoda, "The Evasion of Propaganda: How Prejudiced People Respond to Anti-Prejudice Propaganda," *Journal of Psychology,* 23 (1947): 15–25; Gerald R. Miller and Paula Bacon, "Open-and-Closed-Mindedness and Recognition of Visual Humor" (East Lansing: Michigan State University, mimeographed, 1970).

25. Jenkin Lloyd Jones, "Who Is Tampering with the Soul of America?" *Vital Speeches of the Day,* 28 (January 1, 1962): 180.

26. For instance, Franklin H. Knower, David Phillips, and Fern Koeppel, "Studies in Listening to Informative Speaking," *Journal of Abnormal and Social Psychology,* 40 (1945): 82–88; Joan H. Ulrich, "An Experimental Study of the Acquisition of Information from Three Types of Recorded Television Presentations," *Speech Monographs,* 24 (March 1957): 39–45; Alejandro J. Casambre, *The Effects of Certain Variables in Informative Speaking on Listener Comprehension* (Columbus: Ohio State University, Ph. D. dissertation, 1962).

27. Mary C. McCormick, et al., *Research and Theory Related to Audiovisual Information Transmission,* Interim Report of U.S. Department of Health, Education, and Welfare, Office of Education Contract No. 3-20-003 (Salt Lake City: University of Utah, Bureau of Educational Research, 1964).

28. *Ibid.,* p. 256.

29. *Ibid.,* p. 2.111.

30. James W. Brown, Richard B. Lewis, and Fred F. Harcleroad, *A-V Instruction: Methods and Materials,* 2nd ed. (New York: McGraw-Hill, 1964), p. 386.

7

ONE-TO-ONE COMMUNICATION

7

We have explained what the communication process is and how major components in the process affect it. Now we are ready to see communication put into practice in major forms of one-to-one, one-to-many, and some-to-many communication.

Conversation

Appropriately, we begin with the kind of communication we do more than any other: conversation. In the study by Samovar and his colleagues referred to in Chapter 1, adults reported that of waking hours spent in communication activities, 24.1 percent were devoted to conversation as compared to one-way speaking (15.2 percent) or reading (11.1 percent).[1]

The quality of our conversations may be something else. NBC broadcaster Edwin Newman observes that "Most conversation these days is as pleasing to the ear as a Flash Frozen Wonder Dinner is to the palate."[2] He attributes this partly to overuse of canned phrases like "would you believe?" "just for openers," and "what have you done for me lately," which pass for intellectual exchange between average Americans. The insertion of "y'know" every few words is often cited as a symptom of our conversational sterility. If Emerson was right when he said "The best of life is conversation," then we need to give it our attention.

Conversational habits are difficult to change, but, like other speech communication forms, conversations have some basic principles that should be followed.

Kinds of conversations

Conversations vary from roommates or married couples discussing the day's events to social affairs where almost nobody knows anyone else, from sitting next to a total stranger on an airplane to basking in the intimacy of an inner circle of friends in a student lounge.

Conversation, then, is oral communication between two or more people. Its purposes are as varied as its situations. Many have grown up believing Benjamin Franklin's statement that "the chief ends of conversation are to inform, or to be informed, to please, or to persuade."

Franklin also admonished, "Speak not but what may benefit others or yourself; avoid trifling conversation." This ideal fails to consider another purpose stressed by modern scholars in interpersonal communication, that "the primary function of conversation . . . is to make contact with other people,"[3] or "when one studies the social relations of living beings, one is struck by the unquenchable need among individuals of every species to enter into contact with one another."[4] In an age dominated by technological achievements, the need to relate to fellow human beings increases. Writer John Hersey, analyzing youth of the late sixties and early seventies, made a case that young people need interpersonal encounters. He maintained that youth had committed itself to a war on greed and that "relating and helping are more important than making it. . . . 'Relating' really means being able to give and take."[5] So besides informing, being informed, pleasing, persuading, or being persuaded, another purpose of conversation is therapy.

Preparation for conversation

Some would say that everything we do is preparation for conversation, so we need do nothing special; others admonish us to prepare for conversations as we prepare for more formal speeches. The resolution lies with the individual situation. If you should have occasion to chat informally with a professor or a possible future employer, you would want to reveal yourself as a knowledgeable, clear, and interesting person. Many believe with Publilius Syrus that "conversation is the image of the mind. As the man is, so is his talk." If you are perceived through conversation, then training and practice should follow. A famous conversationalist, Samuel Johnson, recommended four rules: "There must in the first place be knowledge; there must be materials. In the second place there must be a command of words; in the third place there must be imagination, to place things in such views as they are not commonly seen in; and in the fourth place there must be presence of mind, and a resolution that is not to be overcome by failure."

You are accumulating knowledge every day. Unfortunately, you demonstrate your possession of it mostly by writing answers on examinations. You should have already discovered that you learn many kinds of materials better, express them clearer, and retain them longer if you have explained the materials to someone else. To teach is to learn. Seize every opportunity you have to express in your own words what you've learned.

Broaden your horizons by cultivating new reading habits with current news and opinion magazines. These new friends will not only help increase your store of materials for conversations but will help increase your vocabulary. Read with a pencil, jotting down unfamiliar words to look up, and use them if possible within the next week. (Of course, we know that the writing vocabulary is different from our conversational language, so common sense should prevail here.)

Approach conversation with a positive, alert, and accepting attitude. Your mind will be sharper, you will be clearer in organization, word choice, and wit, if you sustain a confident and open perspective. To be sure, your conversational partner may be in different moods at different times. Adjust to them accordingly. Today you may be the listener to the latest funny story or news making the rounds; tomorrow you may be the raconteur.

Activity

The current motto of a well-known news magazine is, *"Time makes everything more interesting—including you."* Explain the double meaning here.

We conclude this section with a basic principle for good conversation paraphrased from the most published authority on conversation in the speech communication field, Robert Oliver: *Determine the purpose of each conversation and adapt to that purpose.*[6]

Elements of good conversation

You could easily compose your own list of elements you consider important to good conversation. Though the list might seem endless, four elements would keep reappearing in one form or another: empathy, clarity, appropriateness, and interest.

Empathy. This concept is perhaps more important in interpersonal association. *Empathy* is the ability to feel "in" with another person, or to walk in his moccasins, as the old Indian saying goes. In conversation it is particularly important to get outside ourselves and try to see what it's like from someone else's perspective. Indeed, if the necessity for contact is as important as noted at the beginning of this chapter, developing this ability is of paramount importance.

Regarded as a social perception skill, empathy suggests the ability to predict accurately the verbal responses of a fellow conversationalist.[7] The ability to anticipate reactions, to judge moods, to be sensitive to a style of thinking, and to appreciate word choice can improve listening—and speaking—in conversation.

Clarity. Developing empathy will create the proper climate for *clarity* —to be understood with ease. One way to achieve this is to use a communication concept called the *feedforward,* which should help counteract misunderstanding.[8] Borrowed from the field of cybernetics, feedforward is made up of goals, expectancies, and contingencies.

The *feedforward goal* is the anticipated end result of the conversation. For example, if you want to talk to an instructor about getting a course grade changed, the goal would be a favorable change.

Feedforward expectancy is the listener's likely reaction at important points in your message. For example, your expectancies in the grade change situation might include: (1) the instructor is glad to check the final exam to see if an error was made; (2) the instructor accepts the fact that a student has the right to ask about a grade; (3) the instructor is defensive about his or her judgment being questioned.

Finally, *feedforward contingencies* are alternate message adaptations to use according to how your listener responds. For example, if the instructor is neutral, you would probably ask to see the final exam, noting that you wrote on the back of one page and thought the instructor might have missed it, that you realize it is tiring to read thirty essay exams, and so on. Anticipating reactions with a format in mind should clarify your approach to such conversations.

Appropriateness. If you have ever had the experience of riding all day with an avid geology major who "converses" tirelessly about synclines and anticlines or the magic of plate tectonics when you cannot tell lava from granite, you probably had a very long day. Or, consider the dinner party experience when a usually successful conversationalist tries to engage her male dinner partner on several topics, but to no avail. When she is about to turn away, he tugs at her arm saying, "Try me on leather."

The informality of most conversations allows great flexibility, but finding an appropriate topic is the key to starting a successful exchange, especially in a group. Politics, sports, "you'll never believe what happened to me today" stories, and everybody's old reliable—the weather—provide possible openers and potential grist for the conversation mill.

If you are in a one-to-one situation, you have many prompters to choose among. As students, information on classes, major, or home town would not be unusual icebreakers. If new on campus, what is this person's impression of the town and campus? Find some common ground as soon as possible—a mutual acquaintance, a musical group you have both heard, a state championship basketball game you both saw. Common ground will lead you into an appropriate topic both of you can explore in depth.

Interest. Psychologist William James declared, "What holds attention determines action." This principle has often been used to guide speakers in keeping audience attention. We suggest a corollary for good conversation: what holds attention contributes to good conversation.

The word that rings a familiar bell brings you warmly into the conversation. "Did someone mention my home town?" you ask, and you are "hooked" for as long as the group will listen. If monotony sets in, change the subject to keep the interchange flowing. High marks will be gained if the subject is novel. The local telecaster who includes in the newscast the oddity (man bites dog) knows the audience enjoys a shift from the routine.

And when you tell the story, avoid starting with "Did you hear the one about . . . ?" Relate the actual happening, keep the events orderly, build suspense holding the punch line as a surprise, and if it is supposed to be funny and no one laughs, do not try to explain it. Resolve to rehearse your story the next time. What seems to be an effortlessly told story is probably the result of serious preparation and several rehearsals.

If you have assimilated the information thus far in this chapter, you should be able to:

1. Start a conversation appropriately with a generalization, as about the weather, a common experience, or the like.
2. Maintain a conversation on a topic discovered to be of mutual interest.

3. Exchange interesting information with empathy and clarity.

The interview

When you are employed in business, industry, government, or the professions, one-to-one communication continues to be as important as it was in school. One form it will take will be more structured conversation, which we call the *interview*.

What is an interview?

The *interview* is purposeful verbal or nonverbal interaction between two or more people directed to a goal held by one or both of the parties involved. This interaction between individuals involves the exchange of information.

It is helpful in understanding the purpose of the interview to distinguish among three types of information: empirical data, logical data, and attitudinal data. *Empirical data* are usually looked on as the interviewer's first responsibility. The interviewer needs to secure "facts." A person's hair is uncombed, the job applicant bites his or her nails or has a speech impediment—these are examples of empirical data. *Logical data* refer not to the specific, isolated observations we have just mentioned, but to conclusions about relationships between observable events. Finally, at the far end of the information continuum, we have *attitudinal data.* This type of information provides subjective insight into a person's values and attitudes. In any interview, it is the accumulation of bits of information that eventually provides the basis for reaching a decision. To do the job well the interviewer must be able to ascertain the difference between objective and subjective information. Both types of information are important, but failure to realize what type of information you are receiving can lead to an unsatisfactory decision.

While all interviews involve exchange of information, the type of information exchanged and the way it is exchanged depend on the particular type of interview. Further insight as to what an interview is can be gained by considering the major types of interviews.

Types of interviews

Employment interviews. The employment interview is probably the most well-known type of interview. In attempting to inject consistency and predictability into selection decisions, businesses have developed devices such as self-descriptive personality inventories, weighted biographical questionnaires, and aptitude tests. However, by far the most common method for selecting employees is face-to-face confrontation. As A. H. Maslow puts it, the selection interview is the process by which an applicant population that presumably contains a proportion of the people with the skills and the abilities required by the employer is separated out from a universe of workers.[9]

The ultimate purpose of the selection interview is to give the interviewer sufficient information to see if the applicant meets requirements for the job; and the applicant should gain sufficient information about the job to see if he or she is interested in accepting if the job is offered. While this process is primarily informative, many selection interviews include elements of persuasion on the part of one or both parties. Competition for competent employees has sometimes become so intense that selection interviewers have to "sell" their companies. Similarly, most college students learn how to present the relevant information about themselves persuasively.

In the majority of cases, the selection interview focuses on the training, experience, and skills of the interviewee. However, in hiring a person for a key position, the interviewer's questions attempt to reveal attitudes, reaction patterns, and personality structure of the applicant. Also, the setting of the interview may vary depending on the position that is open. For example, in most interviews one person interviews the candidate. If the position is important, however, the company may employ what is termed the *serial interview*. This process involves a series of interviews of a single applicant by several interviewers. Some organizations use *panel interview* and have the applicant meet several interviewers at the same time.

The interview is crucial in employment because it obtains information from the applicant and provides information to the applicant. While studies do not always reveal the interview to be a statistically valid method of selecting the best person for the job, it is nonetheless valuable when correctly employed.

You may be interested in knowing that company representatives have cited the negative factors listed in Table 7–1 as reasons for rejecting an applicant.[10]

Performance appraisal interviews. Many organizations have supervisors conduct performance appraisal interviews with their subordinates. The objectives of any appraisal system may be classified as either administrative or motivational. Objectives such as salary increases, promotion, transfer, and demotion fall into the adminis-

One-to-one communication

TABLE 7–1. *Effective Speaking: A Complete Course,* by Arthur N. Kruger, © 1970 by Litton Educational Publishing, Inc. Reprinted by permission of D. Van Nostrand Company.

A. ATTITUDES, BEARING, PERSONALITY	B. INTERESTS, MOTIVATION, APTITUDES, SKILLS
1. Poor personal appearance—haircut, not clean shaven, poor dress or loud or unsuitably dressed.	1. Inability to express himself clearly—poor voice, diction, grammar.
2. Overbearing—overaggressive—conceited, "superiority complex"—"know-it-all."	2. Lack of planning for career—no purposes and goals.
3. Lack of confidence and poise nervousness—ill at ease.	3. Lack of interest and enthusiasm—passive, indifferent.
4. Unwilling to start at the bottom—expects too much too soon.	4. Failure to participate in activities.
5. Makes excuses—evasiveness—hedges on unfavorable factors in record.	5. Overemphasis on money—interested only in best dollar value.
6. Lack of tact.	6. Poor scholastic record—just got by.
7. Lack of maturity.	7. Marked dislike for school work.
8. Lack of courtesy—ill mannered.	8. Loafs during vacations—lakeside pleasures.
9. Condemnation of past employers.	9. Lack of knowledge of field of specialization.
10. Lack of social understanding.	10. Sloppy application blank.
11. Lack of vitality.	11. Merely shopping around.
12. Fails to look interviewer in the eye.	12. Wants job only for short time.
13. Limp, fishy handshake.	13. No interest in company or its product.
14. Lack of appreciation of the value of experience.	14. Unwillingness to go where we send him.
15. Late to interview without good reason.	15. Narrow interests.
16. Failure to express appreciation for interviewer's time.	16. Spends much time in movies.
17. Indecision.	17. Poor handling of personal finance.
18. Little sense of humor.	18. Inability to take criticism.
19. Parents make decisions for.	19. Radical ideas.
20. Emphasis on whom he knows.	20. Never heard of company.
21. Low moral standards.	21. Asks no questions about the job.
22. Lazy.	22. Indefinite response to questions.
23. Cynical.	23. No intellectual curiosity—doesn't read much, little interest in current affairs.
24. Intolerant—strong prejudices.	
25. Unhappy married life.	
26. Friction with parents.	
27. High pressure type.	

The interview

Activity

Sign up for a job or interview with the placement service of your school. If you are nearing graduation, you are probably already doing this. If you are not nearing graduation, look for chances to interview for summer jobs—at camps, recreational areas, and so on. Be alert for notices of these on school bulletin boards. Practice the attitudes, bearing, personality attributes opposite those noted above; try to not show the lack of interests, motivations, aptitudes, or skills in Table 7–1. Evaluate the experience in your own mind. Did you "go over?"

---

trative category. Self-development, improved performance, and increased job knowledge are classified as motivational.

While both kinds of objectives are an integral part of any organization, recent management trends indicate that administrative objectives should be kept separate from the motivational objectives.[11] Administrative objectives and motivational objectives are basically incompatible. Appraisal interviews that attempt to achieve both objectives are likely to fail. For example, an interview attempting to cover both improved work performance and a salary appraisal will essentially become a salary discussion. Because of this incompatibility, we shall be concerned only with the motivational objectives of the performance appraisal interview.

In seeking motivational objectives, the performance appraisal interview should examine past performance in planning for future action and direction. Richards maintains that the modern approach to performance appraisal is to view it as a problem in communication, so the goal is establishment of a constructive communication relationship between the supervisor and the employee.[12] The way job performance information is communicated to the subordinate is critical. One study makes the following suggestions for conducting the performance appraisal interview:[13]

1. Criticism has a negative effect on achievement of goals.
2. Praise has little effect one way or the other.
3. Performance improves most when specific goals are established.
4. Defensiveness resulting from critical appraisal produces inferior performance.

5. Coaching should be a day-to-day, not a once-a-year, activity.
6. Mutual goal setting, not criticism, improves performance.
7. Interviews designed primarily to improve a person's performance should not at the same time weigh salary or promotion.
8. Participation by the employee in the goal-setting procedure helps produce favorable results.

In many cases the subordinate may enter the appraisal interview feeling defensive or suspicious, the idea of defending past performance foremost in mind. To achieve effective communication, it is essential that the superior relinquish authoritarian attitudes. Properly employed, the performance appraisal interview provides a method of feeding back to an employee an evaluation of his or her past performance, and it provides a time for mutual goal setting in regard to the employee's future.

Activity

Did you ever participate in a performance appraisal interview? Boy Scouts do this regularly. Each Scout must have a "personal growth agreement conference," sometimes called a "Scoutmaster's conference," before he can advance a rank. Contact a Scoutmaster in your area and ask what are the most important features and outcomes of such conferences. Check what you find out with the eight points listed in the text.

Consulting interviews. The consulting interview is normally used for problem solving. This type of interview is used to arrive at decisions and to implement them. In this type of communication, ideas are appraised and evaluated by the two or more persons involved. For example, a brain surgeon may call in a colleague for consultation about a rare operation. A company's management may call in an outside consultant for advice in regard to a specific problem.

The purpose of the consulting interview is to analyze a problem through the advice of one or more persons. It occurs when a person or organization is in a situation that requires special information not at one's ordinary disposal. In some cases, a consulting interview may be held simply to verify or check a decision.

Counseling interviews. The counseling interview is normally for matters of a personal nature. It is distinct from the appraisal interview in that it is concerned with job satisfaction and life adjustment rather than job performance or productivity. A study dealing with the counseling functions of companies revealed that 87 percent of the companies surveyed engaged in counseling activities of some type with their employees.[14]

More and more organizations have realized the need for a specialist with the background to deal with employees' personal problems. Large organizations employ several types of counseling specialists, from lawyers who provide financial and legal advice to psychiatrists who can discuss emotional problems. These specialists are needed when an employee's problem reaches the critical stage. Many employee problems can be dealt with by an alert, sensitive supervisor before they reach the critical stage and have to be referred to a specialist.

Most counseling interviews involve either personal problems outside the job—such as family or financial difficulties—or job-related problems that stem from circumstances the employee faces on the job. In the area of personal problems, the supervisor can serve as a "listening post" and can make recommendations to the employee. The supervisor can also serve as a liaison between the employee and higher management, for example, suggesting to management that an employee be given a two-week leave of absence to devote full attention to a personal problem that is hampering his or her work.

Many of the problems an employee faces are related directly to the environment at work. The effective supervisor builds a climate of mutual trust with employees. Likert points out that counseling needs to be done in such a way that in activities and relationships with the company, the employee, in light of his or her background, values, and expectations, will view the experience as supportive and will maintain a sense of personal worth and importance.[15] The supervisor conducting the counseling interview is usually trying to maintain a delicate balance between individual needs and organization goals.

Correction interviews. The correction interview is at times referred to as a *disciplinary interview* or *reprimand*. This type of interview is used to inform the employee that he or she has so violated organizational standards that corrective action has been taken. This type of interview is primarily to give information and to impress on the employee that certain conduct or action is not acceptable.

It is imperative that the correction message be communicated clearly. There can be no double-talk or hidden meanings. The situation puts the interviewee under a great deal of stress, and the tendency to distort the message is probably greater than in any other type of interview. The interviewer needs to make sure the interviewee understands the seriousness of the action but also to minimize the natural hostility the employee will feel.

Grievance interviews. To maintain an effective communication system within an organization, management needs to provide the opportunity for employees to complain about circumstances or conditions they do not like. The grievance interview provides valuable feedback to management on areas such as operations, production standards, and employee morale. Organization leaders need to make sure that the channels of communication are well established and that employees know of their options when presenting a grievance. In addition to the employee's immediate supervisor, other channels should be open in case the employee feels the supervisor is unable to resolve the grievance.

The employee approaching the grievance interview usually feels somewhat aggressive and hostile. Therefore, in the first stage of the grievance interview, the employee usually describes the grievance vividly. As this outburst often serves as an emotional release, it is necessary for this aggressive communication to take place before the supervisor can get down to the real problem at hand. Sometimes this opportunity for emotional release contributes to resolution of the grievance. In any case there is little the supervisor can do except be an empathic listener until the outburst is over. Often the supervisor finds that the grievance first given by the employee is not the real grievance. Only skillful questioning and accurate listening by the supervisor will bring out the real grievance. In all cases the employee must feel that he or she has received a fair hearing. When the grievance is valid, prompt action should be taken to resolve the problem.

Exit interview. The exit interview takes place when an employee leaves an organization. The purpose of this type of interview is to provide an opportunity for management to show its appreciation of the service rendered by the departing employee and perhaps to enable the employee to leave the organization with a positive or at least a neutral attitude toward the organization. The exit interview may reveal the reasons why the employee is leaving the organization, which is critical feedback for most organizations.

The major problem in exit interviews is that employees are frequently reluctant to reveal their real reasons for leaving. For example, an aircraft company reported a 40 percent difference between the reasons given at the time of quitting and the reasons given two to eleven months later. The reasons for quitting given during the exit interview were beyond the control of the company. However, the reasons given by the same people eleven months later were related to internal company problems, such as low pay, slow advancement, and poor supervision. Interestingly enough, the study also reported that 67 percent of those persons who had been out of the company seven months indicated they would be willing to return if a suitable offer were made.[16] Getting the truth in an exit interview is indeed a difficult task.

Sales interviews. Although almost any persuasive interview could be considered a sales interview, we usually think in terms of the professional salesman (or saleswoman) when we think of the sales interview. Salesmen face a variety of situations. Some make several calls a day, while others may spend several days with one potential customer. Some salesmen seek an immediate decision, while others have long-term goals. Although salesmen face a variety of circumstances, a sales interview usually contains the following stages:

1. Establishment of rapport.
2. Dissemination of information.
3. Establishment of the need.
4. Secure the decision to buy.

The first three stages are similar to other types of interviews. However, the fourth stage, commonly called the *closing,* is unique to the sales interview and deserves additional attention.

There are two major types of "closes," termed the "hard sell" and the "soft sell." The *hard sell* is characterized by the insistent salesman who refuses to leave until the sale is made. The salesman is aggressive, presents an abundance of "factual" information, and is dynamic in presentation of material. Until recent years this approach was widely used. This sales approach is now thought to make many people defensive. Gibb maintains that during defense arousal conditions, the listener is prevented from concentrating on the message and, in some cases, may even distort the message received.[17]

The trend in closing during the past fifteen years has been in the direction of the *soft sell.* Salesmen employing the "soft sell" are much less likely to put people on the defensive. When using this approach in the sales interview, the salesman does not attempt to out-talk or force the customer to buy. Instead, the salesman pays

One-to-one communication

careful attention to verbal and nonverbal feedback; he or she attempts to get the customer involved in the sales interview by getting the customer to participate vocally. The advantage of the soft sell over the hard sell has been perceived by most major companies, and as a result more and more sales interviews are in this mode.

Having considered the major types of interviews we are ready to examine some interpersonal communication skills that facilitate effective interviewing. We consider interview structure, styles of interviewing and, finally, the interviewer as a participant and an observer.

Interview structure

Any interview has a beginning, a middle, and an end. The beginning of the interview is the place to establish a workable relationship between interviewer and interviewee. The interviewer attempts to put the interviewee at ease both mentally and physically. The interviewer also gains the attention and interest of the interviewee and eventually provides a clear statement of purpose for the rest of the interview.

The middle, or body, of the interview comprises the major portion of the interview. Here the interviewer attempts to get across the major points the interviewee is to understand. The interviewer needs to be extremely responsive to the interviewee and to the circumstances of the interview. The interviewer who is responsive to the situation gets points across by a combination of making declarative statements, asking questions, and listening.

The end, or close, of the interview should appropriately terminate the interview. There are several ways this can be accomplished. In some situations, it may be appropriate to summarize the important items covered during the interview. Sometimes it is also necessary to discuss necessary action to be taken on each point by either person. On many occasions, one interview is not enough to reach a decision, and when this is the case the interviewer will establish the bases for further conversation in closing the interview. In all cases, the interviewer should indicate appreciation of the interviewee's time and cooperation during the close of the interview.

Critical moments. The structure of the interview is affected by critical moments in each phase. Critical moments are characterized by turning points that can lead either toward or away from the objective of the interview. Critical moments may come about in the following ways: (1) by a response or attitude in the *interviewee* as he or she reacts to the purpose of the interview and the circumstances that led to it and the interviewee's feelings and attitudes toward the interviewer's personality and responses; (2) by the responses of feeling and attitude in the *interviewer;* and (3) by responses stimulated by circumstances over which the interviewer and the interviewee have little or no control.

Let us briefly examine the impact of critical moments on the structure of the interview. In the beginning stage, a critical moment may occur in an initial feeling of uncertainty or awkwardness on the part of the interviewee. The way this critical moment is dealt with largely determines when the interviewer can move to the next stage. The body of the interview usually contains several critical moments. For example, an officer in a large company experiences a critical moment in interviewing an employee to find out the reason for absenteeism. It soon becomes apparent that absenteeism is due to marital problems. As the employee discusses the problems in his marriage he suddenly stops and exclaims, "I can't talk about it any more." At this critical moment the interviewer shifts the interview to a discussion of referral sources for help with family stress, and the interviewer points out that one of the purposes of this service is to make it easier for the employee to attend work regularly.

Critical moments are also connected with the close of the interview. In some cases resistance to agreement becomes so great that the critical moment develops and the best procedure is for the interviewer to close the interview. In other cases, agreement is reached after much argument and discussion. The interviewer needs to realize that a critical moment has arrived and close the interview. Additional discussion after that critical moment may cause the interviewee to change his or her mind, and agreement may be lost. Indeed, much of the interviewer's ability rests upon skill in recognizing critical moments and skill in responding adequately to each critical moment before moving to the next stage of the interview.

Styles of interviewing

Interview style refers to the pattern of communication and interaction used in the interview. Authorities in the field identify three interview styles: directed, nondirective, and the stress interview.

The directed interview. The directed interview is by far the most common type. The format is highly structured. The interview is carefully planned, following a series of direct questions—in many cases following a preprinted checklist to record responses. Since

One-to-one communication

the format is so highly structured, the directive style is the most efficient when the interview needs to be completed within a time limit. This style can best be employed for securing a maximum amount of factual information in a relatively short time. Since the directed interview is so controlled, interaction is limited, and subtle aspects of the interviewee's personality are inaccessible using this style.

The nondirective interview. The nondirective style was developed primarily by Carl Rogers for his "client-centered" therapy interview. Using this style, the interviewer does not take responsibility for deciding what questions will be asked, what subjects will be discussed, or even what should be the solution to the interviewee's problem. Topics, goals, and solutions are viewed as the responsibility of the interviewee. The function of the interviewer when using this style is to establish an atmosphere of acceptance that provides enough security that the interviewee can assume the responsibility of finding solutions to his or her own problems.

The nondirective style is most useful in consulting and problem-solving interviews. In addition to creating a permissive atmosphere, the interviewer attempts to clarify, sharpen, and reflect the ideas the interviewee expresses. This procedure helps the interviewee "hear" what he or she is saying, and in some cases the interviewee will modify his or her ideas and attitudes. This style of interviewing is extremely useful for experienced interviewers to employ.

The nondirective interview cannot be used in all situations, since many interviewees feel uneasy in the unstructured setting. The interviewer may also be tempted to inject too many of his or her own opinions and feelings. Although the nondirective style of interviewing is extremely effective in many situations, its major limitation is that it is much more time consuming than the directed interview.

The stress interview. Usually an interviewer tries to eliminate stress during an interview. However, in some situations the interviewer deliberately introduces stress into the interview by interrupting frequently or by adopting a hostile attitude. Some interviewers introduce stress by remaining silent for long periods of time. In some cases, the interview is planned so that physical discomfort (such as a waitress spilling water on the interviewee's lap) causes stress. Some feel the stress interview is helpful when the interviewee is being considered for a job that will entail stressful conditions.

Obviously, the stress method is best employed by a skillful and experienced interviewer under carefully controlled conditions. The major advantage of this style is that it enables the interviewer to compare the interviewee's behavior under normal conditions with behavior under conditions of stress. The stress style should never be used when the interviewee appears extremely uneasy.

In summarizing the three styles, we should point out that while there may be occasions when one style of interviewing will be used throughout the interview, most interviewers use a combination of the three styles in a single interview. The interviewer shifts from one style to another to accomplish different purposes in the interview.

Interviewer as participant

The effective interviewer functions in a dual capacity as a *participant* and as an *observer*. Let us first consider the interviewer as a participant and examine the interpersonal actions and behavior that make an interview effective. There have been several attempts to classify the communication and interaction that occur in interviews. One of the earliest attempts was by anthropologist E. D. Chapple, who used what he termed the Interaction Chronograph to analyze the content and timing of interview sequences.[18] Later, R. F. Berdie established a method for categorizing statements made by interviewers.[19] More recently, Daniel Sydiaha employed interaction process categories, originally established by Bales for group interaction analysis, to analyze samples of interview conversation.[20] Much work in analyzing interview behavior has also been done by the National Training Laboratories at Bethel, Maine. Although these systems use different terminology, there appears to be agreement on what kinds of communication facilitate interviews. Two major categories are considered here: establishing rapport and communicating appropriate responses.

Establishing rapport. Several factors help the interviewer establish good rapport with the interviewee:

1. *Create the proper climate.* Since the interview is usually conducted on the interviewer's home ground, the interviewer needs to create a climate of permissiveness and support that enables the interviewee to speak freely and fully. The interviewer must inform the interviewee of the ground rules and in most cases of what is expected during the interview.
2. *Permit the release of emotion.* Emotional tension in the interviewee may hamper the interview. If the interviewee has a grievance, it is usually a good idea to provide the opportunity to release emotion at the beginning. After the interviewee is permitted to "speak

his mind," a more intimate relationship can be established between the interviewer and the interviewee.

3. *Reduce tension.* Sometimes permitting the interviewee to release emotion only intensifies the problem. In such a situation the interviewer should attempt to *reduce* tension by changing the subject or by attempting to minimize the conflict. The interviewer takes this approach when the interview becomes so highly charged that an emotional explosion is likely and further interviewing would be impossible.

4. *Encourage participation.* Interaction during the interview is facilitated when the interviewee is encouraged by an interviewer who is receptive to ideas and suggestions of the interviewee. The interviewee can be encouraged by the interviewer's attitude of undivided attention and receptive facial expression.

Communicating appropriate responses. Whether the purpose of the interview is to discuss job performance, counsel a problem employee, or evaluate a job applicant, certain types of responses are helpful in meeting the goals of the interview.

1. *Initiating communication.* In most interviews the interviewer has the responsibility for starting the interview and seeing that it moves toward some specific goal. Under this category the interviewer defines the problem, moves the conversation to a new topic, and guides the interview to a conclusion.

2. *Seeking information.* The majority of time in most interviews is spent seeking information. The interviewer seeks facts, opinions, or attitudes of the interviewee and observes the interviewee's appearance and actions such as eye contact, expression, and other physical characteristics.

3. *Giving information.* The interviewer needs to provide information in order that the interviewee gain an appreciation of the context. It may be necessary to provide the interviewee with factual information and with the opinions and reactions of others.

4. *Providing feedback.* The interviewer must provide feedback so the interviewee knows that statements are not being distorted or misunderstood. Thus, the interviewer rephrases the main ideas and repeats them to the interviewee. Feedback lets the interviewee "hear" what he or she has been saying and helps develop insight into personal ideals and attitudes. The major function of feedback is in reducing erroneous ideas the

listener may be forming because of what he thought he heard.

5. *Summarizing major ideas and main conclusions.* At strategic points during the interview and especially toward the end, the interviewer should summarize the main trends of the interview by pinpointing major conclusions and outlining actions to be taken. This is an extremely important function. Many times two people leave an interview with two completely different ideas about the outcome. Not to summarize the major points of the interview is to lose control of the interview and to permit the interviewee to interpret rather freely what took place.

Interviewer as observer

The interviewer must also listen attentively and observe carefully the actions of the interviewee. It is in this that, in addition to being a participant, the interviewer is an observer in the interview process.

Listening. The ability to listen attentively and perceptively is essential to the interviewer. Effective listening requires concentration on relevant behavior, meaningful perception of what we hear, and accurate assimilation of all we have heard. Let us briefly examine each of these areas. For a more complete discussion of listening and suggestions for improving listening, see Chapter 3.

First, the interviewer must be able to concentrate on relevant behavior in the interview. A good listener develops the ability to separate desired information from "noise." Any interview has a considerable amount of noise that needs to be separated from important information. The interviewee may make statements that supply little or no information, so concentration is required.

Second, the interviewer needs a meaningful perception of what is said. The interviewer and the interviewee need a shared frame of reference. The interviewer needs to understand what values and assumptions the interviewee has. Most of us bring our own values and assumptions to an interview. These pre-sets block out certain kinds of information and may greatly alter the meaning of what we say. In brief, what one *expects* to hear affects what one *does* hear. The interviewer needs to be aware of pre-sets in order to compensate for them when necessary.

Third, the interviewer must assimilate accurately the pieces of information received. Individual statements accurately perceived mean little until the listener puts these statements together into some logical whole. The real test of a good listener is not ability to grasp individual statements but ability to capture the whole idea the interviewee is attempting to communicate.

Observing nonverbal cues. Much information in the interview is provided by what we call nonverbal communication, such as eye contact, facial expression, body movements, and voice characteristics. In some situations, we communicate more through nonverbal communication than we do through verbal communication. In addition to perceiving nonverbal communication as a means of information in itself, the interviewer may want to see if nonverbal communication correlates with verbal information.

Recording information. Since the presence of a tape recorder often inhibits the interviewee, the interviewer should record important information by taking notes. Sometimes the interviewer will have a preprinted form for note-taking, especially in employment interviews. In addition to securing information for use later, note-taking can serve other important purposes. For example, when an employee brings a grievance to a supervisor, the fact that the supervisor is interested enough to take notes does a lot to establish rapport with the interviewee.

The interview

Summary

Conversation is oral communication between two or more people. The purpose of conversation may be to inform or to be informed, to please, to persuade, or the purpose may be therapeutic. To be prepared for conversation, you need knowledge, command of words, imagination, and confidence. Since each conversation is different, you should determine the purpose and adapt to it.

The elements of good conversation are empathy, clarity, appropriateness and interest.

Interviewing involves interaction between two or more persons. Although there are many different types of interviews, the basic interpersonal skills remain the same for all types. An interview, like any form of communication, has a beginning, a middle, and an end. There are critical moments in each stage of an interview; how the interviewer controls these critical moments determines whether the interview accomplishes its objective. The directed, nondirective, and stress interviews are three distinct styles, but most interviews combine elements of all three styles.

Perception plays an important role in the interview situation. Interviewer and interviewee need to understand each other's frame of reference for meaningful communication to take place.

Finally, the interviewer is both participant and observer. Certain kinds of responses facilitate the interview process, and the primary responsibility for interview success or failure rests with the interviewer. However, the same interpersonal communication skills are needed by the interviewee.

QUESTIONS FOR THOUGHT AND DISCUSSION
CHAPTER 7

1. How can Samuel Johnson's four rules for improving conversation be applied to communication you might experience on campus?
2. What role does empathy play in good conversation?
3. How can you make conversation more interesting?
4. What do the interviewer and the interviewee attempt to achieve in an employment interview?
5. How could a teacher use the performance appraisal interview?
6. How could you employ the consulting interview in one of your courses?
7. What are the characteristics of an effective and responsible sales interview?

8. If you are the interviewer, what should you attempt to accomplish in the introduction and in the conclusion of an interview?

9. Compare a directed interview with a nondirective interview.

10. What is meant by "creating the proper climate" in an interview?

EXERCISES · ASSIGNMENTS | CHAPTER 7

1. Without revealing that you are involved in an assignment, make a special effort to engage a friend in a conversation and apply principles suggested in this chapter. Later, write down your evaluation of what went well and what you still need to improve.

2. While in a group, note the quality of the conversation you hear; later, write down your evaluation of the different participants.

3. Visit a local store and shop for a product. Observe carefully how the salesperson performs. Prepare an evaluation of how well he or she did and be prepared to discuss this experience in class.

4. Interview a personnel manager in a local business to determine what role interviewing plays in that company. Be certain you apply sound principles of interviewing during your discussion of interviewing!

5. Conduct an interview with a parent or friend in which you attempt to persuade the interviewee to take a particular position, buy a product, or the like.

6. Plan and carry out an interview of some official in your school or community. (This assignment may be part of the process of gathering information for another speaking assignment in this course.) If you are speaking on an educational problem, interview a faculty member or someone in administration. Sample topics are honor systems, pass-fail grading, open admissions, and curriculum changes. If you are speaking on a local governmental issue, interview the mayor, a city councilor, or the county commissioners. Sample topics are traffic regulation, zoning, and city-county consolidation. In this interview it will be important to *establish rapport*, communicate appropriate responses, listen well, observe nonverbal cues, and record information.

ENDNOTES | Chapter 7

1. Larry A. Samovar, Robert D. Brooks, and Richard E. Porter, "A Survey of Adult Communication Activities," *Journal of Communication,* 19 (December 1969): 305–306.

2. Edwin Newman, *Strictly Speaking,* quoted in Leslie Hanscon, "English: Language Demise Haunts Newsman," *Atlanta Journal and Constitution,* October 13, 1974, p. 20-B.

3. Gerald R. Miller and Mark Steinberg, *Between People* (Chicago: Science Research Associates, 1975), p. 329.

4. G. Revesz, *The Origins and Prehistory of Language,* translated by J. Butler (New York: Philosophical Library, 1956), p. 136.

5. Benjamin DeMott, "Looking Back on the Seventies," *Atlantic,* March 1971: 60.

6. Robert T. Oliver and Rupert L. Cortright, *Effective Speech,* 5th ed. (New York: Holt, Rinehart & Winston, 1970), p. 99. See also Oliver, *Conversation: The Development and Expression of Personality* (Springfield, Ill.: Charles C. Thomas, 1961).

7. Miller and Steinberg, *op. cit.,* pp. 169–170; see also, Frank E. X. Dance and Carl E. Larson, *Speech Communication, Concepts and Behavior* (New York: Holt, Rinehart, and Winston, 1972), pp. 146–147.

8. Linda Heun and Richard Heun, *Developing Skills for Human Interaction* (Columbus: Charles E. Merrill, 1975), pp. 202–209.

9. A. H. Maslow, "Measurement in the Selection and Development Process," in *Behavioral Science Research in Industrial Relations,* Industrial Relations Monographs No. 21 (New York: Industrial Relations Counsellors, 1962), pp. 121–148.

10. Arthur N. Kruger, *Effective Speaking: A Complete Course* (New York: Litton Educational Publishing, 1970), p. 606.

11. For excellent discussions of management theory to satisfy the higher level needs of employees, see Douglas McGregor, *The Human Side of Enterprise* (New York: McGraw-Hill, 1960); and A. H. Maslow, *Eupschian Psychology* (Homewood, Ill.: Dorsey Press, 1965).

12. K. E. Richards, "Some New Insights into Performance Appraisal," *Personnel,* 37 (1960): 28.

13. H. H. Meyer, E. Kay, and J. R. French, "Split Roles in Performance Appraisal," *Harvard Business Review* (January–February 1965): 129.

14. H. Eilbirt, "A Study of Current Counselling Practices in Industry," *Journal of Business,* 31 (1958): 28–37.

15. Rensis Likert, *New Patterns of Management* (New York: McGraw-Hill, 1961), p. 101.

16. Wayne L. McNaughton, "Attitudes of Ex-Employees at Intervals after Quitting," *Personnel Journal,* 35 (1956): 61–63.

17. Jack R. Gibb, "Defensive Communication," *ETC.: A Review of General Semantics,* 22 (June 1965): 221.

18. E. D. Chapple, "The Interaction Chronograph: Its Evolution and Present Application," *Personnel,* 25 (1949): 295–307.

19. R. F. Berdie, "A Program of Counseling Interview Research," *Educational and Psychological Measurement,* 18 (1958): 255–274.

20. Daniel Sydiaha, "Bales' Interaction Process Analysis of Personnel Selection Interviews," *Journal of Applied Psychology,* 45 (1961): 393–401.

SANTINA CURRAN
GOOD DAY! "SUPER SHOPPER"

8 ⌐」

ONE-TO-MANY COMMUNICATION: INFORMING

Daily we seek information on such subjects as birth control, reducing personal expenses, or what a college major in food science is about. This chapter deals with communication that instructs. To inform other people is to share understanding of or information on a topic. Of course, you must first understand the material, and then you need to know ways to communicate your knowledge to other people.

In classes and in the community you will be called upon to clarify or explain concepts, issues, and procedures. Roger P. Wilcox of the General Motors Institute concluded:[1]

> It does not matter whether we are in education, science, industry, business, the professions, the government, or the armed services. As we become proficient in our area of specialization or assume positions of increased responsibility, we shall be called on more and more to convey to others information we have acquired. We may be asked to report on problems, designs, methods, systems, procedures, layouts, policies, or materials. And we may be asked to present our report to supervisors, associates at our own level, or subordinates. In different situations we may be asked to report to all three.

Adapting to an audience

We communicate with many people every day. Often these situations require some strategy for "reaching" an audience. If you have an appointment with a professor to explain why you had to miss the exam, would you not consider before your appointment what the professor's knowledge of your problem may be and how he or she will probably react to your message?

This example shows that much communication to *inform* may also plan to persuade. Many companies employ speakers who provide informational programs to social and civic groups on the companies' products or services; these speakers are also expected to create good will and thus more customers. In 1971 a CBS television program, "The Selling of the Pentagon," explored how the United States Department of Defense disseminated information favorable to that department. Senator J. William Fulbright wrote *The Pentagon Propaganda Machine* that described the "military information apparatus." Part of that apparatus is a program of public speaking on "informative subjects." As the *Army Information Officers' Guide* says, "There is no substitute for personal contact in public relations. . . . The most effective way to tell the Army's story is through the Army's public speaking program."

So we must keep in mind that much "informative" communication's ultimate goal is to persuade, but we also believe there is a need for speaking primarily designed to instruct.

Influence of audience on subject and purpose

The nature of your audience will help determine your subject, your purpose, and your treatment of the subject. Audience analysis, then, must begin the moment you decide to speak, and must continue during the preparation and actual delivery of the speech. The reason for communication is to produce some effect upon an audience. This chapter emphasizes speaking in the hope of *enlightening* an audience.

You may learn whom you will speak to before you know your topic. If in speech communication class, you know you will be speaking to your classmates and the instructor. If you are invited to address the local garden club, you know you will speak to gardening enthusiasts. If you are elected to a state or national office, you could be heard by a much larger audience. Your challenge is to select a subject and purpose that suit the audience and your own convictions. What you say and how you say it contributes, in an informative speech, to the audience's reception, understanding, and retention of your materials.

Sometimes, of course, personal conviction requires you to talk on a topic regardless of audience interest. The task becomes how to treat the subject in order to be as meaningful as possible. For example, your listeners may initially have little interest in hearing about some aspect of foreign relations; however, by linking their personal safety and economic welfare to the world community, you may win an attentive response to your ideas.

Common sense tells us that information presented in an appealing way will be learned more efficiently, and scientific studies tend to support this conclusion. With some exceptions, experimental studies in speech tend to support the contention that speakers using what experts call "good delivery" convey more information than do those using "poor delivery." A wealth of educational research testifies to the fact that *meaningfulness* (appeal based on utility) is a large factor in learning and retaining information:[2]

> There is a large body of convincing evidence which shows how poorly students retain information which is not related to significant problems and which has a low degree of perceived internal relationship. In contrast, results obtained with well-organized and meaningful materials may show actual gain rather than decrease with a passage of time. Meaningful learning may suffer only slightly with a passage of time. Ability to apply principles, solve problems, and interpret experimental data are examples of the kind of activities which are very resistant to the ravages of the forgetting process.

As a speaker, you need to provide your listeners with a rationale that will make them want to learn. You must get the audience interested in your subject. Do this in the introduction of your speech and maintain that motivation throughout the speech. The way to do this is through good delivery, clear organization, visual aids, and specific and meaningful information.

You will often be speaking to your speech classmates, who are bright and well educated; most are also in school to learn. Students can become interested in just about any topic. You may have to use imagination and creativity, but you can probably come up with a strategy that will create interest and relate your subject meaningfully to classmates. Ask yourself: "Of what use would this information be to my audience? How can I make it interesting? Would they find it interesting because it can save them money, make them more successful in careers, or give them a sense of personal fulfillment?

Adapting to audience information levels

Because informative communication involves explaining and clarifying, try to discover what the audience knows about your subject.
At the end of your speech the audience should have learned something they didn't know before.

If you fail to anticipate the audience's understanding and information level, you could miss the mark in one of two ways. First, you
may tell the audience what they already know. An example of giving
an "informative" speech that did not inform occurred in a speech
class at the University of Nebraska. The student speaker stepped
to the front of the room and displayed an object he identified as "a
football." Then he said something like this: "Today I'd like to tell
you about the game of football. It is played by two teams of eleven
players each. The football field is one hundred yards long, and the
object is to get this ball past the goal at one end of the field. When
you do this you score what is called a 'touchdown,' and it is worth
six points. . . ." The speaker was presenting this "information" to
rabid fans of the Nebraska Cornhuskers. Aghast at the poor response to his speech, the student protested that he had given a
"speech to inform," since it contained information. The instructor
pointed out that a "speech to inform" is not defined solely by what a
speech *contains,* but by what *effect* it has on the *audience.* His
speech provided the audience with no information it did not already
know.

On the other hand, you may fail to inform your audience because of a second reason; you may assume the audience knows
more about the topic than they do. To inform, you must build upon
the audience's existing understanding and take them through a
learning experience.

An interesting example of a speech that assumed too much
knowledge of the audience was given by a student who explained
very carefully how to make the "short club" bid in bridge—advantages of the bid, conditions under which it should be made, and how
one's partner should respond to it. At the end of her speech, the
instructor asked for a show of hands from those who knew enough
about the game of bridge to play it. Two hands went up. Asked if
they knew how to make the "short club" bid, both responded "yes."
Thus, the student's speech can be classified as what some people
call, "Clear Only If Known" (or COIK): the speech was unintelligible
to those who did not play bridge. The speech did not *inform,* despite the fact that it contained information.

How can you discover how much an audience knows about
your subject? Opportunity to investigate a potential audience varies

with each speaking engagement. A candidate for governor will probably hire people to travel in the state investigating what people know and want to know about potential issues in the campaign. But most of us work without benefit of organizations and large budgets. If you are going to talk to a local group, ask specific questions about that organization: Who belongs to this group? How many usually attend? What topics are usually discussed? What will the audience expect from your speech? What subjects will or will not interest this audience? How much do they know about certain subjects?

There are other sources you can use. Look in official publications published or supported by the sponsoring group to find what its general philosophy is. Browse through local newspapers for information relating to the group's community involvement. Determine what experience it has had with a topic. On some occasions you can use questionnaires or polls to measure the audience's knowledge.

A few specific audience characteristics may provide more insight into an audience's understanding and knowledge of speech topics.

Age. The age of people in your audience may indicate something of their interests or experience with a particular topic. Twelve-year-olds can be as excited about proposed playground improvements as their parents, but for different reasons. Persons over eighteen will be more concerned about marriage or choosing a career than those much younger. Age can indicate knowledge, level of formal education, and experience.

Sex. Audience reaction may also be influenced by the sex of the audience members, but sex roles are changing, so be cautious in generalizing about males and females. Traditionally, more men than women have been involved with auto mechanics, but you would be wise not to make a blanket assumption. Study the particular audience you will address before jumping to conclusions. You may discover, for example, that a group of men are not interested in stock market investments, and a group of women are.

Level of education. The general level of education is an important characteristic of an audience. Education usually improves a person's resources for making comparisons, drawing conclusions, and possibly making informed decisions about general topics. A well-educated person can probably understand new materials and ideas more easily than an audience with little background knowledge to draw on.

Knowledge of the subject. Listeners' knowledge of your subject is a key factor in communication. The audience's knowledge of the subject, for example, will determine where you begin your discussion. If the audience is unfamiliar with an issue, you will have to devote the introduction to an orientation. Do not move too quickly into the main body of your speech until you are certain the audience understands the meaning of technical terms and knows clearly what you plan to do. These are critical choices which only an alert speaker can make when analyzing an audience.

Personal experience. Knowledge of a field may not depend solely on formal education. Personal experiences are also important. To experience something is to have an excellent opportunity to understand it. To speak before persons who have had wide experience with the subject is a real challenge. Such listeners will soon perceive whether you have a practical understanding of the subject. In such a circumstance be willing to learn from your audience.

Activity

Make a list of things a speaker, speaking on any subject, would have to do in order to adapt to *you* as an audience member; for instance, "The speaker would have to speak on a topic of interest to me."

Next, write down a list of things a speaker on some *specific topic*—such as photography, mountaineering, or life in outer space—would have to do in order to adapt to you as an audience member.

Studying the occasion

Study carefully the circumstances surrounding your speaking occasion to identify the purpose of the meeting and the role you are expected to perform. Why are the people meeting? What topics are appropriate for the occasion? What physical arrangements will influence your speech? What is the size of the room, the quality of the acoustics, and the amount of lighting? Is there a reliable public address system? How will seating arrangements affect what you do? Will the audience be filled with children?

When analyzing the occasion, investigate what requirements and choices it places on you in your role as speaker. Some characteristics of each occasion can only be discovered by studying that particular event.

On the other hand, some stock questions you can ask will help prepare you for nearly any occasion: What led to this situation? Who were those involved in bringing it about? What are the key issues? What self-interests are involved? What groups are concerned? To what extent are religious, economic, political, and social forces at work? What expectations are inherent to this occasion? Must I be formal or informal in dress, use of words, and delivery? Are there physical factors to consider? How will the time of day and amount of time allotted for the speech affect my speech? What is the purpose of the meeting? What role am I expected to play? What do my personal convictions require me to do?

Creating a speech

To reach its full potential as a means of communication, a speech should be an *original* discourse prepared by the speaker for a particular purpose, audience, and occasion. At least since Antiphon wrote speeches for his Greek customers centuries ago persons have written speeches for other speakers. Today a team of ghostwriters aids the President of the United States. An important business executive is likely to have a speechwriter on call. When practical, however, you should prepare your own original discourse. (Of course, you should always prepare your own assignments in speech class, because the purpose is to help *you* develop the art of speechmaking.)

What is an original speech? An original speech is created by a speaker for a specific purpose from reliable materials obtained through personal experience and careful research.

Inventing the speech

Suppose you are a senior in college and a teacher in your former high school asks you to return and inform a senior high school class on what a college education is all about. You agree to speak and begin to consider what to say.

You check the *Reader's Guide to Periodical Literature* for general articles and the *Education Index* for more specialized materials. One article is ten pages in the *Reader's Digest* on "What a College Education Is Really Like." Your first reaction is, "Man, I'll duplicate that article and simply present it orally to the audience!" After looking over the article you discover it does not contain many points *you* have learned to be true and important about college life today. Also, you know the teacher wanted to hear from *you*. Thus, you wisely decide not to steal someone else's work but to write your own speech.

After gathering your thoughts and carefully searching the library, you have materials from two general sources: (1) your own knowledge based on nearly four years at college and (2) quotations, statistics, and ideas from books and articles. Your task now is to select materials from both sources and categorize them in clusters to be most interesting and informative to your high school audience. We illustrate this *process of invention* in Table 8–1, in which the items represent the ideas and supporting materials you will use to write your speech.

Outlining the ideas. The ideas listed in Table 8–1 are the raw data you will use to create your own discourse to a particular high school

TABLE 8–1. Collecting ideas from two sources for writing a speech on your college experience.

MATERIALS FROM YOUR OWN EXPERIENCE	MATERIALS FROM BOOKS, ARTICLES, INTERVIEWS
1. Cost	a. Data on academic requirements
2. Study time required	b. Income of college graduates relative to nongraduates
3. Food	
4. Housing	c. Available jobs for college graduates
5. Library	
6. Advising	d. Expectations of parents
7. Intercollegiate sports	e. Kinds of colleges
8. Being away from home	f. College rankings in different fields
9. Social life	
10. New friends	g. Adjustments college students have to make
11. Variety of styles of life	
12. Flunking out	h. Effects of peer pressure
13. Teachers	i. Tests that measure interests and abilities
14. Advisers	
15. Normal course load	j. How to study
16. Part-time jobs	k. Cost of college education
17. Scholarships	l. Role of "minor sports" in college
18. Loans	
19. Intramural sports	
20. Fraternities and sororities	
21. Religion	

class. Notice that the items are listed in no particular order. You must now choose topics from both columns that cluster around *main ideas* or *conclusions.*

Look through the items and determine which ones relate to each other; for example, several items relate to entertainment. You can try to develop this theme by taking from column 1 items 7, 9, 10, 19, and 20, and from column 2 item I. The six items will probably remind you of other items that fit the category but that you had not thought of until now. This kind of analysis is an aid to thinking of additional ideas, for example, rock concerts, college drama productions, or a favorite "hang-out" for students.

When put in outline form, the categorization process results in the core of a theme for your speech. The outline may look like this:

I. College life can be great fun.
   A. Those who enjoy sports will find much to watch and do.
      1. Colleges often have active intercollegiate competition in a number of sports. (Item 7 in column 1)
      2. "Minor sports" provide a wide variety of choices (Item I)
      3. Intramural sports offer each student an opportunity to participate. (Item 19)
   B. Social life gives the student an opportunity to escape the grind of classes and develop as a total person.
      1. There are many opportunities to meet new friends. (Item 10)
      2. Fraternities and sororities are active on some campuses. (Item 20)
      3. Churches sponsor many social activities. (Item 21)
      4. The student union offers a wide variety of social activities. (Thought of at last minute)
   C. Special events are provided for the entire campus community. (All were recalled after the above items were listed.)
      1. Rock concerts abound!
      2. The Drama Department puts on several plays each year.
      3. There is an active ballet troupe on campus.
      4. All students are invited to join or listen to the Glee Club.
      5. The orchestra provides an opportunity for advanced students of music to play and for all students to listen.

After studying the remaining items in Table 8–1, you discover a second theme:

II. College life is difficult for some people.
    A. Many students have financial difficulties.
        1. Cost of college is great. (Items 1 and k)
        2. Many students have to work part-time. (Item 16)
        3. Some students have to assume the responsibility for a loan. (Item 18)
        4. The number of scholarships is decreasing. (Item 17)
    B. College life requires personal adjustments.
        1. High school students often lack discipline necessary for studying. (Items 2, 12, and j)
        2. Being away from home for the first time is difficult for some students just out of high school. (Items 8 and g)
        3. The wide variety of life styles may conflict with your values. (Item 11)
        4. Expectations of parents and peers are not always easy to handle. (Items d and h)
        5. Apathy of some teachers and advisors can make college life difficult. (Items 13 and 14)

These selections for the two points above (college can be fun and college can be difficult) are initial choices. You may discover you need more information, so you return to the library or you interview the dean of students.

After making initial choices, you should consider ways of improving the organization and development of the topic from your outline. For example, does "High school students often lack discipline necessary for studying" (II, B, 1) fit best where it is? You must ask other questions: Can I cover all this in the thirty minutes allotted? If I were a high school senior again, are these the topics I would want to hear about? Is any of this already known to the audience? Have I presented a fair picture of college life?

By drawing from your own experiences and from reliable library sources, you can *invent* an original speech that is informative and appropriate for your audience.

Organizing a speech

Importance of organization

In communicating your thoughts to others, "message structure is an important element in effective speech."[3] To learn effectively, whether from a speech to inform or from printed material, the information should be well-organized. An impressively large number of studies in the field of learning psychology demonstrate that human beings learn well-organized material more easily than they learn disorganized material:[4]

> Schooling is more efficient when learning is well-organized and there is a psychologically sound basis for materials, methods, and processes of instruction. So strong is the tendency to learn in an organized way that even when material is presented in a disorganized or relatively meaningless fashion, pupils tend to develop an organization of their own.

The effect on immediate recall of organization in speeches to inform has not been studied as often, and the findings are somewhat less consistent. However, two studies by Thompson have found that well-organized speeches do produce greater immediate recall of information than do poorly organized ones.[5] Perhaps an even more important point is made in the excellent summary of the literature by Petrie: "Several studies suggest that generalizations or major ideas are better comprehended and retained than are details or specifics and that the better developed the generalizations are, the better they will be retained."[6]

This provides support for the belief that informative speaking should be limited to messages that depend more on the learning of a few general principles than on remembering a lot of specific details. For instance, the person who gives a speech on "Twenty-two helpful hints on wintertime driving" will be lucky indeed if the audience can later remember an average of four or five of these hints. But if the speech were based on two main ideas, the speaker ought to be able to design it so the audience will understand, believe, and remember the two generalizations:

1. Successful operation of your auto in winter requires putting it in top condition by professionals.
2. Winter driving requires more caution and patience than summer driving.

Choosing a purpose

Decide what your subject will be and what specific purpose you want to achieve. For example, your general subject could be interviewing, and your specific purpose could be to tell the speech communication class how to conduct a successful job interview.

The challenge now is to organize your materials successfully. These materials are from your own experience and from your library search. Organizing is part of creating a speech, as we have seen. How can you best organize the materials to explain the topic clearly? What *parts* of this topic must be developed if the audience is to understand the whole subject? How can you best arrange individual parts so they will be interesting and informative?

Discussion

Plato's statement that "every discourse, like a living creature, should be so put together that it has its own body and lacks neither head nor feet, middle nor extremities, all composed in such a way that they suit both each other and the whole"[7] is still a good fundamental principle. It is a good idea to begin work on the body, or discussion, before developing the introduction and conclusion.

There are numerous ways to develop the main body of your speech. You may find it useful to combine several types of organization. Look for imaginative ways of organizing a speech from the nature of the subject and audience. The principles discussed below are to be considered fundamental to more creative procedures.

Chronological order. The main body of your speech can be discussed on the basis of time. Some topics lend themselves to such development. Time is particularly suitable when presenting historical events, narrative themes, and descriptions of processes. You might report the chronological events of a vacation you have taken, the involvement of the United States in World War II, or how to operate a Polaroid camera for instance:

  I. First, I will teach you how to load the camera.
  II. Second, I will teach you how to take a well-focused picture.
  III. Lastly, I will show you how to develop and permatize the picture.

Topical order. Your main subject may also be partitioned on the basis of subtopics. Some topics are traditionally thought of in terms of categories. Football is discussed in relation to offense and defense. Government is divided into local, state, and federal. Fine arts include music, sculpture, and drama. Look for natural divisions and show how they relate to the whole; for instance:

Thesis: One should know a country's customs, for then one would know much about that country.

    I. Some customs have a legal basis.
   II. Some customs have a religious basis.
  III. Some customs are imported from other countries.
     etc.

Spatial order. In some instances, you may want to divide and discuss your ideas on the basis of geography or other physical dimensions. For example, a library could be discussed by its different subject sections, reading rooms, and other facilities. A modern moon missile might be explained by discussions of the launching pad, nose cone, the fuel cells, and so on. Or some other physical entity can be explained in this manner:

Thesis: Today I will explain the structure of the egg you may have had for breakfast this morning, from outside to inside.

    I. Just inside the outer shell is the outer shell membrane with an air space at one end.
   II. The white and yolk are separated by the vittelline membrane; two Chalaza protrude from the yolk through this membrane.
  III. Inside the yolk and attached to the vittelline membrane is the egg's germ cell.

Problem–solution order. This arrangement is most often used in a *persuasive* speech; the speaker argues that a problem exists, that the proposed solution will solve the problem, and that this solution is the best and most practical solution available (see Chapter 9). But the plan can also be used *to inform,* usually in the kind of informative speech that explains how a problem *in the past* was solved. For instance, consider the following arrangement for a speech to inform:

Thesis: The present city lake at Pinckneyville, Illinois, solved a crucial community problem and has had other advantages.

    I. Prior to 1948, Pinckneyville suffered from water supply shortages four out of the past previous five years.
   II. Since the new city lake was built by constructing a dam between Deerslide and Little Deerslide hills, the town has never had a water problem.

III. In addition to providing an abundant and inexpensive water supply, the lake provides recreation for people in the area.

Chapter 9, on persuasive speaking, takes up the use of this organizational pattern for persuasive speeches.

Cause–effect order. Some topics are appropriately organized on the basis of cause and effect. If you were informing an audience on poverty's impact on society, you could study how poverty causes children of poor families to receive inadequate pre-school training. In an informative speech your basic goal is to explain this happening. Often, however, you will go beyond just informing to advocate something be done about it, a process explored in Chapter 9.

When using causation as a means of organizing your thoughts, there are many possible patterns. You can first discuss the effect and later take up the cause, for example, beginning with the problem of crime (effect), then moving to the causes of crime.

Induction or deduction. As defined in Chapter 5, induction reasons from specific instances to form a generalization. In the informative speech, inductive reasoning is useful to explain how a principle, attitude, or belief was reached. For example, you could show inductively how some people have developed attitudes toward people of Irish descent in the United States by pointing out how specific life experiences led to those attitudes.

When developing your message deductively, begin by stating your conclusion early. As a method of outlining an informative speech a chief service of deduction is to define a concept or to show how others have defined an issue. This process can enlighten an audience on how attitudes and perceptions work in society. Often, however, like problem–solution and cause–effect order, when you use induction and deduction as means of organizing communication, you go beyond just informing to persuading.

Introduction

The introduction, like the conclusion, of your speech is an important part and should be carefully conceived to stand alone, while at the same time should be closely connected to the main body of your address. Studies reveal that information discussed early and that discussed late in a speech are often better remembered than information given nearer the middle.[8] There is no clear agreement among researchers whether one should place strongest arguments first or last,[9] so you probably should mention your best materials early and again late in the speech.

The introduction should make a few points the speaker considers primary. Ideas are retained significantly better when the introduction directs the audience's attention to particular parts of a speech.[10] Studies indicate, however, that when one reveals early the content that opposes a position an audience holds strongly, the audience may be less apt to respond favorably than when not told in the introduction what is to follow.[11] On the other hand, if the speaker is well liked by the listeners, and if the audience feels this is reciprocated, the speaker may be well advised to state his or her intentions in the introduction.[12]

So there is more than one way of introducing a speech. It seems clear to say, however, that in an informative speech you will do well (1) to win the attention of the audience with a quotation, vivid statement or story, reference to the immediate occasion, humorous illustration, rhetorical question, comparison, or the like; (2) to express concern and good will for your audience and indicate knowledge of their interests; (3) to orient the audience to your topic by providing necessary background, explanation, and definition; and (4) to preview the purpose and thesis and call attention to the main points to be developed.

Conclusion

The conclusion should be as carefully planned as the introduction. Of course, you must use your own judgment to meet this moment appropriately, but a sound rule is to find some way to tie together the main ideas developed earlier. The conclusion should accomplish two goals: it should clarify briefly in a fresh and interesting way the ideas discussed in the body of the speech, and it should help the listener retain the main points by summarizing them. This is a final opportunity to link your thoughts with the interests of your audience.

Organizational aids

Listeners appreciate a speaker who is easy to follow. Listeners like to be able to "see the outline" in the speech. Speakers do not have the visual organizational aids writers have to guide readers through a message, such as chapter headings, white page space, headings, or even paragraph indentations to show where new ideas are presented. The speaker must substitute *oral* organizational aids, of which there are several kinds.

Transitions. The transition is to help the audience members mentally "shift gears" by saying, in effect, "OK, we have finished talking about this idea; now let's go on to another, but related, idea." The transition re-states or summarizes the main ideas just covered and forecasts the next main point. Some examples are: "So, you see, it really *is* a simple operation to load the Polaroid camera. Now, the next step is pretty easy too—to frame, focus, and take the picture." Or "Now that you understand the water supply problems that led to Pinckneyville's decision to create a large lake by damming up the valley across from Deerslide to Little Deerslide hill, let me talk for just a minute about the extra advantages this lake brought to the community."

Such transitions undoubtedly help listeners understand oral messages. Thompson has found that the "addition of statements to highlight relationships among units in a speech can enhance comprehension. The value of transitions in oral communication has been supported empirically on two occasions."[13]

Internal summaries. When a main idea is composed of several smaller points or is more than usually complicated, it helps audience understanding if an internal summary of what has gone on so far can be made, for example, "So there were several causes of the Pinckneyville water shortages: a more or less protracted lack of rainfall caused the lowering of Beaucoup Creek; an increase in population; and an increase in the amount of water used per person."

Guideposts. Often what is required in a speech is not a substantive internal summary or transition but simply a quick cue as to where you are going next. You may indicate that you must digress a moment to explain something you failed to mention earlier ("And that reminds me of something I should have said earlier"). Or it could help the audience remember by numbering: "My second point is that . . . ," "My third step is to . . ." Even enumerating points on your upraised fingers can be considered guideposts.

Outlining

Outlining helps discipline your thoughts. It serves as a check that you have chosen ideas that help achieve your specific purpose. A few main points inherent to an understanding of the whole subject can be selected. Those main ideas can then be arranged to explain or support a particular theme. Each main point is then divided into subpoints.

Your outline will be determined in part by the method of organization you select (chronological, topical, problem-solution, cause-effect, induction, or deduction). Since the outline is the blueprint of what you want to get across in your speech and is useful in your rehearsals to learn the sequence of ideas you want to follow, your outline should follow certain "rules."

Rules of outlining. First, in addition to a title for your speech, at the top of your outline write a sentence that states the purpose—what response you will be seeking from the audience. For example, the purpose is to convince my audience that capital punishment should be ruled unconstitutional as a "cruel and unusual punishment" or the purpose is to teach the audience the differences between crocodiles and alligators.

Second, organize the outline into three separate parts: introduction, body or discussion, and conclusion.

Third, use a consistent set of symbols to denote descending order of generality.

Fourth, show the logical relationship and subordination of ideas in terms of descending order of generality by indenting headings, such as:

  I. Main idea
     A. Support for I.
     B. Support for I.
        1. Support for B.
        2. Support for B.
           a. Support for 2.
           b. Support for 2.

Fifth, number items in each part of the outline separately. That is, the first main point of your introduction would begin with main idea *I.* Then the first main idea of the body or discussion is numbered *I;* and the first main idea of the conclusion is *I,* also.

Sixth, write your outline in complete sentences. This process may at first seem unnecessary to you, but reflect: this is to be your plan for arranging *ideas.* And can you remember what was probably the first definition you ever learned of a "complete sentence"? It probably went something like, "A complete sentence is a group of words that express a *complete thought.*" Complete sentences—a subject and predicate logically related to one another—encourage complete thoughts.

For instance, how complete can your thinking be if you think only in terms of a noun-like subject without some action or state-of-being verb-like predicate being involved? For example, think of your best friend. Do you think of him or her in the abstract, doing nothing or having nothing done to him or her—or in no specific state of being? You probably think of him or her talking, playing tennis, or reading, smiling, or being happy or sad.

Nor can you think very intelligently about an action in the abstract without some subject doing it. Can you think of *running* in the abstract? Not really—you think of a boy running, or a car, or water, or a horse. So make your outline contain complete thoughts by using sentences.

Another benefit of complete sentences is that they are a diagnostic aid for your instructor. As you give your speech, it may be that your instructor can tell that your speech is not very well organized but cannot tell *why.* When you turn in your outline, the instructor can find out the cause of your poor organization.

Seventh, write each main head as a simple sentence, usually with an active verb. In fact, it is a good idea to phrase the main heads orally before writing them down to ensure simplicity of oral style.

Eighth, check to make sure that main heads are logical, that they do not have excessive overlap, and ensure a consistent, simple thought pattern.

Rule nine is to check that the main heads you have chosen, if accepted and/or understood by your audience, will *sustain your purpose.* Since rules 8 and 9 go together, let us look at two examples illustrating both these rules:

EXAMPLE 1

Purpose: The purpose of this speech is to teach the audience how to operate the Polaroid Land Camera.

Main Ideas:

   I. You load the camera in three easy steps.
  II. You also use three easy steps to take the picture.
 III. Developing and finishing the picture is easy, too.

EXAMPLE 2

> *Purpose:* The purpose of this speech is to convince the audience that our county should build a new reservoir west of town.
>
> *Main ideas:*
> I. Our present water supply will be inadequate ten years from now.
> II. A new reservoir west of town would supply us with plenty of water.
> III. A new reservoir would be the most efficient and practical way of improving our water supply.
> IV. The new reservoir would provide additional recreation for the county.

Tenth, in outlining, if you have an *A,* you ought to have a *B.* If you have a *1,* you ought to have a *2.* In other words, don't divide and have just one part left over.

Eleventh, make sure that subheads at each level develop the heading just above them. That is, check to make sure that each subhead directly explains and/or proves that heading under which it is indented.

Rule twelve is to word headings and subheadings as you would say them conversationally. Do not write heads as notes to yourself. For example, write "The point is well illustrated by the story of the coffee-drinking mountaineer," not "Tell the story of the coffee-drinking mountaineer at this point." (If you later want to write a little note in the margin of your outline to remind yourself of something, that is all right, like the politician who jotted in the margin of his speech: "Argument weak here; raise voice!") But address your outline headings and your statements to your audience.

Thirteen, include supporting materials in the outline. Include also the transitions and guideposts.

Below is a model outline illustrating these rules.

> *Title:* How to Organize a Speech
> *Specific purpose:* To inform the speech communication class how to organize an informative speech.

Introduction

I. Lively organization can help both speaker and the listener.
II. Organization of an informative speech involves three basic concerns.

A. The main discussion of the speech is developed.
B. The introduction and conclusion are carefully conceived.
C. Organizational aids are used to help convey one's thoughts.

Discussion

I. The main body of a speech can be organized in at least three ways.
   A. Chronological order is helpful when going from one step to another.
   B. Problem-solution development is suitable for treatment of many social evils.
   C. Many subjects can best be divided topically.
Transition: Now that we know how to organize the body, let's take up the beginning and end of the speech.
II. The introduction and conclusion serve important functions in a speech.
   A. The introduction helps one get off to a good start.
      1. The introduction serves to gain the attention of the audience.
      2. In the introduction one reveals concern for the subject and audience.
      3. The introduction includes a preview of the items to be discussed.
   B. A conclusion also plays an important role in communication.
      1. The conclusion is a good place to summarize the main points of a speech.
      2. In the conclusion one can make a last appeal for action or approval.
Transition: Organization of the body, the introduction, and the conclusion is made clearer through the use of organizational aids.
III. Organizational aids help the audience understand your message.
   A. Transitions alert the audience for a change of direction.
   B. Definitions help explain what the speaker means.
   C. Internal summaries ensure the audience understands one point before a different point is discussed.

Conclusion

I. There are three chief considerations involved in good organization.
   A. The main discussion of the speech must be carefully developed.

B. An introduction and conclusion should help tie the entire message together.
C. Organizational aids should be used when needed.
II. Good organization can help ensure meaningful results.

Supporting materials

When preparing an informative speech, remember to use personal experiences and information discovered during your library search. Chapter 6 explains the kinds of supporting materials you can use, and the section in this chapter on "Creating a Speech" illustrates how those findings are used as raw materials to invent your speech. One final reminder: in the informative speech, supporting materials are used to *explain* and *clarify,* whereas in persuasion they often become forms of *proof.*

Kinds of informative speeches

There is information in just about every kind of speech, including those that persuade or entertain. But speeches to inform are meant strictly to provide information. Types of speeches to inform are those on *processes, products, organizations,* and *concepts.* Another kind of speech to inform, the *oral report,* is treated as a distinct type.

Speech to inform on a process

Process here means a coordinated series of events that logically forms a meaningful whole. A "process" speech describes *how* to do something, how something is made, or how something evolves into something else. Here are some examples of possible topics for speeches to inform on various processes:

How window draperies are made
Navigating an airplane by dead reckoning
Artillery range-finding
How a thermostat works
Refinishing furniture
Transmission of photographs by radio
How a tropical storm becomes a hurricane

How to find a magazine article
The functions of the liver
Making maple sugar in Vermont
How to identify counterfeit money
How narcotics addiction begins
What makes an airplane fly
The minting of coins
Artificial respiration
How to splint a broken leg

The main ideas of such a speech are generally arranged chronologically, the first major step of the process coming first, and the last step of the process coming last in the speech. Occasionally, the speech on a process will be organized along a topical sequence. For instance, in discussing artificial respiration you could take up various means of artificial respiration as *topics:* the back pressure method, the back-pressure-arm-lift method, and the mouth-to-mouth method.

Speech to inform on a product

The speech to inform on a product tells *what* something is, although it is sometimes related strongly to the process speech and may also tell *how* the product works.

For instance, a speaker in one of the author's classes brought in an automobile trunk lid borrowed from a local junk dealer. On one-third of the trunk lid the speaker had already applied a new brand of car wax; on another third he demonstrated how easily the new wax went on; then he used the remaining third to contrast the old dull finish to the shiny third waxed with the new product.

New products are continually coming off the assembly lines. If you discover a truly new product the audience is likely to have little or no experience with, a speech on that product and how it works would be timely and useful. Topical order or, if a "how to" type of speech, chronological order, is the most likely method of organizing such a speech.

Speech to inform on an organization

Americans apparently love to join together in organizations. As a result, there are multitudes of organizations to learn something interesting about. A speech to inform on an organization is likely to tell *what* it is—its purpose and membership—but might also tell *how* it operates, recruits members, and so on. Your speech on an organization might focus on a topic, such as its hierarchical structure, its membership, its goals and activities, or its history.

You should concentrate on aspects of the organization that would be most interesting and useful for your audience. For instance, in discussing the Thomas A. Dooley Foundation you might stress the work of the organization, the healing of the poor and sick in Southeast Asia, and its role in making Asian friends for the United States that could never be "bought" with foreign aid. In speaking on the local credit union, you might stress the processes of how one can join and how one borrows money cheaply from it. In speaking on the United Nations, you could mention the complexity of its decision-making apparatus or the strengths and weaknesses of its capacity for maintaining world peace. In a speech on the local Lions Club you might discuss community services the organization provides.

Speeches to inform on a concept

Speeches explaining concepts are basically speeches of definition, telling *what* and *why*. Usually, such a speech explains the concept from a theoretical or cause-effect standpoint, then applies the concept to specific instances. For instance, a speech on the refraction of light would explain how light rays bend as they leave one medium and enter another; the practical means of finding objects submerged in water are then presented.

The oral report

The oral report has four distinct features:

1. The person who presents the report has usually been assigned the responsibility for making it.
2. The report is often assigned by the audience that will hear it, either by one person or a group.
3. The content tends to be specialized and technical, usually based on some specific investigation.
4. Because of its peculiar content, the oral report seems to fit best into its own unique pattern of arrangement.

Speaker. What kind of person makes an oral report? Examples include an industrial chemist who reports an experiment that tests glue for the manufacture of furniture; the head of a fraternity committee who reports on his committee's investigation and recommends what furnishings should be obtained to outfit the new club room; a company vice president who reports on why it takes an average of five days from the time an order comes into the plant until it is shipped to the customer. These examples indicate the variety of people who make oral reports.

Audiences. The audiences for oral reports usually comprise the persons who assigned the reports in the first place. The chemist and the vice president were probably given their tasks by their superiors.

The fraternity furnishings committee was probably elected by the full membership and given its task, perhaps with a specific date on which to report its findings. Oral reports may be shared with a wide variety of audiences, and not always with the group which requested the study be done.

Content. The oral report is usually concerned with a somewhat original *investigation* carried out for the purpose of providing information or solving a specific problem.

Organization. What kind of arrangement best suits the oral report's contents? The specific organization is unique to the oral report because of the relationships among the arrangement, the reporter, the audience, and the content.

As with any other speech, the oral report should consist of three parts, the introduction, the body, and the conclusion.

The introduction should establish interest and attention, and should clearly state the thesis, or at least the subject, of the report. A bit of history as to why the investigation was carried out might be included. In fact, since the audience is presumably already highly interested in the content of the report, having assigned the study on which it is based, how the investigation came to be conducted might suffice to arouse interest. The history in this case leads logically to the statement of the report's thesis or subject.

The data or findings are the meat of the report and are presented in the body of the speech. Since the usefulness of your findings is directly related to how carefully they were arrived at, the body should begin with an explanation of how data were gathered.

Suppose I were to report that I had taken a poll of students at your campus and found that two-thirds of them favored raising tuition at your college. You would probably give me a skeptical look and ask how I conducted my poll. If I told you I had asked three students, and two of them happened to be on tuition scholarships, you would dismiss my poll results as worthless.

So you must tell how materials were selected and gathered. Also, you need to state your standards or criteria for evaluating the results. If reporting on a survey, you will tell how you picked the sample polled, how the questions were chosen and worded, who asked the questions, and under what conditions were they asked.

After you have introduced your report, stated how your data were gathered and evaluated, and given the results, you are ready to draw a conclusion. The conclusion can take one of three forms.

First, your conclusion might be in the form of a recommendation on what action should be taken: "Therefore I recommend that glue from Process 437 be substituted for the glue we now use," or "So our committee recommends the package plan of furnishings offered by Hennings Department Store." As you can see, an oral report may result not only in information but also in persuasion.

But perhaps your employer dislikes having employees make recommendations. Your conclusion then might simply be a brief evaluation of the investigation and its findings, leaving the decision of what the findings suggest to others.

Your conclusions could also consist of a combination of the evaluation and the recommendation: "The tests we conducted were rigidly and thoroughly controlled under various combinations of heat, humidity, and stress. Therefore, I recommend that glue from Process 437. . . ."

A skeletal outline of the oral report might look like this:

Introduction:
  I. History of the problem or other interest material.
  II. Thesis statement, or purpose of investigation.

Body:
  I. How the investigation was carried out.
  II. Standards for judging results.
  III. Results.
      A. Data.
      B. Implications of data.

Conclusion:
  I. Evaluation of study, or
  II. Recommendations, or
  III. Both.

A model speech to inform

This chapter concludes by presenting a model speech to inform. Beginning students often say that it would be helpful if they could be exposed to a good speech of the type that is assigned so they can know what is expected. Read the following speech and the explanation after it explaining why this is considered a good speech to inform.

Radio by day and by night

Most of you listen to the radio from time to time. But have you ever wondered why radio reception at night is different from radio reception during the day? You've probably noticed that at night you can get stations from much farther away, stations you can't pick up during the day. For instance, at night in Miami you can listen to radio station KMOX in St. Louis. But along with this, you may have also noticed that you sometimes get more static interference at night than you do during the day. Ever wonder why? Or have you ever wondered why some radio stations go off the air at sundown and don't come back on until the next morning after sunrise? Did you know that all three of these phenomena—the longer nighttime range of radio stations, the increased static at night, and the licensing of some radio stations for only daytime broadcasting—are attributable to the same cause?

The basic reason why daytime broadcasting differs from nighttime broadcasting is my topic for today. I intend to explain the role played in the transmission of radio waves by a layer in our upper atmosphere called the *ionosphere.*

During the day, about all you receive on your radio are what we call *ground waves.* These ground waves are radio waves that go out from the transmitting antenna and follow the curvature of the earth close to the ground, as shown in Figure 8–1. You're likely to get very clear reception fairly close to the transmitting antenna, but farther away the signal gets weaker and weaker. The energy of the wave drops off rapidly because of the earth's gravity; the energy is "soaked up" by the earth, so to speak, very much like a rolling ball is slowed down by friction with the ground. For this reason it takes an extremely powerful transmitter to send a ground wave over any great distance. The U. S. Navy has a transmitter on the west coast which can push a ground wave all the way around the world, but it is the world's most powerful transmitter. In fact, it broadcasts with a power of 1.2 *million* watts of energy—and that is twenty-two times more powerful than any U. S. commercial radio station!

At night the conditions for the propagation of radio waves change drastically. The ground wave continues to follow the curvature of the earth and to be damped out by the force of gravity; but now the *ionosphere,* a layer of our upper atmosphere, begins acting as a giant mirror, which refracts and reflects radio waves that have gone up into the sky and sends them back to earth.

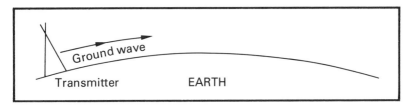

FIGURE 8–1. Ground Wave Radio Propagation, Daytime

A model speech to inform

During the day these waves that head skyward, referred to as *sky waves,* are mostly absorbed by what is called the *E layer* of the ionosphere, much the same way in which the force of gravity absorbs ground waves. But at night we get the conditions you see demonstrated in Figure 8–2. With the setting of the sun, the lower E level of the ionosphere disappears; and the next level, the *F level,* which is about ninety miles high, refracts and reflects the "sky waves" back.

Some rays approach the F level of the ionosphere at too great an angle, as does ray T1, and thus it is not bent enough to come back to earth. These rays continue going up, and die out in space. But beginning at shallower angles, at about ray T2 in Figure 8–2, the rays are bent and reflected back to earth, where you can pick them up on your radio.

Radio waves lose far less energy travelling through the air than they do travelling along the ground. Therefore, a sky wave can go a lot farther than a ground wave on the same amount of energy. The net result is that the range of radio broadcasting stations is greatly increased at night, when sky waves are available to carry their signals much farther than their ground waves can carry them. The range of some radio stations doubles, trebles, or more.

Because radio stations can broadcast much farther during the night than during the day, you can pick up stations from farther away at night. But you're likely to get more static then, too. The reason for the increase in static is that electrical storms give off the same kind of electrical energy as do radio stations; and at night you can

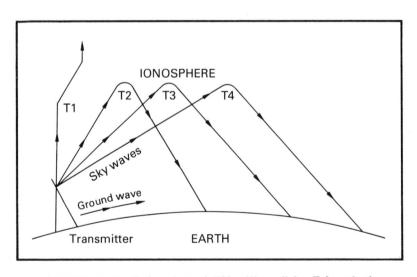

FIGURE 8–2. Refraction of "Sky Waves" by F Level of Ionosphere

One-to-many communication: informing

pick up electrical interference from a much greater distance through "sky waves" of static.

Also, there are radio stations broadcasting on the same frequency from different locations in the country. The locations and power of radio stations are controlled and limited so that during the day, the signals of stations on the same frequency do not overlap. To keep the more far-ranging signals of the same frequency from overlapping at night, some stations on a frequency are only licensed to broadcast during the day.

So, now when it gets dark enough for your local daytime-only stations to go off the air and you tune in that distant station you can't get in the daytime, but have some difficulty with more static than you'd like, you know the reason. The F layer of the ionosphere is "doing its thing."[4]

Evaluating the speech

The above speech, adapted from a U. S. Air Force course for radio operators, exemplifies several features which you as a speaker might employ in your speeches to inform.

First, the speech concerns a limited aspect of the overall topic of radio. In other words, a small subdivision of the subject was selected to be covered thoroughly and in detail, which lends interest to the presentation. And the one aspect of radio chosen for coverage is one that can be related to the audience. It explains why certain phenomena which they have all experienced occur and how. Thus, the introduction capitalizes on personal experience and uses it as a rationale for audience interest and attention to the subject.

The second paragraph clearly states the thesis and can be considered the end of the introduction. This paragraph explicitly tells the audience what the speaker is going to tell them.

The speech is then divided into three main ideas—two on the theory of radio wave propagation and the third applying the theory to show the effect upon actual broadcasting and licensing. The body of the speech might be outlined this way:

I. Daytime radio wave propagation is limited because it must rely on ground waves.
II. At night radio waves travel much farther by reflection off the ionosphere as sky waves.
III. The difference between daytime and nighttime radio wave propagation produces three noticeable effects upon radio broadcasting and its licensing.

The speech uses clear, simple visual aids and other specific supporting material. The loss of energy from the ground wave to the force of gravity is compared to the friction of the ground on a rolling ball, a literal analogy since the two things compared are alike in principle. An example of how much power a ground wave requires is given in the case of the U. S. Navy station, and its power is contrasted with the most powerful commercial radio stations. The example of being able to hear radio station KMOX, St. Louis, in Miami makes concrete the distance that nighttime radio can cover. The specific names of the applicable ionospheric levels are given, and the height of the F level is specified.

The conclusion aptly summarizes the three effects and indirectly restates the thesis of the speech. The last short sentence rounds the speech off with a snap.

In short, this is a speech to inform on a well-limited aspect of a subject related to audience interests and experiences. It explains the subject in easy-to-understand language and with adequate supporting material. It is organized into three clearly distinguishable main ideas. And, most importantly, it depends for its effectiveness upon learning a single concept—the difference between daytime and nighttime radio wave propagation and the concrete results stemming from that concept. Even if audience members should forget the

One-to-many communication: informing

actual effects of ionospheric wave propagation, they could easily reconstruct them by remembering the concept.

The above speech is a useful model for your own informative speaking—not to merely one to copy or imitate, but one you would do well to emulate.

QUESTIONS FOR THOUGHT
AND DISCUSSION
CHAPTER 8

1. When your purpose is to inform an audience, what consideration should you give to audience analysis and adapting to the audience?

2. What specific audience characteristics can you study to determine the probable reaction to one of your speeches?

3. What questions should you ask to determine the influence of the speaking occasion on your speech?

4. What basic steps are involved in creating a speech?

5. This chapter discusses several ways you can organize the main body of your speech (chronologically, topically, and so on). Which method would be best for the topic, "finding your way around in the campus library"? Explain why the method you chose is most appropriate.

6. What should you accomplish in the introduction of an informative speech? What about in the conclusion?

7. When should an internal summary be used in discourse?

8. Cite the kinds of informative speeches one might hear, and give an example of each from campus life.

9. What distinguishes an oral report from other kinds of informative communication?

EXERCISES · ASSIGNMENTS | CHAPTER 8

1. Using recent speeches in *Vital Speeches of the Day* or *Representative American Speeches,* find actual examples of the following: introduction, conclusion, main ideas in body of speech, cause–effect relationship, chronological organization, topical organization, spatial organization, problem-solution, internal summary, transition, definition.

2. Listen to a speaker (teacher, preacher, salesperson) and evaluate whether it was easy to follow the pattern of thought. Determine why.

How could the speaker have improved his or her organization and thus improved communication with the audience?

3. Prepare a three- or four-minute report on an experiment (reported in a journal) concerning the organization of an oral message.

4. In *Vital Speeches* or *Representative American Speeches* find an example of one of the kinds of informative speeches discussed in this chapter. Be prepared to discuss it in class.

5. Try to find an informative speech that does not persuade an audience.

6. Prepare a three- to five-minute informative speech in which you clearly explain the basic steps in a process. Use visual aids when appropriate.

7. Prepare a three- to five-minute informative speech in which you discuss a manufactured product.

8. Prepare a three- to five-minute oral report in which you explain the organizational structure of a business, church, government, school, or other institution.

9. Prepare a three- to five-minute statement in which you define an abstract concept, such as liberty, love, brotherhood, democracy, prejudice, or freedom.

10. Attend a speech on campus and write an analysis of the audience from what you can observe. How well did the speaker adapt to the audience?

11. Prepare a three- to five-minute report analyzing your speech class as a potential audience. What should you consider when adapting to this group?

12. Prepare a three- to five-minue statement concerning the results of an experiment dealing with audience analysis. Use a source such as *Communication Monographs* or *Journal of Communication.*

13. Prepare a three- to five-minute analysis of yourself, citing characteristics which any speaker would do well to consider if directing a message to you.

ENDNOTES | Chapter 8

1. Roger P. Wilcox, *Oral Reporting in Business and Industry* (Englewood Cliffs, N.J.: Prentice-Hall, 1967), p. 6.

2. Glenn M. Blair, R. Stewart Jones, and Ray H. Simpson, *Educational Psychology,* 2nd ed. (New York: Macmillan, 1967), pp. 236–237.

3. Ernest Thompson, "Some Effects of Message Structure on Listeners' Comprehension," *Speech Monographs,* 34 (March 1967): 52.

4. Blair, Jones, and Slmpson, *op. cit.,* p. 236.

5. Ernest Thompson, "An Experimental Investigation of the Relative Effectiveness of Organizational Structure in Oral Communication," *Southern Speech Journal,* 26 (Fall 1960): 59–69; and "Some Effects of Message Structure on Listeners' Comprehension," *op. cit.,* pp. 51–57.

6. Charles R. Petrie, "Informative Speaking: A Summary and Bibliography," *Speech Monographs,* 30 (June 1963): 80.

7. Plato, *Phaedrus,* translated by W. C. Helmbold and W. G. Rabinowitz (New York: Liberal Arts Press, 1956), p. 53.

8. Percy H. Tannenbaum, "Effect of Serial Position on Recall of Radio News Stories," *Journalism Quarterly,* 31 (1954): 319–323.

9. Carl I. Hovland, Irving L. Janis, and Harold H. Kelly, *Communication and Persuasion* (New Haven: Yale University Press, 1953), pp. 100–105.

10. R. Carter, "Writing Controversial Stories for Comprehension," *Journalism Quarterly,* 32 (1955): 319–328; Mark A. May and Arthur A. Lumsdaine, *Learning from Films* (New Haven: Yale University Press, 1958).

11. Jane Allyn and Leon Festinger, "The Effectiveness of Unanticipated Persuasive Communications," *Journal of Abnormal and Social Psychology,* 62 (1961): 35–40.

12. Judson Mills, "Opinion Change as a Function of the Communicator's Desire to Influence and Liking for the Audience," *Journal of Experimental Social Psychology:* 2 (1966): 152–159.

13. Ernest Thompson, "Some Effects of Message Structure on Listeners' Comprehension," *op. cit.,* p. 56.

14. Sources for this speech include: Keith Henney and Glen A. Richardson, *Principles of Radio,* 6th ed. (New York: John Wiley, 1952), pp. 508–511; "Ionosphere," in Vol. 12 of *Encyclopaedia Britannica,* 1966 Edition, p. 501; and "Navy Radio Circles the Globe," *Life,* 35 (November 30, 1953): 129–132.

ONE-TO-MANY COMMUNICATION: PERSUADING

Persuasion is a general purpose of speech communication. *A persuasive speech* attempts to influence feelings, beliefs, or behavior. It is sometimes called *advocatory speaking* since the person asking for change is the advocate of a new position. Materials for persuasion include not only the facts and principles used in informative discourse but also authoritative beliefs, opinions, and arguments.

The topics of persuasive speeches may vary from urging the formation of a world government to urging classmates to take a course in black rhetoric. The communicator seeks to win the audience's allegiance, to move them some distance on the continuum of belief that runs from complete disagreement to wholehearted endorsement, and to get them to act in a particular way.

Audience analysis

In informative speaking you must be aware of the audience's information level and understanding; in persuasive speaking you have to consider much more. People have their own convictions and ways of behaving, and changing them is not easy. To understand audience involvement in a persuasive situation, we first consider audience behavior.

Audience behavior

Human belief and behavior stem from personal desire or *motivation.* We often believe what we want to believe and do what we want to do.

Put another way, we believe in and do things that are personally satisfying. Of course, we often do things we do not want to do, such as pay taxes or take required courses. But we do these things because we would rather do them than suffer the consequences of *not* doing them.

Berelson and Steiner, two social scientists who have catalogued a substantial number of conclusions about motivation and human behavior, conclude that: "People tend to select, organize, and interpret stimuli in line with existing motives; their thoughts and memories are similarly channeled and modified according to what is important or gratifying to think and remember."[1] When attempting to convince an audience of the veracity or worth of a particular proposition, you need to do something besides tell the audience what you want them to accept and believe: you must show them how acceptance will personally gratify them.

Since the way we perceive and process information, and thus form attitudes and behavior patterns, is often based on self-interest, there is a tendency for strong *consistency* among one's attitudes and behaviors. In fact, to paraphrase Berelson and Steiner, if sufficiently motivated, a person's perception of the world can be distorted to conform with that individual's beliefs.[2] In a study by Festinger, for instance, 553 people were asked if they thought the link between cigarette smoking and lung cancer had been established. Among nonsmokers, 29 percent believed such a connection had been established, and 55 percent did not; but only 7 percent of heavy smokers admitted there was proof of a connection between cigarette smoking and lung cancer, and 86 percent felt it was not proved.

Several "balance" theories of motivation are now popular in social psychology and communication. An important one is the *cognitive dissonance* theory of Leon Festinger.[3] *Balance theories* rely on a model of humans as creatures who seek to maintain their thoughts and emotions at a stable level. Simply stated, when cognitions and attitudes are all relatively consistent, a person is at ease because of a lack of any self-contradictions. If, however, the person should contact some information (an event, an experience, a message) that the person recognizes as true but which conflicts with his or her cognitions and attitudes, the person would experience cognitive dissonance. That is, several items of information regarding a particular subject would be in conflict, producing discomfort. This discomfort would energize one into some sort of physical or mental action to get rid of the uncomfortable dissonance and to return to a homeostatic (balanced) condition.

Suppose Mrs. Jones is a middle-aged, financially successful businesswoman. She voted straight Republican in the last election.

She is opposed to expansion of the federal bureaucracy, feels she is overtaxed to support too many able-bodied people on welfare, believes in "rugged individualism," and has other conservative positions. Now, suppose a high Republican official, for whom Mrs. Jones voted and whom she likes and respects, proposes vast upgrading of the welfare system and proposes to spend large sums to achieve it. This is likely to provoke cognitive dissonance in Mrs. Jones. A man whom she admires has come out in favor of a program repugnant to her. She has dissonance to dispel but how does she dispel it?

One obvious way is to change her attitude toward welfare programs, reasoning from authority: "Republican Smith says we should expand welfare; I believe in taking Republican Smith's advice; therefore, I now believe we should expand welfare."

But becoming persuaded to change attitudes is only one of the ways of reducing dissonance. Mrs. Jones has other options. She could change her opinion of Mr. Smith: "Republican Smith favors a policy repugnant to me and to Republicans generally; Smith is not a 'real' Republican; therefore, I will no longer heed the advice of Mr. Smith."

Mrs. Jones can distort reality further. For instance, she might simply "forget" that Republican Smith made a statement favoring expansion of welfare. Freud called this *repression* and it happens to the best of us. If successful at "forgetting," she will relieve herself of dissonance.

There are other weapons in Mrs. Smith's arsenal. She can distort. She can purposely misunderstand what Smith proposed: "Oh, he's for expanded welfare, all right, but he's for a system that would combine *work* with getting payments, and I agree with that kind of system." Or she might put an "innocent" interpretation on it by rationalizing: "Oh, sure, Republican Smith *says* he is for expanding welfare—but he doesn't really mean it—he's just saying that to get votes so he can continue his fine record of public service."

It is the persuasive speaker's job to create dissonance in audience members so they will become energized to escape its discomforts. But you must present your speech so that it is by your solution (changed attitude or willingness to act) the audience chooses to reduce that dissonance rather than by some other means, as forgetting, distorting, or rationalizing the dissonant information, or derogating the source of the information. Specific ways for doing this will be taken up in the section of this chapter dealing with the content and organization of the persuasive speech.

Audience perception

If you were to say in a speech, "What we ought to have in the White House today is another Dwight Eisenhower," what would this mean to your audience? It would mean different things to different people, depending on their individual perceptions of Eisenhower as a president. One listener decides you mean that we need a strong leader of high moral courage; another thinks you mean the country is tired of activist government and is ready for four years of a "do-nothing" president; a third concludes that you mean we should have a president concerned with principle and disdainful of party politics.

What you have done with your single statement is to tell each of three people a different thing. You said the same words to each, but each interpreted them in light of his or her own perception of the idea, "Dwight Eisenhower as president."

By *perceptions* we mean those cognitive and emotional reactions the listener associates with a person, act, or concept. Different people perceive things differently because they differ in age, education, religion, geographical roots, political affiliation, values, beliefs, and so on. Is a college graduate likely to feel the same toward a new school bond issue as would a high school dropout? Would a serious Roman Catholic and an atheist see eye-to-eye on the subject of birth control?

One way audience perception affects the response to your speech is through the deductive reasoning that takes place *between speaker and listener.* Reasoning deductively involves going from a general belief to its application in a specific instance. We can illustrate that deductive process by putting it in the form of a syllogism:

> Listener believes: All Americans love wealth.
> Speaker states first: John is an American.
> Listener concludes: John loves wealth.

Most people have formed opinions about the Republican party, Girl Scouts, French people, laborers, abortion, and sex education, for instance. When such subjects are discussed ("John is an American"), most persons automatically supply their preconceived general beliefs ("All Americans love wealth") and draw conclusions ("John loves wealth") based on these beliefs. When members of an audience supply the same basic beliefs as the speaker, they are in agreement. When they supply opposing premises, there is conflict with the speaker.

Members of a group who hear a statement may supply different basic beliefs, thus react differently. For example, you say in a meeting that "House Bill 1-A is a sales tax." Two of your listeners respond as follows:

LISTENER 1

Listener believes: All taxes are bad.
You say first: House Bill 1-A is a sales tax.
Listener concludes: House Bill 1-A is bad.

LISTENER 2

Listener believes: Taxes are necessary for better public services.
You say first: House Bill 1-A is a sales tax.
Listener concludes: House Bill 1-A is necessary if we are to have better public services.

This is how deduction works in our daily lives, and understanding this process teaches us to anticipate all kinds of reactions to our words and our ideas. We all have basic beliefs about many subjects, and when a subject is discussed and the belief is strong, we supply our own conclusions. Thus we may *answer for ourselves* what we believe about an issue.

A communicator faces a difficult challenge to crack these beliefs enough to get a fair hearing. One can see how critical it is to analyze the audience—to anticipate what conclusion listeners are likely to supply when confronted with a particular topic. While you talk, they are "talking to themselves." After you identify what probable premise they will impose on your *subject,* you will know better how to direct your discussion and supporting materials.

In the case of Listener 1, above, you would have to consider ways of getting that person to rethink the belief that all taxes are bad. To persuade Listener 1 you might argue that "None of us likes taxes. But you would not like to think of a fire gutting your home and realize there were no firemen to help. It takes money to pay for a fire department. And the money must come from a tax such as Bill 1-A." Anticipate the fundamental reaction of your audience to your message and search for honest ways of convincing your listeners to reconsider their initial judgment. Look for areas where there may be agreement between you and your audience.

One researcher, after surveying the research on attitudes and beliefs, concluded that "one of the best-established findings of social psychology is that individuals who have well-established attitudes and beliefs act so as to maintain them; the more extreme the attitudes, the more difficult they are to change." He also warns that "individuals will reject communications which urge too much attitude change."[4] Communicating with persons who have different beliefs from your own is not easy. You will do well to develop your patience and a sense of respect for and understanding of the other person before you seek ways of changing actions and beliefs.

Audience characteristics

Chapter 8 discussed audience traits of age, sex, level of education, knowledge of subject, and personal experience. When preparing a persuasive communication, review these characteristics and ask yourself how these factors could influence an audience member's attitudes, beliefs, and perceptions. Three additional characteristics of an audience may be particularly important in a persuasive situation.

Cohesiveness. The relative unity of a group is an important characteristic to consider when analyzing an audience. Is the audience composed of persons bound together by a common purpose or is it a heterogeneous group? For example, members of a church may be so committed to a particular belief that they are able to overcome minor differences that may exist among them. On the other hand, a second parish may be so divided that the church splits into separate denominations. When analyzing an audience, then, explore the degree of cohesiveness among the members. Determine why a particular group is united. These findings will provide valuable information concerning audience attitudes and beliefs.

Responsiveness. When preparing your speech, anticipate whether your audience will respond in some way before, during, or after your presentation. In the 1950s one would enter an auditorium, sit on the stage, be introduced, then lecture to a silent audience. The 1960s taught us that speaking situations can be more explosive than that. Politicians visiting campuses may be met with hostile signs, comments, and questions. On some occasions audiences may not be willing to wait until after the speech to ask questions; they want a response at the time a statement is made. In these kinds of speaking situations, the speaker at some point becomes a listener, and the listeners become speakers.

Such conditions have important implications if you hope to

communicate meaningfully in those situations. For example, you cannot plan a prepared text and assume you will not be interrupted. Your word choice, organization, and delivery must be flexible so if someone jumps up and asks a question or yells, "You are wrong!" you can stop and deal with the situation. The audience may not allow you to slip by with broad generalities and weak arguments. You either understand your topic, or, under the pressure of questions and comments from the audience, you will be revealed as one who does not know what he or she is talking about.

Beliefs and values. In our search for security, status, happiness, wealth, comfort, and other goals, we have built up beliefs and values concerning how to go about achieving them. Beliefs and values may be acquired from education, religion, society, personal experiences, and the like. When you confront an individual or a group, you are face to face with persons who have strong feelings and thoughts and who often believe they are right—whatever their education, level of competence, experience, vocation, or religion.

For example, you may honestly believe from your study and experience that "anyone who wants to work can find a job, and welfare programs should be abolished." On the other hand, the person you are addressing—who has experienced job discrimination, lives in poverty, has had little education, and has no contact with prosperity—also knows that many people who want to work can't find a job. How can this situation be resolved? Both sincerely believe they are right. To increase understanding between the two persons, there has to be a *sharing of the different perceptions* that are as real to the two people as are their different environments. The speaker should attempt to anticipate these differences and discover some common reality to establish communication and possibly resolve conflict.

Activity

1. An advocate wishes to convert you to another religion. What would that advocate have to do to adapt to *your* behavior, perceptions, or characteristics? Make a list.
2. A politician wants your vote. What would that politician have to do to adapt to you? Make a list.
3. A salesperson is trying to sell you a used 1971 Volkswagen. What would that seller have to do to adapt to you? Make a list.

Adapting to audiences

Now that you have studied the behavior of audiences, audience perception, and audience characteristics, how can you adapt to an audience? There are at least three types of audience reaction which the persuasive speaker will confront.

The favorable audience

If your audience already favors a point you are going to make, you can either pass quickly over the point to dwell on other areas; or you can amplify the point of agreement to heighten your common ground with the audience.

For instance, you are going to argue that the United States should adopt a policy of universal military training. Now with many audiences there is one relevant proposition on which there will be pretty much general agreement—the "need" issue. Most people agree that there is a *need* for a standing military force. So with many audiences you could pass over this aspect quickly with the mention that "we all agree we need a standing army," and then get down to the problems caused by maintaining that standing army.

You may find yourself talking to an audience that already agrees with your general thesis and with *all* the main points you had planned to make. In this situation, you can really "lay it on thick!" Since the audience will hardly be arguing with you, you can spend your time and energy heightening these beliefs and attempting to energize them into action. A speech to an audience of this kind, rather than being one to convince, becomes a speech either to *stimulate* or to *actuate.* A later section of this chapter takes up these persuasive speech types in more detail.

The hostile audience

Occasionally you will need to advocate a proposition you know the audience already disagrees with. For instance, if you were to try convincing your classmates that your college should raise tuition or to convince workers at a particular plant to put in an hour or two overtime without pay in order to achieve some company goal, you would find the audience opposed, even hostile, to your entire purpose. Against such odds, is it possible to succeed at the persuasive task?

Evidence from experience and from experiments in communication has shown that audiences opposed to ideas can be won over. Last-ditch barnstorming tours have affected elections the pollsters had given to the opposition. Tired football players have become conquering heroes by the coach's pep talk. Balky legislatures and irate bands of taxpayers have been persuaded to vote, however grudgingly, for tax increases and bond issues to build schools, roads, and sewer systems.

You cannot convert hostile audiences by beating them over the head with their lack of insight or stubbornness; you cannot overcome them by outlasting them. You will have to use an appropriate strategy and adapt to each situation as events dictate.

Invest some time pointing out what areas you and the audience already *agree* on, such as common goals. Develop in your audience an awareness of areas of agreement. For instance, you are going to give a speech asking voters to approve a tax increase in order to raise teacher salaries and purchase new textbooks and equipment for the public schools. You could point out that you and the audience are proud of the community. Assert that quality education is one of the most important means of preparing youth to face the future independently. Point out that your community's schools have been doing a good job of preparing its youth and that "all of us" want them to continue that fine job. You have now demonstrated relevant areas where you and your audience have common interests.

As you are building areas of agreement, you are also establishing yourself as one worthy of belief. People tend to believe the speaker who seems to agree with them. So when you get to the proposition on which opposition originally existed, your audience is more apt to respond favorably both to your proposition and to *you.*

Now you must persuade audience members to set aside their objections. Here is where you need clear, reasoned, and specific *information*—your facts and figures, your illustrations and comparisons, your specific instances and testimony—all delivered in a reasonable, fair, and enthusiastic manner. Describe specific benefits the audience will obtain by adopting your plan.

The agreeable but unmotivated audience

How does one persuade an audience to *do* something? Suppose you want to induce a group of people to give a pint of blood apiece to the Red Cross. If you were to question directly each person in the audience whether he or she really *ought* to perform this humanitarian act, the person would probably agree that he or she should. So why should the Red Cross be so habitually short of blood? Because while audience members might agree with the idea that they should contribute, they do not really *want* to; they have no motivation to donate blood. They may foresee no reward for themselves in the act of giving blood. So it falls to the speaker to discover what appeals can be used to motivate the audience to go to the Bloodmobile, sleeves rolled up.

Providing the proper appeals will usually not be enough. Even if listeners were stirred to *want* to give blood, they might still balk because of their objections. An *objection* is any reason that would keep someone from performing a particular act. With giving blood, one objection might be fear of expected pain. The speaker must remove the objection—must convince the audience that there is little pain. Audience analysis will help you anticipate what objections a particular audience will have so you can overcome them in your speech.

Activity

List three persuasive speech theses for which *you* would be a *hostile* audience. List three for which you would be a *favorable* audience. List three for which you would be an *agreeable* but *unmotivated* audience.

Organization and purposes of persuasive messages

Chapter 8 explained the basic principles of organizing and outlining messages and defined ways to organize a speech: chronological, topical, spatial, problem-solution, cause-effect, and induction or deduction. Here the emphasis changes from organizing informative messages to the strategies for organizing persuasive speeches.

A chief difference between informative and persuasive organization is that the main ideas of the persuasive speech are not just "divisions" of the content in terms of topicality or chronology but are actually major *arguments* or *conclusions* which, taken together, form the case for accepting the thesis. A second difference is that supporting materials in the persuasive speech are not merely for explanation; they are also *evidence* that constitutes *proof* of the conclusions which they purport to support.

The way these arguments or conclusions are ordered is more a direct result of the speaker's specific purpose than of any other consideration. So we must discuss these specific purposes and the organizational pattern most suitable for each.

Fotheringham has written an excellent book explaining persuasion as a *campaign* in which preliminary purposes are to establish effects. On these preliminary effects are built other effects by other messages until, finally, the persuader's goals are accomplished.[5] Fotheringham thus thinks that *purpose* is too vague a word to use for the anticipated outcome of a persuasive speech. He prefers two distinct subconcepts: *instrumental effect* and *goal.* His grounds for differentiating these concepts rest on the idea that a persuasive message is *part* of an overall persuasive campaign. In the campaign any individual message attempts to achieve a particular *instrumental effect;* but the overall *goal* is to achieve some *action* from the audience. Achievement of the instrumental effect will help the persuader attain the goal at a later time.

To illustrate, suppose John Doe wishes to get elected to Congress. He is unknown to the electorate, so he would probably launch a campaign to become known. He would begin giving speeches attacking the record of the incumbent legislator he hopes to replace. It might be diagrammed according to the schema adopted by Fotheringham:

> *Message source* (speaker): John Doe, candidate for Congress.
> *Message receivers* (audience): the electorate.
> *Instrumental effect sought:* To become known to the electorate.
> *Goal:* To get elected.

There are a number of ways to categorize the purposes of persuasive speeches. Fotheringham's approach teaches us the complex nature of achieving a particular goal and how it is wise to be realistic in our expectations.

The general purposes of persuasive speeches can be classified into three kinds: speeches to *convince,* speeches to *actuate,* and speeches to *stimulate.*

The speech to convince

The speech to convince generally assumes the audience does not already agree with the speaker's thesis; thus, the speaker's job is to convince the audience of the thesis. The thesis of any speech to convince can be classified as one arguing the truthfulness of a proposition stemming from one of three kinds of issues: *fact, value,* or *policy.*

Issues of fact. An issue of fact is a question about whether a particular event occurred, or whether it occurred a certain way, or whether a certain entity exists or ever existed. A speech to convince on an issue of fact argues for a *proposition* of fact: that an event did or did not occur, or occured a certain way, or that the particular entity exists. One should not argue over matters of fact that are easily documented. It is foolish to argue over what the highest mountain in the world is or in what year Dwight Eisenhower was born. These are matters of public record and can be looked up in standard sources.

But some issues of fact cannot be answered by looking up the answer in the library; and we may discuss these in persuasive speeches. To answer controversial issues of fact, you must gather your evidence, apply your reasoning ability, and attempt to show the probable truth of the proposition that you choose to support. Here are some examples of controversial issues of fact:

Did Christopher Marlowe, and not William Shakespeare, write "Shakespeare's" plays?

Did Lee Harvey Oswald alone assassinate John F. Kennedy?

Is crime really increasing faster than the population?

Is God dead?

Are sightings of "flying saucers" entirely explainable as natural phenomena?

Is it likely that there is intelligent life elsewhere in the universe?

Was Hitler insane?

Do some people have extrasensory perception?

Do most Americans believe the federal government is doing a good job?

Is the theory of evolution correct?

Discovering the main arguments for most questions of fact will not be easy. The main line of argument for most propositions of fact stems directly from the nature of the content of the issue of fact. For instance, in order to prove that Marlowe and not Shakespeare wrote "Shakespeare's" plays, you would have to argue, as did Hoffman:[6]

1. Marlowe did not die when history says he did—his death was a "put-up job." (If he *did* die when history says he did, he died too early to write the plays.)
2. Marlowe was better equipped by education and experience to write great literature.
3. Shakespeare's plays are written in a style much like that used by Marlowe in the plays we know Marlowe wrote.
4. Clues within the plays allude to Marlowe's actual authorship; these clues are cleverly imbedded by Marlowe himself, writing from exile.

Issues of value. An issue of value asks what interpretation or value we should place upon some concept or event. This issue frequently takes the form, "Which is best among the alternatives?" We are faced with many issues of value in our daily lives, and these issues can lead to a surprising variety of speeches to convince. Consider the following list of such issues:

Has self-reliance gone out of style?

Is a college education a necessity today?

Is the city manager type of government superior to the elected mayor type?

Has state government gotten too large?

Was Senator Joseph McCarthy a hero or a menace?

Is gambling morally wrong?

Can one find life in the Army valuable?

Is the Forkner shorthand method superior to the Gregg method?

Are the Communists in Latin America a threat to our security?

Are American-made cars better bargains for Americans than foreign cars?

Is modern art really Art?

The above list shows that there are two types of issues of value: one type poses a question about the application of a value judgment, and the other asks for a comparison between two or more concepts or things. In developing a speech to convince on either type of issue of value, there are two stock issues you should develop.

I. "These are the criteria or standards on which X and Y should be judged or compared."
   A. Support for choosing these criteria.
   B. Further support for choosing these criteria.
II. "X does (or does not) meet the criteria or standards,

above. (Or, according to the standards, X is superior to Y.")
  A. Support; application of standards.
  B. Support; further application of standards.

It is important that your first main idea define the grounds for the evaluation or comparison; for if you and your audience cannot agree on *how* to evaluate, you can hardly agree on your evaluation. This is why the examples indicate that you may have to use support in order to get the audience to accept your criteria.

Issues of policy. An issue of policy concerns what policy (rule, or law) should be adopted to solve a particular problem. Some examples of policy issues are the following:

Should the jury system be abolished?
Should we adopt a negative income tax to solve the problem of poverty?
Should radio and television licenses be awarded on a different basis than now?
Should grades be abolished at your college?
Should desegregation of the public schools be achieved through busing?
Should the college build a new library?
Should we legalize marijuana?
Should the states adopt uniform marriage and divorce laws?
Should our state adopt "right-to-work" laws?

There are three stock issues inherent in any issue of policy. To convince your audience your thesis is correct, you must generally organize a speech on a policy to deal with each of these three stock issues:

1. Is the new policy *needed?* That is, under present circumstances and without the new policy, does a *problem* exist—are people being treated unfairly, getting hurt, wasting resources, and so forth?
2. Is the proposed policy *advantageous?* Will it solve the problem?
3. Is the new policy *practicable?* That is, can we afford it? Will it be enforceable? Is it efficient? Will it create other problems?

How are these stock issues inherent in any issue of policy? If I wish to convince you that the country should appropriate a million dollars to dam a river a few miles away to create a new city reservoir, your first inclination is to say "No, it will be too expensive." Your first question would probably be, "Why do we need a new reservoir?" I then point out that we will outstrip our water supply within ten years at the present rate of use. Your next question might be, "OK, but will the million-dollar dam give us an adequate water supply?" "Yes," is the answer, and I pull out my facts and figures to prove it. Finally, you ask, "All right, but how can we get the money?" And I respond with a plan for a bond issue.

So you are at last convinced that there is a problem with the water supply, that my proposed solution will solve the problem, and that the solution is practicable. You now agree with my thesis: We should dam the river to create a new city reservoir.

Note that to prove that a new policy should be adopted, you must satisfactorily answer all three stock issues. No matter how practical or advantageous a new reservoir might sound, no one is going to vote for it if the present water supply is adequate (no need). No matter what the need is, the audience will not be in favor of my proposal if the new reservoir won't solve the predicted water shortage. It makes little difference whether a need exists and my proposal will solve the need if it is too expensive, does not fit our present concept of what is fair and moral, cannot be achieved in time to do any good, and so forth.

Concomitantly, it is relatively easy to prove that a new policy should *not* be adopted by creating doubt in the minds of listeners on only *one* of the issues. Perhaps this is why a very small proportion of the bills submitted to a state legislature or the United States Congress ever becomes law. It is much easier to be against change than to devise and propose needed, advantageous, and practical solutions for problems we face.

Solutions to obvious social problems are not always easily found. This condition was sounded by Senator Thomas F. Eagleton, who, like many other people today, is concerned over the amount and availability of pornographic literature, but confessed an inability to write particular legislation which would at once stop smut and maintain freedom of speech and of the press.[7] Senator Eagleton also believes that guns are too plentiful and too readily available to would-be killers but admits that, among the many bills proposed, he has not seen any that would solve that problem without denying free access to firearms by those who use guns in sports.

If you are going to argue against adoption of a particular policy, try to avoid "putting all your eggs in one basket" by arguing just "no need" or just "no advantages" or just "impracticability." Instead, argue all three issues:

I. There is no need for the new policy (or the need for the new policy is quite minor).

II. *Even if* there were a need for action, the proposed policy would not solve the problem.

III. Even if there were a problem and the proposed plan would solve it, adoption of the plan would involve too much expense and could not be implemented without causing additional problems.

Introducing and concluding speeches to convince

Introductions. The introduction to a speech to convince, in most cases, should perform the same functions as does the introduction to the speech to inform (see Chapter 8). It must capture the attention and interest of the audience and should provide a rationale as to why the subject is important to the audience. With one exception, detailed below, the introduction should also reveal the speaker's purpose or thesis and should preview the main ideas to be covered in the body of the speech. If such an introduction is successfully carried out, the audience is then disposed to listen to the body of the speech.

The only situation in which you would *not* want to reveal in the introduction your purpose and the main ideas that support it is when you expect your thesis to be so unacceptable to your audience that its revelation would cause the audience to argue against you throughout the speech. In such a situation you would delay mentioning your thesis until late in your speech, after you have prepared the audience for it (see "The Hostile Audience" earlier in this chapter).

Conclusions. Concluding a speech to convince is again like concluding the speech to inform (Chapter 8). Clarify the ideas, summarize your main points, and round out the speech by restating the thesis in an interesting way. A former student of one of the authors once presented a speech advocating that the United States had a responsibility to help feed the hungry peoples of the world. She concluded her appeal something like this:

> And so, you see, it is not only the humanitarian thing to do, it is the practical thing to do. Hunger is very real in the world; the United States can greatly alleviate that hunger; we can only benefit from feeding the world through creating, thus, a safer, more peaceful world. For as the Roman author, Seneca, wrote centuries ago, "A hungry people listens not to reason, nor cares for justice, nor is bent by any prayers."

The speech to actuate

When your persuasive task is to get the audience to *do* something, the purpose of the speech is *to actuate* them. The task of actuating an audience is quite different from convincing them; the latter merely involves obtaining belief, whereas the former involves actual behavior. The difference between the tasks of actuating and convincing an audience rests on two basic differences between belief and action.

First, the beliefs and the behavior of an individual may very well differ, for the former is private and the latter is public. Berelson and Steiner conclude, from their review of the scientific literature:[8]

> Behavior, being visible, is more responsive to extreme pressures and accommodations. OAB's [Opinions, Attitudes, Beliefs], being private until expressed, can be maintained without even being subject to question or argument. And there is no necessary reason for OAB's and behavior to be in harmony: we are polite to acquaintances we really don't like, we go along with the majority·in a committee action rather than make a fuss, and we go to the polls even though we really don't care about the outcome.

Second, unless your listeners are strongly ego-involved or otherwise committed to their belief or attitude, it might be less difficult to alter their attitude or belief measurably than to get them to *do* something about it. In other words, each of us holds a great many attitudes and beliefs about which we *do* practically nothing. For instance, we may disagree heartily with the editorial position of the local newspaper without writing a letter to the editor in rebuttal; we may greatly appreciate a television network's public service program without implementing the lesson of the program; we may harbor strong feelings about a pending decision on a school redistricting or land use zoning without bothering to attend the public hearing on the issue.

To persuade someone to *do* something, you must make the person think that an expenditure of energy will be worthwhile, and you have to generate the energy for him or her to take action.

If we turn again to the model of humans as creatures who consistently strive toward homeostasis, we may consider this example. Suppose you are in favor of a particular tax bill pending in the state legislature, and you are fairly confident that it will pass. Then you read in the newspaper the text of a speech by a prominent legislator attacking the bill. Now you become afraid the bill may be in trouble. You want it to pass because it seems an equitable law, and it will save you some money. You begin to worry. You find it difficult to sit still for very long when thinking about it. Finally you write your state representative urging him or her to fight and vote for the tax measure. You stamp and seal the envelope and post the letter. You sigh and assure yourself that you have done your part in saving the bill; you have the matter "off your chest" and can return to a state of homeostasis.

Activity

Think back to the last time you became so steamed up over something that you were as restless as in the example above. What did you do to restore your balance?

Your task in a speech to actuate, then, is to create in members of your audience an imbalance (a nonhomeostatic state) and then to direct them to the goal that will restore the balance. You must energize the audience and direct them to expend that energy by taking particular action.

A highly useful strategy for achieving the goal of actuation has been the *motivated sequence* popularized by Alan H. Monroe.[9] Its five distinct steps are arranged to conform to the ways people are known to decide to *act.* This makes the sequence most applicable to the speech to actuate. Here are each of the five steps in order.

The attention step. When you walk to the front of the classroom to begin your speech, you must first get the attention and interest of your audience—you must do what psychologist H. A. Overstreet called "crossing the deadline of interest." This can be accomplished by arousing curiosity with a rhetorical question; with humor; by referring to the importance of the subject or to special interests of the audience; or by honestly complimenting the audience; or a number of other ways. Nancy Endruschat, a student at St. Lawrence University, once began a speech by going to the chalkboard and writing in large print letters S E X. Then she turned to her audience and said: "Have you ever seen this word on a schoolroom blackboard? Probably not, since sex is not often brought up in classrooms. That is why I would like to speak to you today on why we should institute sex education courses in our public schools." She was dealing with an interesting subject, but her introduction enhanced the audience's attention to her thesis.

The need step. After you have the audience riveted to your subject or to you, the next step is to upset the audience's homeostasis. This lack of equilibrium will make the audience receptive to the source of action you will propose. This is the step Holm calls the "want phase" of the speech because it is designed to make the audience *want* what you have to offer.[10] The needs or wants you create in this step of your speech will be one of two kinds: a physical or psychological need, or some unfulfilled desire.

Before his vivid challenge for Americans to "ask what you can do for your country," John F. Kennedy stated the need for action in broad sweeping terms:[11]

> The world is very different now [than 175 years ago]. For man holds in his mortal hands the power to abolish all forms of human poverty and all forms of human life. And yet the same revolutionary beliefs for which our forebears fought are still at issue around the globe—the belief that the rights of man come not from the generosity of the state but from the hand of God.

The "threat" type of need step is used by the insurance representative who asks you to think of how your family will manage once you, the breadwinner, are "out of the picture"; it is used by the manufacturers of shock absorbers and mufflers to make you think your car is unsafe; and it is used by the American Cancer Society to remind you that cigarettes kill.

The need step illustrating unfulfilled desire is also used in public speeches to actuate. A student at the University of Nebraska, in an effort to get classmates to give blood to the Red Cross, used a need step something like this:

> We Americans like to be generous. Generosity is part of our ethic. We are taught it almost from the cradle. But, with many generous acts, we deprive ourselves of things we want and desire. If we give to charity a five-dollar bill, that's five dollars we don't have to spend on ourselves. Give some unfortunate the shirt off your back and you need a shirt yourself.
>
> But did you know there is a way to be generous without costing yourself a red cent or a stitch of muslin? Did you know that you can give the most valuable and precious of all things—even life itself—to others, without an iota of loss to yourself? Did you know that you can give what

cannot be manufactured, compounded, or formulated by anyone but you? Did you know that you personally, could become partially responsible for the saving of a life in Vietnam's rice paddies or County Hospital? Or could become an indispensable part of a team effort at open-heart surgery? Well, you can do all these things—by giving blood.

The satisfaction step. After focusing your listeners' attention and creating a state of internal need within them, they should be receptive to your suggestions for returning to a balanced state. In the satisfaction step you tell them exactly what they should do. Provide as much information as they will need in order to do what you ask. Your purpose may be to get them to buy and read *Gone with the Wind.* Tell them where it can be purchased and how much it costs. You want them to attend the address by a visiting lecturer? Be sure to mention the time, date, and place. You wish them to take Art Appreciation 103 next term? Tell them when and where it meets, who teaches the course, how the course is conducted, and so on.

In addition to giving the audience all the information, you must perform the all-important job of overcoming audience objections to doing as you ask. If audience members have reservations about doing as you ask, they will probably not do it, no matter how strongly you attracted their attention and created a need, and no matter how clearly you have explained what they should do. Quoting statistics from studies at Cornell on the relative chances of surviving an automobile crash with and without seatbelts will not get many people to "buckle up for safety" if you cannot overcome their feeling that seatbelts are too confining or they're just too much of a nuisance to buckle every time. You will never sell audience members on the idea of making their next car a Volkswagen beetle, no matter how logically it fits their basic transportation *needs,* unless you can convince them that their objection to its lack of space is not justified.

The visualization step. The fourth step in your speech to actuate is primarily designed to increase desire for attaining the satisfaction step. This step is aptly named, for you paint a picture for the audience so it can "see" the future results of accepting or not accepting your suggestion. This step might even be called "the projection step" since you ask audience members to project themselves, through their imaginations, into the future.

There are basically three types of visualization steps: negative, positive, and combination (negative and positive combined). The *negative visualization* step pictures the unpleasant circumstances that will result if the speaker's proposal is not accepted. In extreme form, the forecast of disaster is made by the prophet of doom ("unless the people of this country wake up . . ."). The *positive visualization* step projects a picture of how happy and satisfied the audience will be if the speaker's proposal is accepted. The *combination* step simply combines the two processes, usually with the negative part before the positive.

In a classroom speech at the University of Nebraska in 1968 John Andreason urged audience members to use their seatbelts each time they drive a car. A paraphrase of his combination visualization step follows:

> (*Negative*) Oh, I know it's easy to make up excuses to not buckle up on every little trip. Well, just keep on making those excuses, and you might have the kind of "minor" accident Walter H. Cameron of Indianapolis had. Forced off the road and into a concrete abutment at twenty-five miles per hour, Mr. Cameron crashed into the steering wheel with the same force as falling two stories. A broken jaw, three fractured ribs, a cracked elbow, and fourteen stitches in the face and neck were the price he paid for a dangling, unused seatbelt.
> (*Positive*) But develop the seatbelt habit, and each time you climb behind the wheel the solid, reassuring metal click of your seatbelt reassures you that you are safe—safe from injury, and a safer driver because you have once again reminded yourself that driving is a serious and risky business. As you drive, the gentle tug at your lap will be a constant reminder of your new status as a safety-conscious, safer driver, which can become a source of real personal pride.

The action step. The conclusion of the motivated sequence speech is called the *action step* because it states precisely what the audience is to do to solve a problem. We should be quite specific in prescribing the action, for if the audience does not know or remember what to do or believe, it can hardly be expected to respond.

There has been little scientific research on whether the speaker should explicitly or implicitly draw the conclusion, but the bulk of research that has been done supports the *explicit* prescription.[12] If the previous steps have successfully energized audience members to act, you must now tell them exactly what to do. You can do it in several ways.

A simple call to action, or a challenge to the audience, is the most direct. "The book I recommend is presently on sale in paperback at the college bookstore for only $1.75. Get your copy right away. Read it and experience a whole new world opening up for you." Or, "This is for you one of the most important pieces of legislation your legislator will ever vote on. Do you wish him or her to vote without writing how you feel about the matter?"

You can end your speech with a statement of personal commitment and perhaps an invitation: "By next year's election I will be registered to vote; I intend to study the candidates and issues carefully; then I intend to vote for the candidates I think are the most qualified and who support the sides of the issues I think are best for all Americans. Won't you join me?"

You can end your speech with a quotation, as did Charles Schalliol:[13]

> If we ignore air pollution it will loom ever larger. In the words of Professor Morris B. Jacobs, former director of the Department of Air Pollution Control, "It is now time to end this plague. Time to look beyond narrow vested interests, to awake from slumbering too long—and save ourselves. We had better act now. It will soon be too late."

A speech can be concluded in other ways. You can present an emotional appeal, summarize, use a literary quotation or an illustration. But make your action step *explicit*—point directly to the action you wish audience members to take.

The speech to stimulate

The speech to stimulate, or to inspire, seeks to heighten and emotionalize some belief already held or to produce greater effort in what is already being done. The most easily recognized examples of the speech to stimulate are the inspirational sermon, the pep talk, and the patriotic Fourth-of-July-type speech.

The sermon is not usually trying to *produce* belief. The clergyman can assume that members of the congregation already believe in God, are committed to the tenets of the particular sect, believe in "brotherly love," and so on. The sermon attempts to cause the congregation to believe these concepts more vigorously. It attempts to light a lamp of zeal and dedication to the ideals the listeners have held long but without fervor.

Some sermons seek not to actuate the congregation but to urge greater effort in behavior the minister or priest assumes is already being performed. Thus, the sermon does not urge contributions to the financial upkeep of the church but urges *larger* contributions.

In the same vein, the pep talk by the football coach at half-time does not seek to actuate the players to try to win. The coach assumes the players *have* been trying to win; but greater effort is sought. To do this the coach must mobilize and energize the players —in fact, inspire them.

The Fourth of July orator assumes that anyone who chooses to come outside to listen to a speech must already have some love for the country. The speaker's job has traditionally been to rejuvenate that love of country through inspirational recounting of past, present, and future glories.

Because of the nature of the task, the speech to stimulate is a difficult one to do well. The difficulty stems from three principal qualities usually present in the successful speech to stimulate.

First, the speech to stimulate is frankly emotional. Since it seeks to emotionalize the audience, the speaker often must speak, feel, and act emotionally during the speech. In an era when "blowing your cool" is considered by some to be anathema, many speakers restrain their emotionalism and thus fail. On the other hand, the speaker who does really "let it all hang out" may appear too fanatical. In this type of speech, the successful speaker must honestly feel and communicate emotional intensity while also demonstrating reasonable constraint.

Second, the speech to inspire usually must rely upon especially vivid language, such as figures of speech. Figurative language must be fresh and imaginative and must stir the audience's imagination and spirit. It takes much skill, imagination, and effort to consistently —or even occasionally—devise imaginative, stimulating language when members of your audience already agree with you. If they have already heard it before, what you thought was a carefully polished gem of wisdom will turn out to be a tired cliché. It is not often that a Winston Churchill can capture the spirit of an era as he did in coining the phrase "iron curtain" in 1946 at the beginning of the Cold War. Considering the vast number of words voiced in speeches, few stand out as memorable and telling phrases. An example is Patrick Henry's "Give me liberty or give me death" or Winston Churchill's stirring call for British courage, "Let us, therefore, brace ourselves to our duties, and so bear ourselves that, if the British Empire and its Commonwealth last for a thousand years, men will still say, "This was their finest hour."

Third, the successful speech to stimulate must usually contain some *content* that is new to the audience. Parishioners may have heard the story of the Good Samaritan many times, so retelling it will hardly stimulate brotherly love within their hearts. But perhaps narrating how a small host of followers of the late Tom Dooley have selflessly fought disease, ignorance, poverty, and privation in order to help the desperate people of Asia can inspire similar humanitarian thoughts and actions.

Even though the speech to stimulate is difficult to master, you may occasionally wish or need to make such a speech. How do you go about it?

In general, the motivated sequence is also recommended for speeches to stimulate, as you are faced with the same kind of psychological task: you must secure attention, create an imbalance or need in the audience, and specify how that need can be satisfied; you must help the audience visualize the results of following your advice; and you must clinch your goal with a final appeal to action or commitment.

Persuasive appeals

Chapter 6 defined kinds of supporting proofs you can use in persuasive discourse. Now we will categorize persuasive appeals into three types. For over two thousand years, speech theorists have stated that there are three general means of inducing belief and action, or three *modes of proof*. Most speech communication theorists today are satisfied with the names Aristotle used for them: ethos, pathos, and logos.

Ethos is proof that resides within the speaker. It is made up of the qualities of the speaker that cause the audience to accept or reject the speaker's ideas. Factor analysis by McCroskey has revealed that the two factors that most reliably comprise ethos are *authoritativeness* and *character*.[14] In other words, how audience members perceive the speaker's knowledgeability or expertise (authoritativeness) and the speaker's honesty and friendliness (character) affect whether they will believe or act simply because the speaker says they should.

Two other dimensions of ethos should be mentioned. *Prior ethos* is the influence the speaker brings to the speaking situation. We might call this kind of ethos *reputation*. *Developed ethos* is created by the speaker through delivery, appearance, ideas, and evidence while speaking. It would be nice to enter each speaking situation with the knowledge that your reputation has preceded you and that your audience is ready to believe you. Of course, the reverse would be catastrophic; if your reputation is very bad, the audience will not believe anything you say! Student speakers are not generally blessed or cursed with extremes of reputation, so they must rely on speaking delivery, content, and organization to *develop* ethos while speaking.

Aristotle advised many years ago that each speaker, regardless of previous reputation, should develop ethos for each speech: "This kind of persuasion [ethos] like the others, should be achieved by what the speaker says, not what the people think of his character before he begins to speak."[15]

Pathos is "emotional proof." We say pathos resides within the audience, because people share certain common motives that can constitute a basis for belief or action. If I can get you to increase your fire insurance by appealing to your fear that you may lose more than you are presently covered for, I have used pathos. I also use pathos when I sell you a dandruff shampoo by appealing to your natural desire to attract the opposite sex.

Logos is the form of proof residing in the speech itself. Logos might be considered another name for "supporting materials." Logos is what the speaker "finds" in some way and places into the speech. Logos is sometimes called *logical proof.*

These three forms of proof are interrelated. For instance, one's use of pathos and logos is apt to influence one's developed ethos. And, even though it is useful for purposes of analysis and clarity to call them separate concepts, audiences cannot distinguish among them, and even experts cannot always agree in classifying arguments or appeals as belonging to one of the three modes.[16] Most communication experts agree that successful persuasion is aided by good use of all three modes of proof.

Ethics of persuasion

Ethical questions are involved when one person attempts to influence the thinking and actions of others. For example, does the end justify the means? If you feel strongly that a particular position is right, does this justify using any method that will work to win others over to your point of view? Many persons judge the success of communication strictly on the basis of whether it is effective—whether the communication achieves the speaker's goal. Effect is certainly important, whether trying to inform or persuade; however, the means one uses to gain that effect are also important.

Individuals often must determine for themselves what is the personal and social responsibility of a communicator. Most responsible citizens agree that it would be wrong to distort or falsify information, evidence, reasoning, or ideas just to be persuasive. Not only would such practices be wrong, but in the long run they also will not be effective. A person who sells a product (or an idea) by lying should not expect many customers to return. Such practices will harm one's *ethos.*

There are also means of persuasion we would agree are acceptable ways of influencing people. For example, a persuader should be encouraged to use informed analysis of social problems in order to implement a solution the speaker is convinced would remedy some situation. Any citizen who has studied all sides of an issue has the right to take a strong stand on behalf of his or her conviction.

Between the two extremes of lying and the most conscientious problem-solving are many methods of persuasion that may be ethical or unethical, depending on how they are used and who is judging them. For example, how much emotional proof is appropriate in persuasion? Should the speaker use emotion only or balance the message with facts? You should confront these questions candidly and consider carefully what are ethically acceptable means of persuading listeners.

A good place to begin in your search for ethical guidelines is to avoid behavior that might hurt others. Search for methods of persuasion that improve the human condition. There exists in human society an unlimited potential for good and for individual and group growth. In our search for improving human society, however, we need a sincere respect for the other person. As Nilsen concluded, "freedom of speech, which includes the freedom to persuade, imposes on everyone who exercises that right an obligation to use speech so that it becomes a carrier of freedom."[7]

QUESTIONS FOR THOUGHT
AND DISCUSSION
CHAPTER 9

1. What special problems does the *persuasive* speaker confront when considering how to adapt a speech to an audience?
2. Considering what "balance" theories teach us about human behavior, what kind of reactions should a speaker expect from the audience?
3. When determining how perception will influence audience reactions, explain why it is possible for different persons to react differently to the same message. How should this possibility influence the way you communicate your ideas?
4. What should you do differently when addressing a hostile audience as compared with a favorable audience?
5. How can you motivate an unmotivated audience?

6. What special considerations should you give to organizing persuasive messages?
7. Distinguish between the following kinds of persuasive appeals: *ethos, pathos,* and *logos.* Which one is more likely to be found in a library?

EXERCISES · ASSIGNMENTS | CHAPTER 9

1. In *Vital Speeches of the Day* or *Representative American Speeches* find samples of speeches designed primarily (a) to convince, (b) to actuate, and (c) to stimulate. Why do you classify each as you do?
2. Find in speeches examples of *ethos, logos,* and *pathos.*
3. Prepare a brief analysis of how well some speaker supported his or her main arguments.
4. See if you can find a sample speech in which the speaker used the motivated sequence organization and development. Was the method used well?
5. Evaluate a persuasive speaker and determine why the speech was well organized (or why it was not).
6. Prepare a brief analysis of yourself as a member of an audience, and determine what attitudes and beliefs you have which a persuasive speaker would do well to consider.
7. What methods of persuasion do you consider ethical? What means do you consider unethical? Why?
8. Using *Education Index,* locate several articles on the general topic of "sex in the schools" and determine what probable attitude toward the position taken in each article the following persons would have: your speech communication class, your parents, members of a particular church, and your state legislators. In what way does the theory of cognitive dissonance help you answer this question?
9. Prepare a persuasive discourse on a topic you know will make your classmates feel hostile. Be prepared to explain later the persuasive strategy you used to try to overcome this hostility and win support for your position.

ENDNOTES | Chapter 9

1. Bernard Berelson and Gary A. Steiner, *Human Behavior: An Inventory of Scientific Findings* (New York: Harcourt, Brace & World, 1964), p. 266.
2. *Ibid.*

3. Leon Festinger, *A Theory of Cognitive Dissonance* (New York: Harper & Row, 1957).

4. Gary. Cronkhite, *Persuasion: Speech and Behavioral Change* (Indianapolis: Bobbs-Merrill, 1969), pp. 139–140.

5. Wallace C. Fotheringham, *Perspectives on Persuasion* (Boston: Allyn and Bacon, 1966).

6. Calvin Hoffman, *The Murder of the Man Who Was Shakespeare* (New York: J. Messner, 1955).

7. Senator Thomas F. Eagleton, in keynote speech before the Central States Speech Association's annual convention, St. Louis, April 18, 1969.

8. Berelson and Steiner, *op. cit.,* p. 576.

9. See Alan H. Monroe and Douglas Ehninger, *Principles and Types of Speech Communication,* 6th ed. (Glenview, Ill.: Scott, Foresman, 1974).

10. James N. Holm, *Productive Speaking for Business and the Professions* (Boston: Allyn and Bacon, 1967), pp. 363–368.

11. President John F. Kennedy, Inaugural Address, January 20, 1961.

12. See Stewart L. Tubbs, "Explicit versus Implicit Conclusions and Audience Commitment," *Speech Monographs,* 35 (March 1968): 14–19.

13. Charles Schalliol, "The Strangler," in *Winning Orations* (Detroit: Interstate Oratorical Association, 1967), p. 57. Reprinted by permission of the Interstate Oratorical Association.

14. James C. McCroskey, "Scales for the Measurement of Ethos," *Speech Monographs,* 33 (March 1966): 65–72.

15. Aristotle, *The Rhetoric,* translated by W. Rhys Roberts (New York: Modern Library, 1954), p. 25.

16. See Samuel L. Becker, "Research on Emotional and Logical Proofs," *Southern Speech Journal,* 27 (Spring 1963): 198–207.

17. Thomas R. Nilsen, "Free Speech, Persuasion, and the Democratic Process," *Quarterly Journal of Speech,* 44 (October 1958): 243.

10

SOME-TO-MANY:
MASS
COMMUNICATION

10

So much information on mass communication is available that a single chapter on the subject is something of a challenge. To illustrate: the Henry Grady School of Journalism at the University of Georgia offers no less than sixty-six undergraduate courses dealing with some aspect of mass communication; and the cumulative index of doctoral dissertations in the field of mass communication through only 1972 contains seventy-two *pages* of doctoral dissertation titles, each page containing between fifty and seventy titles. Obviously much has been written about mass communication. Faced with the task of selecting what material should go into a single chapter, one must know how the mosquito felt who found its way into a nudist camp: it knew what it wanted to do but hardly knew where to begin!

Material for this chapter was chosen by answering the question: What concepts would probably produce a more efficient *consumer* of mass communication? For, although the readership of this book might harbor a budding Johnny Carson, Barbara Walters, or James Reston, certainly all readers will be *customers* of mass communication all their lives.

Mass communication defined

Mass communication is usually defined as having certain characteristics that distinguish it from interpersonal communication: media used; relatively impersonal contact between sender and receiver; relative heterogeneity of the audience; the delayed nature of feedback between receiver (audience) and sender; greater selectivity practiced by the receiver, especially in exposure and attention; and the "group nature" of the senders.

Media.   The means of mass communication are usually either broadcasting or print.   The broadcast media are radio and television, sometimes supplemented by relay stations or satellite transmitters. The print media are mostly newspapers and magazines, although some would include outdoor advertising (lighted signs, skywriting, billboards), paperback books, direct-mail advertising, and graffiti.

Impersonality of contact.   Most contact between mass communicator and receiver is impersonal.   Usually the message sender does not even see the receiver.   Of course, some media are more personal than others.   Some television performers, for instance, report that strangers walk up to them and chat as if they were old friends, simply because the performer has been in the stranger's home so often. President Franklin D. Roosevelt had the knack of making people feel, via the medium of radio, that he had actually dropped in for a "fireside chat."   And some people come to "know" certain columnists, like James Reston or Art Buchwald, by reading their columns for years.   But most mass communication establishes far less personal contact between sender and receiver than, say, between store clerk and customer, or between speaker and questioner at a public forum.

Heterogeneity of audience.   Mass media audiences tend to be large, heterogeneous, undifferentiated groups of people.   Of course this varies considerably from one medium to another, because a particular medium of mass communication may have a certain audience in mind and may tailor its output for them.   In this way, "Top Forty" radio stations address themselves to teenagers, while other stations appeal to those who like classical music; *Popular Photography* magazine is directed to serious photographers.   But once a message is communicated through a mass medium, it is available to a wide and diverse audience.

Delay in feedback.   A person conversing with one or just a few persons gets immediate feedback, verbal and nonverbal.   Even the public speaker who is face to face with the audience gets some kind of immediate feedback, mostly of the nonverbal kind.   But the producers of mass media messages usually must wait hours, weeks, or months to learn whether their messages were effective.   A new advertising campaign for a product may not affect sales of the product for months.   Even when a controversial item in the news brings quick popular reaction, this feedback is often "incomplete." For instance, in August 1975 Betty Ford, the First Lady, mentioned during a television interview that she would not be surprised to learn someday that her daughter was having an affair. The ensuing telephone calls and letters were almost certainly from those who felt a strong desire either to support Mrs. Ford or to attack her for her statement; the large number of people who were neither dismayed by nor supportive of Mrs. Ford did not bother to call or write.

Receiver selectivity. A person engaged in some form of interpersonal or face-to-face communication is apt to have deliberately chosen to communicate and to pay active attention to what is said. This would be equally true of a family discussion of the budget and an open meeting of the County Commission. With mass media, however, the receiver not only chooses to be exposed or not but must choose from a bewildering array of possible media. And, while reading a newspaper or magazine, watching television, or listening to a radio, if something more important comes up, the communication can easily be shelved or turned off, whereas one would hardly get up and leave in the middle of a family conversation or a public speech. Much more will be said about receiver selectivity and the mass media later in this chapter.

Group nature of senders. Most face-to-face communication is produced by one person at a time. Mass communication material is usually the result of several people's efforts. Television newscasts employ cameramen, writers, tape editors, reporters, directors, assistant directors, advertising people, and so on. Newspapers and magazines are produced by large staffs. Even a single speech by a single individual, if important enough for broadcasting on television, may result from hours of work by a whole team of ghostwriters and advisers.

Mass communication in the United States

In many countries the only mass media are owned or operated by the government and are used as extensions of the government. A government can control its populace by controlling what information is disseminated. At the time of the writing of this book, for instance, the People's Republic of China had not disseminated the information that the United States had put men on the moon and brought them back. Apparently the Chinese government did not want its populace to know of such sophisticated American technology.

American mass media, on the other hand, are privately owned and are relatively free to operate as they wish. There are some restraints, of course. Broadcasting is more subject to governmental control than is print. This is primarily due to the idea that the airways are public, so use of them must be regulated. The Federal Communications Commission (FCC) began operating in 1934 and regulates broadcasting in three specific ways:

1. Since the broadcast frequency spectrum is limited, use of each frequency (and the power allotted for use) is a pressing problem. The FCC must allocate frequency ranges to various uses: one band is reserved for commercial broadcasting, another for police use, another for amateur radio "hams," another for Citizen's Band radio and so forth.
2. The FCC licenses each broadcaster within a particular classification for specific frequency and for amount of power that may be used. This regulation serves primarily to keep stations and broadcasters from overlapping and producing "interference" (noise).
3. The FCC also regulates and oversees broadcasting stations to ensure that they follow FCC rules and technical requirements. In general, stations are licensed to operate "in the public interest," and, if a station is found not to so operate, it can be fined; it can also be reprimanded, be issued orders to cease a certain practice, or it can lose its license to broadcast. Each licensee must show at license renewal time just how the station has met the public interest through its programming.

Some other general rules of the FCC regarding broadcasting are listed below.

Fairness. If a station editorializes by presenting one side of a controversial issue, it is obligated "to afford reasonable opportunity for the discussion of conflicting views" on the issue. This has been called the "fairness doctrine."

Political appearances. In general, if a candidate for political office is allowed to use a broadcasting station, all other official candidates for that office must be allowed equal time. For instance, Lar Daly, an otherwise obscure citizen used to perennially run for the offices of both mayor of Chicago and president of the United States. To the consternation of network officials and Chicago broadcasters, Daly would demand all the free air time given to his competitors for those offices. The FCC forced Chicago stations to give Lar Daly air time equal to that given Mayor Richard Daley, which the former used to espouse such causes as legalized gambling and elimination of public schools. When in 1956 Daly demanded equal network time with Dwight D. Eisenhower in the presidential campaign, his protest went all the way to the United States Supreme Court before it was turned down.[1]

A more recent example involved Ronald Reagan, former governor of California. When he announced his candidacy for the Republican nomination for president in 1975, he had to give up broadcasting his radio show, "Viewpoint." Stations even decided not to rerun his old Hollywood movies or episodes of the old television show, "Death Valley Days," which Reagan had hosted. For some presidential elections Congress has suspended the "equal time" rule. The first such suspension was in 1960 and allowed presentation of the debates between candidates John F. Kennedy and Richard M. Nixon.

Advertising. The FCC does not regulate advertising except that it limits the number of minutes per hour that can be devoted to non-program material. The FCC can force a station to cease using what the FCC considers false and misleading advertising.

Quiz shows and payola. Quiz shows that are rigged by giving contestants the answers in advance are prohibited. Disc jockeys who are paid money to "plug" certain records must make such payments public knowledge.

Obscenity and fraud. Stations may not broadcast information or schemes that the station's managers know to be fraudulent. They also may not broadcast "obscene" language.

Station management. Although the FCC does not monitor all broadcasts, it does require that each commercial broadcaster keep a log of what program material and commercial announcements actually were broadcast.

Networks. The FCC has passed rules limiting the amount of program material that television or radio networks can supply to their individual stations.

Media: extension of the business world

By 1974 the average American was spending an average of just over three hours per weekday watching television, with an extra one and a half hours per day each weekend.[2] A study in Philadelphia indicated that teenagers there average almost *four* hours of television viewing per day and spend another two hours listening to the radio.[3] People who spend this much time attending to broadcasting as entertainment may become annoyed at over-commercialization, at the inanity and repetitiveness of many advertisements, and at network scheduling of *three* television specials at the same hour.

The commercialization and competitiveness of the networks and local stations stem from the fact that broadcasting is not an extension of the entertainment world but the business world. The people who pay for broadcasting are businesses who advertise their services or products. If people would sit before their sets and do nothing but watch commercials, television would broadcast little else *but* commercials, but of course people will not do this. So in order to get you in front of the set, entertainment is provided so you will be there when the commercials appear. Understanding the nature of broadcasting may not make you any happier about commercials and competitive scheduling, but at least now you know its rationale.

Of course, it is the commercial nature of broadcasting that also causes it to be competitive in other, mostly beneficial, ways. For instance, there is constant station and network competition to build "image" by broadcasting quality shows and to boost the news department's credibility by featuring comprehensive and accurate reporting. Sometimes the race to get news on the air first may result in distortion through sheer haste, but by and large most Americans would probably rather have business pay the broadcasting bill than have the government control it.

Print media are somewhat less an extension of the business community than are the broadcast media, but the publication that can sustain itself by subscriptions alone is rare. Some expensive professional journals exist without including advertisements, and so does *Mad* magazine. But the wide-distribution magazine or newspaper whose advertising revenues decline is heading for extinction.

Media versus the government

Because in the United States freedom of the press is guarded by the First Amendment to the Constitution, the mass media and the government have an unusual arrangement. Government officials and politicians want to use the media to further their programs and political fortunes, so they try to maintain good relations with reporters, columnists, and media executives. Likewise, the media people, who wish to extract news stories from government officials and politicians also try to maintain good relations. However, the news-gatherers have traditionally been assigned a "watchdog" role to sniff out and expose corruption, misdeeds and plain foolishness by elected and appointed officials. We have recently seen some dramatic examples of the combat between government and the media.

In 1971 CBS television produced a one-hour documentary, "The Selling of the Pentagon" that exposed the vast and costly public relations efforts of the military establishment to influence public opinion. Even though the program was based entirely upon unclassified materials available to anyone willing to search them out, military officials and politicians who support the Pentagon's viewpoints objected strenuously to the show. Some government officials demanded to see "out-takes"—film not actually used in the program —presumably to catch CBS using classified material. CBS was finally coerced into telecasting a postscript to the program that contained critical reactions to the program by Vice President Spiro Agnew, Secretary of Defense Melvin Laird, and Chairman F. Edward Herbert, of the House of Representatives Armed Services Committee.

Another example of the government-media conflict from the same era is Spiro Agnew's running argument against broadcast media and selected newspapers (before he resigned the vice presidency in disgrace), in which he made statements such as, "A narrow and distorted picture of America often emerges from the televised news."[4]

And who can forget that it was primarily the investigative reporting of two hard-working reporters for the *Washington Post* that led to a unique event in American history: the resignation of a president in office.

Breadth and depth of media news coverage

In general, the press covers news events in both greater breadth and greater depth than does either television or radio. The usual network television news program covers the "news of the world" in under thirty minutes. Few people could read "all the news that's fit to print" (the slogan of *The New York Times*) in that short a time. A half-hour news broadcast may show a twenty-second film of a thirty-minute speech, and summarize the rest of the speech in less than a minute; the *Times* would probably print the entire speech and the reaction to it by the audience and by various important people.

There are some interesting exceptions to the generalization that the press covers more stories in more depth and breadth than do broadcast media. In 1975 John J. McCloy, friend and adviser to many United States presidents, was incisively interviewed on television for two hours by CBS commentator Eric Sevareid, providing viewers with the memoirs which Mr. McCloy has said he will not write. A baseball game might get three column-inches in the newspaper but be broadcast from start to finish on radio and television.

"Gatekeeping" and access to the media

Two concepts of major concern today are "gatekeeping" and access to the media. "Gatekeepers" determine what topics are allowed exposure and how much exposure these topics get. Access to the media is important because so many different voices wish to air their points of view on television or radio, or in the press.

Gatekeeping. It is impossible to print or broadcast every event in the world. So someone or some group must choose what information is broadcast as news. The general process of deciding what will be disseminated (and how much time will be spent on any one aspect) is known as *gatekeeping;* those who do the choosing are called gatekeepers.

There are a number of reasons why some items of information are chosen and others are not chosen for dissemination in the mass media. First, some items must be left out for time or space reasons. Therefore, information that appears to be the most important or newsworthy is disseminated. Since the more unusual news item gets reported, it is often the case of aberrant behavior that is reported, which perhaps gives a distorted view of things. When a dog bites a man, that is not news; when a man bites a dog, *that's* news! Reports of fires, rapes, muggings, murders, and riots abound in the news, while the fact that millions of people go quietly about their business, obey the law, and get the work of the world done is hardly ever mentioned.

Rules and regulations and laws sometimes necessitate gatekeeping. The National Association of Broadcasters (NAB) voluntarily limits the advertising of alcoholic beverages to wine, beer, and other malt beverages. The Television Code of the NAB forbids "profanity, obscenity, smut and vulgarity," attacks on religion and religious faiths, and a number of other practices, such as showing the inhumane treatment of animals. It is presently prohibited by law to advertise cigarettes and in most states it is illegal for any news media to give the names of minors arrested or tried in criminal cases.

The wishes of advertisers sometimes influence gatekeeping practices. This is less prevalent in the print than in the broadcast media for several reasons. First, most newspapers receive about 30 percent of their revenue from sales and subscriptions, whereas the broadcast media have practically no income from this source. Second, newspapers sell advertising to a wide variety of advertisers, large and small, including individuals. On the other hand, a radio or television show may be sponsored by a single large company. No advertiser wishes to offend a significant number of potential customers, so few advertisers will sponsor a program that is controversial. It is probably the commercial-supported nature of television (and somewhat true of radio) that is responsible for the fact that no truly critical satire or analysis is broadcast, whereas newspapers are less apprehensive. This leads to newspapers' printing the stinging political cartoons of Herblock, Oliphant, Szep, and others and the biting columns of Art Buchwald, Art Hoppe, and Russell Baker.

One of the most laudable reasons for withholding material from the mass media is the gatekeepers' belief that withholding certain news will be in the best interests of the public. Two incidents of this kind were reported by Summers.[5] While he had been a member of the NBC programming board, certain bad news items about the progress of World War II were "softened" and were sometimes broadcast so that some *good* news might be available to give a balance. Summers also pointed out that a particular radio drama set in the future was not aired at all because it was felt that it might be misinterpreted by some in the radio audience. The play—a love story—took place at a time when Germany had invaded the United States and occupied New York City. It was "killed" because it was feared that some people might think Germany had actually occupied New York; the board remembered the panic caused by Orson Welles's radio production of *The War of the Worlds,* when many listeners mistook the drama for an on-the-spot broadcast of an invasion from Mars.

Perhaps the kind of gatekeeping that should disturb us most is that which stems from pressure and threats from federal or local government, from special interest groups (some businesses and corporations), or even from small groups or individuals. Since newspapers enjoy wider freedoms than does broadcasting, and since, unlike broadcasters, newspapers rely very little on big national advertisers and need no license to operate, newspapers are probably less subject to pressure and threats. However, some reporters ceased their investigative reportings of the infamous Manson "family" out of fear for their own lives.[6]

An interesting example of probable gatekeeping was noted in the capitol city of a midwestern state several years ago. One of the authors and his wife had attended a play and were driving to an after-theater party. An announcement on the car radio reported that an elderly couple crossing the street next to the capitol building had been struck and killed by an automobile. Details were to be provided later. Although both the broadcast media and both city newspapers were attended to diligently for the next few days, not another mention of this accident could be found. One suspects that the driver of the car was a person of some prestige who could get the story "killed."

An interesting attempt at gatekeeping by advertisers was made in summer 1975. CBS television had produced a documentary, "The Guns of Autumn," that depicted people who hunt animals for sport as rather brutish and savage. American hunters, with the help of the National Rifle Association, were able to put enough pressure on all but one of the program's sponsors to cause them to withdraw their sponsorship. CBS broadcast the show anyway and used the vacated commercial time slots to promote the network's new fall shows.

Access to the media. Because a country like the United States is based on the idea that its people will be exposed to a free market-place of ideas, several problems are more or less constantly re-curring.

One of these problems is the problem of multiple ownership of the media. There is a general fear that if all or most media are owned by a few companies or a single company, variety in messages will be reduced or destroyed. In recent years the FCC and the courts have discouraged consolidations of media ownership. For instance, the FCC approved the acquisition of a Chicago FM station by the Chicago Tribune Company. However, since the Tribune Company already owned a television station, an AM radio station, and two daily newspapers, the FCC decision was appealed. The appeals court sent the decision back to the FCC, which finally ruled against the Tribune Company's acquisition of the FM station.[7]

Another problem related to media access involves the *fairness doctrine:* when "a person's honesty, character, or integrity is at-tacked on the air, the station must notify the person attacked, submit a tape or transcript of the offending program, and offer him free time for a reply."[8] Various court cases over the fairness doctrine have firmly established the "right of reply," but the kind of attacks that deserve reply are not easy to determine.

Broadcasting stations must provide a balance to controversial and political viewpoints, including exposure of political candidates on the air. But *how many* different political positions or candidates must be allowed exposure? Who should reply to broadcasts made by the president has never been entirely settled; and the question of how balance should be applied by broadcasting stations when one candidate or political party has much greater sums of money to spend on broadcast time has not been answered.

In short, the principles of multiple ownership, fairness, and balance are pretty well established, but the nuts and bolts operations of these principles—how they are to work in practice—are still unsolved.

There is one other media access problem, which became all too evident in the turbulent 1960s: what can an impoverished person or organization do to get a message broadcast? How can a small, poor, and perhaps radical group get access to media they feel will be powerful enough to effectively portray their point of view? All too often the tactic has been to raise the devil.

Knowing that television crews, who, with their lights and equipment, are highly visible in a neighborhood and are always looking for action to film, it became commonplace in the 1960s and 1970s for radical groups to invoke or provoke violent behavior for the purpose of getting their message televised. Some people, at least, believe televised violence in one city has led to subsequent violent protest in other cities. Some also believe that when Lynnette Fromme pointed a pistol at President Ford in September 1975, she was trying to draw media attention to herself and her antipollution, anti-tree-felling campaign. In fact, it was her defense contention that she intended not to shoot the President but to attract attention to her causes.

Effects of the mass media

Much of the research done on the mass media studies what results the media produce, accidentally and deliberately. Researchers generally agree on certain media results and do not agree on others. Two media results on which there is substantial agreement are that information is transmitted and that advertising sells products.

Information transmission. Without doubt, our mass media—especially electronic media—make possible almost instantaneous transmission of information all over the world. Today's student may consider unthinkable that it took a month for news of the signing of the Declaration of Independence to reach Savannah, or that many lives were probably lost after Lee surrendered at Appomattox because news of the event could not reach all commanders of the North and South simultaneously. It has been estimated that half a billion people in forty-nine countries watched Neil Armstrong's first step on the surface of the moon.[9]

Advertising sells products. There is also little doubt that mass media advertising—especially television advertising—effectively induces people to buy certain products or services. It was estimated that by 1975 advertising expenditures on television amounted to almost $3 billion.[10] This amount of money would not be spent unless it produced results. Lestoil, a cleaning detergent, offers a dramatic example of the impact of television advertising. Advertising it in newspapers seemed to have no effect, so the advertising was moved to television. The rapid rise in sales took Lestoil from obscurity to a position of leadership in the field.[11]

However, advertising results should not be taken to mean that the persuasive force of television is all-powerful. After all, when you buy a laundry detergent, you must buy some particular brand, and you are likely to buy the one you have heard advertised most often or the most persuasively. You must already have a desire to buy *some* laundry product, and you must simply select one. As Krugman says of television advertising, "persuasion as such, i.e., overcoming the resistant attitude, is not involved at all and it is a mistake to look for it in our personal lives as a test of television's advertising impact."[12]

Let us now turn to some areas where experts do not agree.

Linguistic habits. Some people feel that television is dramatically changing our use of language. For instance, in 1968 CBS produced a one-hour program entitled "The Strange Case of the English Language." In one section the narrator used a blackboard covered with words and phrases that had recently become popular and had already faded into obscurity. Many of these words became popular through television. Jack Paar's "I kid you not" was one example offered, as were television-news words such as *enclave*. On that program linguist Mario Pei declared that he felt that the impact of television had been tremendous in obliterating regional dialects, hinting that all Americans would soon be speaking a kind of Standard American Television English.

Pei could be correct, but many regional dialects are still quite distinguishable. One particular dialect, called "black English" and used by many black Americans, has remained particularly resistant to obliteration, even though its users expose themselves to television a great deal.[13]

Social behavior. Media effects on individuals' social behavior have been the subject of much concern to humanitarians and social scientists. This concern has manifested itself in a great deal of research, especially studies of television's effects. A survey by Comstock and Fisher of some 2,300 studies of television, for instance, indicated that 60 percent of these studies concerned television and young people.[14]

The vast amounts of data from the studies of the effect of the mass media on human social behavior (including attitudes, opinions, and beliefs) have led to greatly varying conclusions about the media's impact. Some experts are certain the impact is tremendous, while others think the effect is fairly minor.

One who believes the media effects are strong is Marshall McLuhan, author of several books and articles on the media, for instance, "This new electronic environment, which almost eliminates time and space from human experience, changes the images we have of ourselves and of others. . . . Instant electric information creates the 'mass man' by involving everybody in everybody."[15]

Experts who look at the scientific information about media impact on social behavior and minimize it include Berelson and Steiner,[16] and Joseph Klapper.[17]

Berelson and Steiner's overview of the evidence, at least through the early 1960s, indicates little effect by the mass media on human behavior. Their conclusions about media effects can be summarized as follows. First, people generally expose themselves only to congenial information (selective exposure). If people only expose themselves to viewpoints with which they already agree, little change is to be expected.

Second, however, it is not possible entirely to avoid exposure to uncongenial information. The high availability of some messages ensures that at least some opposing information will reach people, if even by accident. When this occurs, selective perception operates, and the message is interpreted according to the predispositions of the audience.

One interesting example of selective perception involves the television program, "All in the Family." This show derives much of its comedy through ridiculing Archie Bunker for his narrow-minded ethnic and religious prejudices and his ignorance. Research shows that those who agree with Archie's prejudices and the views he expresses in the program generally think his ideas are more palatable than are those of the people he argues with. Even though many people *disagree* with Archie's ideas, they tend to *like* Archie as a person.[18]

Finally, even if non-congenial information accidentally reaches someone, and even if it is not misperceived, its effect is likely to diminish through the decay of selective retention.

Since one is more likely to be exposed to, perceive, and remember congenial information, this information does tend to have an effect. However, it cannot change attitudes, opinions, or beliefs; it can merely reinforce them.

This summary draws more or less the same conclusions as Klapper, with one main addition. Occasionally, the mass media do seem to cause the audience to change either in attitude or in behavior. Klapper cites a 1940 voter study that indicated that probably 5 percent of the voters' minds were changed during the campaign by the mass media.[19] Klapper explains that such effects happen because some people were already ripe for change. For instance, they may have been subject to "cross pressure" or may have held weak attitudes in favor of a particular candidate or party which were overcome by repetitious exposure to competing messages.

Communication research has uncovered the fact that in many situations *personal influence* is superior to persuasion from mass media, whether the goal of persuasion is conversion or reinforcement. During World War II Kate Smith appeared in an eighteen-hour radio marathon for the purpose of selling War Bonds. During that period she was astoundingly successful: thirty-nine million dollars in bond sales were pledged. A follow-up study of why this broadcast was so successful revealed that the personal appeal and believability of Kate Smith seemed to account for the pledges, not the fact that she was heard on radio.

Personal influence is also a strong mediator for the influence of the mass media. Much has been written on the "two-step flow" (or "multi-step flow") of information from the media through opinion leaders who then personally effect change. This process seems to work well, since mass media are an efficient means of getting information to opinion leaders.

An interesting example of the two-step flow of information (or persuasion) happened to one of the authors. He had heard a particular anti-dandruff shampoo advertised on the air many times but had dismissed the claims, having had poor experiences with other anti-dandruff shampoos in the past. One day a particularly good student gave a persuasive speech in class urging use of this brand of shampoo to control dandruff. The personal influence of the speaker lent credence to the advertising, and this writer is now a regular user of that shampoo.

A topic of special concern has been the effect of media on children, especially the impact of television *violence* on them. This concern is probably due to the great deal of exposure children today have to television and the fact that their perceptual machinery is not as well developed as that of adults. Young children, it is presumed, are almost "blank slates" on which can be written television's message.

The studies do not produce consistent results. However, a recent comprehensive review of studies on the subject caused Comstock to draw four broad generalizations:[20]

1. The very experience of viewing television is an addition to the life of a youngster. Children view television quite a bit, form definite tastes, and tend to learn to distrust commercials, for instance. They also learn to think of television news as highly credible.

2. Evidence suggests that television does affect the beliefs and behavior of young people. Children learn a lot of information from television, and they tend to imitate behavior they see on television, but the behavior they learn to imitate can be both antisocial behavior and good behavior.[21]

3. Whether or not television violence produces aggressive and antisocial behavior is most controversial. Comstock quotes many different conclusions on this hypothesized effect, showing a wide range of opinion on the topic. Although a number of actual experiments demonstrate that television violence produces aggressive behavior and attitudes in the young, social science methodology may not have yet successfully isolated television violence from other contributing factors. For instance, syndicated columnist Sidney Harris has this to say: "It is not the violence in television that engenders violence in children, but the passivity in the act of watching for so long; the child becomes violence-prone because he has no outlet for his normal aggressive energy he should be working off in creative activity.[22]

4. While disagreement on the findings exists, more disagreement does exist on how serious the matter is. A study, let us say, indicates that after viewing three hours of violent television, the average number of "aggressive acts" or "aggressive verbalizations" of a group of youngsters is greater, on the average, than those of a comparable group who watched three hours of nonviolent television. The questions now become how aggressive were the "aggressive acts," and how many more aggressive acts, on the average, is "too many?" Linked to those questions are these: by what standards are we to judge the severity and num-

ber of aggressive acts and words, and when can we agree that the effects are so serious that possible remedies should be reviewed?

Comstock offers no useful means of determining how to develop and assess criteria to judge the seriousness of the effects of television violence on children. But he concludes that, even if it had not been found that television violence can make children unruly (especially aggression-prone children), public pressure might still be brought to bear on networks to reduce the level of such broadcast violence.

Some conclusions

This chapter has briefly attempted to define mass communication, to explain the nature of the media of mass communication as they operate in American society, and to summarize a great deal of research and speculation about media impact upon the audience.

One more important point is that we know little about the long-term effects of *any* communication, especially of mass communication, simply because long-term studies have yet to be conducted. As Klapper says, "Next to nothing is known as yet regarding the social effects of mass communication over periods of, let us say, two or three decades."[23]

To end on a philosophical note, when we speak of "mass communication" we are generally talking about the *physical means* by which messages are transmitted—inked sheets rolling off high-speed presses or messages broadcast through the airways. Mass communication differs from interpersonal communication in that it is usually the product of a group rather than of an individual. But it must be remembered that the processing of messages for either sending or receiving is still a remarkably *human* transaction. High-speed presses and electronic broadcasting appeared on the scene quite recently, but human neural and perceptual machinery for processing messages has not changed since Adam.

QUESTIONS FOR THOUGHT
AND DISCUSSION
CHAPTER 10

1. What mass media have you observed in the past week?
2. What factors influence the audience that might be prone to observe a particular mass media speech or program?

3. What are the differences between a speaker addressing an audience in an auditorium and a speaker addressing an audience via television?
4. In what ways are the media regulated by government in the United States?
5. Are media in the United States free to say what they want?
6. Why is the "fairness doctrine" important?
7. How does the "fairness doctrine" affect what is communicated in the media?
8. How is broadcasting an extension of the entertainment world?
9. How is broadcasting an extension of the business world?
10. What role did the mass media play in uncovering the Watergate scandals?
11. Of what significance is the concept of "gatekeeping" to people in the United States?
12. How can one determine what is the "best interest" of the audience?
13. In what ways do United States citizens have access to the media?
14. In your own experience, is television advertising effective?
15. In what ways do mass media influence human behavior?
16. How does violence on television affect children?

EXERCISES · ASSIGNMENTS | CHAPTER 10

1. Keep a diary of your media viewing or reading for one week. Prepare a written report in which you categorize the type of media observed (television, newspaper, etc.), specific programs or materials witnessed, and amount of time devoted to each.
2. Observe a television set in a home or dormitory and see if you can determine whether the programs selected are in agreement with the viewers' attitudes or repugnant to them. How can you tell?
3. Observe a child watching television during the "cartoon" period when the child can choose the channels. Determine the nature of the material the child chooses—violent, funny, dramatic, and so on.
4. Study a speaker who is addressing both a live audience and a radio or television audience. In what way did the speaker attempt to adapt to the audiences? Did the speaker ignore one audience?
5. Interview an editor or station manager of a local newspaper, radio station, or television station and ask what their primary purpose is—to entertain, to make a profit, to serve the community? Then personally observe that medium for one week and determine what the purpose is.
6. Select a television program you thought was worthwhile but was taken off the air. By reading articles and interviewing station management,

determine why that program was cut. What does this tell you about decision-making in television programming?

7. Interview the manager of an educational television station. Explore with that person the differences in purpose, decision-making, and so on between commercial television and educational television.

8. Are the shows you find on a local radio or television station, in your judgment, in the best interest of the audience?

9. Do political campaign commercials on radio and television help voters make enlightened choices?

10. Compare one week's coverage of some important event by radio, newspapers, and television. Which medium provides the best coverage? What criteria do you use to make this decision? What are the advantages and disadvantages of each medium in covering the news?

ENDNOTES | Chapter 10

1. "Free, Equal and Ridiculous," *Time,* March 30, 1959: 65.

2. Bradley S. Greenberg, "Mass Communication and Social Behavior," in *Communication and Behavior,* edited by G. J. Hanneman and W. J. McEwen. (Reading, Mass.: Addison-Wesley, 1975), p. 269.

3. *Ibid.,* p. 270.

4. Reported in *U. S. News and World Report,* November 24, 1969: 10.

5. Lecture by Dr. Harrison B. Summers in Speech 652, Summer 1959, The Ohio State University, Columbus.

6. Reported in *Time,* September 15, 1975: 10.

7. Wilbur Schramm and Janet Alexander, "Broadcasting," in *Handbook of Communication,* edited by Ithiel de Sola Pool, et al. (Chicago: Rand McNally, 1973), p. 607.

8. *Ibid.*

9. *U.S. News and World Report,* July 28, 1969: 21.

10. R. Wayne Pace, Robert R. Boren, and Brent D. Peterson, *Communication Behavior and Experiments: A Scientific Approach* (Belmont, Calif.: Wadsworth, 1975), p. 104.

11. *Ibid.*

12. *Ibid.*

13. Much of the research on "black English" is summarized in Elissa De Barone, "Toward Mutual Understanding: Differences in Black English and Standard English—A Perspective on Transracial Communication" (Athens: The University of Georgia, unpublished M.A. thesis, 1974). Heavy exposure of black Americans to television is documented in B. S. Greenberg and B. Dervin, *Use of the Mass Media by the Urban*

Poor (New York: Praeger, 1970); and J. Lyle and H. R. Hoffman, "Children's Use of Television and Other Media," in *Television and Social Behavior,* Vol. IV: *Television in Day-to-Day Life Patterns of Use,* E. A. Rubinstein, G. A. Comstock, and J. P. Murray, (Washington, D.C.: U.S. Government Printing Office, 1972), pp. 129–256.

14. G. A. Comstock and M. L. Fisher, *Television and Human Behavior: A Guide to the Pertinent Scientific Literature* (Santa Monica, Calif.: Rand Corporation, 1975, R-1746-CF).

15. Marshall McLuhan, "At the Flip Point of Time–The Point of More Return?" *Journal of Communication,* 25 (Autumn 1975): 104–105.

16. Bernard Berelson and Gary Steiner, *Human Behavior: An Inventory of Scientific Findings* (Harcourt Brace and World, 1964), chapter 13.

17. Joseph Klapper, *The Effects of Mass Communication* (Glencoe, Ill.: Free Press, 1960). For more recent rendering of Klapper's views, see "The Social Effects of Mass Communication," in *Messages: A Reader in Human Communication,* edited by Jean M. Civikly (New York: Random House, 1974).

18. Stuart H. Surlin, "The Evaluation of Dogmatic Television Characters by Dogmatic Viewers: 'Is Archie Bunker a Credible Source?' " (Paper presented at the International Communication Association's annual convention, Montreal, April 1973); and Neal Vidmar and Milton Rokeach, "Archie Bunker's Bigotry: A Study in Selective Perception and Exposure," *Journal of Communication,* 24 (Winter 1974): 36–47. For more popular discussion of these two studies, see Leonard Gross, "Do the Bigots Miss the Message?" *TV Guide,* 23 (November 8, 1975): 14–16ff.

19. Klapper, *The Effects of Mass Communication, op. cit.,* p. 62.

20. George Comstock, "The Evidence So Far," *Journal of Communication,* 25 (Autumn 1975): 25–34. This article was part of an eleven-article symposium on "The Effects of Television on Children and Adolescents" in that issue.

21. See Rita Wicks Poulos, Eli A. Rubinstein, and Robert M. Liebert, "Positive Social Learning," *Journal of Communication,* 25 (Autumn 1975): 90–97.

22. Sidney J. Harris, "Thoughts at Large," *Athens Daily News* (Athens, Georgia), December 4, 1975: 4.

23. Klapper, "The Social Effects of Mass Communication," *op. cit.,* p. 257.

11 ⊓

SOLVING PROBLEMS THROUGH SMALL GROUPS

People have many different ways of satisfying their needs and solving their problems. For example the United States chose military draftees by "chance" by drawing birthdates from a barrel during the war in Vietnam. Others have solved problems by relying on authority (parent, boss, or clergyman) or debate (on the floor of the Senate or in a P.T.A. meeting).

This chapter explains small group discussions as one workable method of making decisions. We define *small group communication* as communication that occurs when three or more people gather in a face-to-face situation and through interaction attempt to reach a solution to a common problem. Although three people are a minimum, a group usually functions best when it includes between five and nine members.

An important point is that small group communication requires oral interaction. We are concerned with groups that are physically together in a way that they can communicate directly with each other. For the group to function efficiently, there must be communicative interaction among members. Each member of the group should be free to initiate and react to communications.

The final point in our definition is that group members have interest in a common problem. Frequently it is a problem that brings the group together in the first place. Acceptance of common goals usually contributes to better communication interaction and increased cohesiveness of the group.

Reflective thinking

Small group problem solving has been greatly influenced by the work of John Dewey, in particular, his book, *How We Think*.[1] In this book Dewey attempts to describe the thought process of a person facing a problem. Concerned with analyzing reflective thinking appropriate for the problem-solving process, Dewey began by maintaining that when a person faces a problem he or she experiences a feeling of perplexity or confusion. To alleviate this feeling, the individual must follow a rational procedure, which Dewey described as reflective thinking.

Reflective thinking is characterized by deliberation and an attempt to keep one's mind open to the greatest possible number of solutions. The reflective thinker resists impulsive decisions. Reflective thinking, according to Dewey, is a process that requires discipline and effort. The reflective thinking process consists of five phases:

1. Recognition of a problem.
2. Definition and analysis of the problem.
3. Raising suggestions for possible solutions to the problem.
4. Selection of the best solution for the problem from the many solutions that have been suggested.
5. Carrying out the solution.

The problem-solving process

The process of reflective thinking forms the basis of the method used by many small groups to solve a problem. Sharp and Millikin found "that the quality of the group's decision was related to the reflective thinking ability of group members, adding additional support to the conclusion that reflective thinking ability is one important determinant of the product of problem-solving discussion."[2]

To demonstrate this method of decision making, we discuss the process under three main headings: the problem, the solution, and implementation of the solution.

    I. Problem
       A. Definition and limitation of the problem
          1. What specific topic are we to discuss?
          2. Are there words within our stated topic that need defining?
          3. How should we limit our topic?

B. Analysis of the problem
    1. What is the history of our topic?
    2. What recent events led up to this problem?
    3. Do serious problems exist?
    4. What caused these problems?
    5. What is being done to solve existing problems?
II. Solution
    A. What criteria must be kept in mind in seeking a solution?
    B. What are possible solutions that will satisfy existing needs?
    C. Reaching a solution
        1. What are the advantages and disadvantages of suggested solutions?
        2. Which solutions meet the established criteria?
        3. Which solutions best remove the causes?
        4. Would it be useful to combine several of the suggested solutions?
        5. What solution will we support?
III. Implementation of the solution
    A. Who will be responsible for implementing the solution?
    B. What audience has power to implement the solution?
    C. What situational factors must one consider?

The problem

Whether you are concerned about the sales of hard drugs in your community or the decline of membership in your favorite organization, the first step is to study the problem.

Definition and limitation of the problem. Too often in society and in courses in communication, persons rush to offer advice or persuade an audience to take a specific action before they understand whether there is a problem or what the problem is. On occasions the problem is obvious. A building's roof is leaking and is impossible to ignore. A private school yearly goes further into debt. With such conspicuous situations there is agreement concerning the difficulty.
On occasions it is difficult to communicate to others that a need exists. A soldier may observe misconduct on the part of fellow soldiers in a war zone, but communicating that activity not only takes great courage but also considerable strategy. Organizations and individuals resist public communication about their own failures. A worker in a political campaign who witnesses illegal campaign tac-

tics or an executive who learns of illegal transactions may confront powerful obstacles when simply attempting to communicate these observations. Achieving recognition of a problem can be complicated.

Defining the problem, then, is important. Life is too complex to study as a whole, but we can take one segment at a time and improve society. Limit and define the need carefully and your group will be working toward the solution of the same problem. Later in this chapter we mention again how to limit a problem and cite examples of how to word the problem in the form of a question.

Analysis of problem. To understand a problem the group must analyze it. To analyze a problem is to partition it into inherent parts and to discover its causes. Can you imagine a physician taking a quick look at a rash on your left arm and, without further inquiry, prescribing surgery to remove your limb? Such an example sounds absurd, but some approach social problems in this manner. On the basis of little study and consideration of causes people conclude that all welfare programs should be abolished, or the government should guarantee each family an income of $6,000. Too often people prescribe instant remedies for complex situations without prior analysis. Communication that ignores causes is not likely to be as successful as it could be.

Analysis of causes is critical to your group's understanding of human events and to the successful analysis of social problems. What you perceive to be the cause of an event will determine to some degree what you recommend to improve the situation. What would you believe if you saw a youth throw a brick through a window? If you immediately said, "That mean bum should be locked up," your understanding of the event is evidently that meanness caused the youth to throw the brick. This reasoning would then help determine how you would solve the problem: either you would look for some way to rid the youth of "meanness" or you would advocate getting the youth off the streets and into jail. But what if you had perceived that the brick-throwing was caused by deep personal frustrations? This frustration might be caused by indifferent parents, inadequate schools, unemployment, or some other situation beyond the youth's control. This perception of the event would influence you to advocate quite different solutions from the first, perhaps providing the youth a job.

Finding the causes of a problem often involves studying the history as well as the present conditions of a situation. Suppose a group wanted to do something about traffic congestion in a large city. The group must ask: When did the problem begin? What was done earlier to control traffic better? Why didn't these plans work?

Why weren't certain actions implemented? Do the same obstacles still exist? If so, can something be done now to overcome the obstacles? Finally the group works up to the present situation: Why do serious problems now exist? Is the traffic problem caused by the number of vehicles? Is it the kinds of vehicles? Is it the roads? Or is the source of the difficulty the attitude of the public? What available solutions are being tried or ignored? Why?

In determining the cause of the problem, there are certain tests one can apply. In the case of the person with a rash, the physician might discover that a certain food caused the rash. Thus, the doctor knows how to cure the rash. With social and economic problems, however, isolating causes is seldom easy. What are the actual causes of poverty, human frustration, and political corruption? The difficulty does not change the aim: we should search diligently for causes so our recommended solutions will be sound.

When testing possible causes of a problem, ask the following questions: Can a cause-effect relationship be demonstrated? Is the alleged cause adequate to produce the effect? Are there possibly several causes of the problem? Are there forces preventing a probable cause from causing the problem? Such tests are vital to the success of the problem-solving process.

How group members understand what a problem is and what caused it will determine to a large degree what solution they will recommend. A mistake in the analysis of causes of the problem will be reflected in the results of the problem-solving process. Do not rush to advocate a position you really don't fully understand, but approach complex problems with some sense of humility. There will be times when you must admit that you have not found the best solution. Then your goal becomes to persuade others to join the search for a better understanding of the problem and for the most appropriate solution. The first step of the problem-solving process, then, is careful study of the problem and its causes.

The solution

After the group has a thorough knowledge of the problem and its probable causes, it is in a position to consider alternative actions. As noted above, perception of the problem and its causes will influence the line of reasoning and solution suggested. For example, after one of the urban riots in the 1960s, some persons advocated more policemen. Later it was discovered that one cause of the unrest was the inability of people in the area to find transportation from their neighborhood to places of work. While more policemen may have been necessary to treat the *effect* (the riot), a long-range solution would also have to consider the causes, one being the matter of transportation.

Considerations of criteria. One must also ask what standards the group's solution should meet. For example, if you were considering a way to repair a leaking roof, you would have to weigh cost, time, looks, labor, extent of damage, age of the roof, and insurance coverage. Some criteria, such as cost and time, are so common to so many different problems that they might be called "stock criteria." Other criteria grow out of the nature of the particular problem; for example, the criteria to consider when raising taxes not only includes economic matters but also public opinion.

If you do not consider causes and criteria during the solution stage, you will confront them when you later attempt to implement a solution. Then, however, they will be obstacles to implementation. For example, if you decided to use a rare material for the new roof without concern for the criteria of cost and availability of materials, when you go to purchase the material it may be too costly or not available at all. Time invested in careful deliberation on the causes of a problem and the criteria for solutions is time well spent.

However, some research indicates one should not get locked into criteria prior to a discussion of all possible solutions. Studies show that deciding on criteria too early may prevent creative discussion when the group takes up solutions. Brilhart and Jochem investigated whether more and better ideas for solutions would be generated if they came up before or after the establishment and application of criteria. They found that student groups came up with more and better solutions before criteria were established and evaluation took place.[3]

Weighing alternative solutions. After defining the problem and studying criteria by which you will judge solutions, you are now ready to consider all possible solutions. The purpose here is to gather as many ideas and alternatives as possible—welcome all suggestions. Most persons will attend a group meeting with personal preferences as to what should be done. It takes self-control to be willing to listen fairly to the preferences of others, yet this is an important aspect of problem solving. The person who develops an attitude of inquiry and cooperation and is open to all suggestions is less apt to be ruled by prejudice and poor information.

After possible solutions are exhausted, the group is ready to weigh each suggestion and combination of alternatives to determine whether they treat the causes of the problem and are reasonable in view of your chosen criteria, such as cost and time.

Choosing a solution.   Finally in the solution stage of the problem-solving process the group decides on one best solution.   This may mean modifying one's own thinking or that of several persons.   What you or the majority in a group believe to be the best decision may cost too much or may take too long to implement.   The solution that best removes the causes of the problem and meets solution criteria is the one you can defend with confidence.

Implementation of solution

The third step in the problem-solving process is implementation of the selected solution.   It is one thing for a group to reach a decision in theory and something entirely different to have that decision adopted.

What if a group decided on a way to stop a particular factory from pouring pollutants into a river near your homes?   Or what if you had been meeting with other people periodically for six months and had decided on a specific plan to reduce crime in your community?   In the first example, the group is confronted with the tough task of convincing managers of the local factory to make decisions which may add to their expenses in order to stop polluting the river.   Not an easy job!   In the second case, the work of simply identifying all the necessary people and agencies concerned with crime would be a challenge.   Would you work through the town council or the county commissioners?   At what point would state and federal laws and officials have to be considered?   Unless your solution is only something like "Everybody write your legislator," the task of implementation will involve as much work as planning, organization, and communication as the discovery of the solution.

The group is faced with the challenge of communicating its recommendations to the appropriate decision-making person or body. If the group that reached the solution has the authority to implement it, the solution is easier, but group members still must convince others that it is an improvement over present procedure and deserves support.   Usually, however, solutions have to be sold to a board of directors, the person next up the chain of command, or to the public.

In addition to the solution which must be explained and advocated, three other factors are critical to the implementation of a solution: persons who want a change, persons who must be influenced if the suggested change is to take place, and situational factors that should be considered.

Persons advocating the solution.   After going through the first two stages of the problem-solving analysis (consideration of the nature of the problem and the best solution) the people who want a change are in a confident position. Unlike the persons who act with little understanding of their subject, your group is well informed. They are not disturbed by tough questions, since most of these questions have already been confronted by the group earlier during the problem-solving process. Those who now advocate a solution welcome the opportunity to share their insights and findings with those who may not have their background or knowledge. When persons work long and hard on a project, they are delighted with the chance to show what has been accomplished. One can be open and candid and willing to listen to suggestions by others. After all, the purpose is not to win points but to improve human society.

The best strategy and most convincing argument may be simply to explain as carefully and as candidly as one can the definition and nature of the problem, its causes, some of the solutions considered, and why a particular solution was chosen. In other words those advocating a new program take the audience on a verbal tour of the analysis they went through in getting to their present thinking on the subject. There may be, however, a more appropriate method of organizing one's presentation of the solution (see Chapter 9 on persuasion).

Role of audience. This brings us to the second aspect of the implementation stage: those who must be influenced if the suggested change is to take place. The person or persons with final decision-making authority may vary greatly. If only your group members are involved in the entire problem-solving process, they only have to convince their group. When others are involved, you first must discover who has the authority to make the final decision. This may be the president of a company, the faculty, students, a chamber of commerce, or a body of government. Public opinion, possibly involving a vote, may be the final arbiter.

After deciding who has decision-making power, your group will attempt to convince that person or persons that your suggested solution will remedy a recognized solution and thus merits adoption. Your strategy will depend upon how your audience perceives the situation.

If those who have power to make a change do not view the situation as a problem, you must first demonstrate that there is indeed a problem. If you have followed the problem-solving process carefully, you know the nature, extent, and probable causes of the problem. You now have to share those findings with the decision-making board. If, however, you are unable under rigorous questioning and deliberation to demonstrate a justification for a new way of looking at a problem, you will likely fail in your attempt to have your recommendation adopted. Remember, the decision-makers may perceive the entire subject differently than you do because of self-interest, tradition, ignorance, cost, public pressure, lobbyists, sincere concern for people, or different personal experiences relating to the topic at hand.

Communicating with persons with perceptions different from your own about complex problems is extremely difficult under the best of conditions. Even after convincing yourself of the worth of a particular solution on the basis of long hours of research and reflection, you will have to explain your thinking in such a way as to ensure your plan a fair hearing. Unless the situation is of crisis proportions and easily recognized, people tend to avoid or ignore it. See Chapter 9 for more help with how to adapt to audiences.

Situational factors. The third aspect of the implementation stage concerns situational factors. Of course, audience reactions could be considered a factor of the speaking situation; other factors are social or political forces at work at the time, economic conditions, interests of different parties, personal prejudices, others' knowledge of the subject, quality of the solution, the occasion, personalities involved, concern for quality of life, intensity and immediacy of the problem, your ability to communicate, and so on. These examples are listed to illustrate the wide variety of determinants that can influence whether even a good solution can be implemented. Some of the factors may seem more reasonable than others, but any or all could prevent the adoption of the solution or assist in its passage. In Georgia in 1975, for example, the teachers were given a 5 percent pay raise. Many teachers even received contracts confirming their increased salaries. Before schools opened in the fall, however, salary raises had been rescinded, due to a decrease in tax revenues. Thus, situational factors prevented the implementation of action already decided on after much discussion, debate, and persuasion.

There is no prescription that will guarantee desired results. Each speaking situation is one of a kind. Look for factors inherent to the situation and to your subject that will influence how your solution will be received. At every step in the problem-solving process important judgments have to be made concerning these situational factors. If you have analyzed the nature and causes of the problem, have carefully weighed all possible solutions, and have, on the basis of the causes of the problem and the criteria established, selected what seems to be the best solution, you can have considerable confidence in your understanding of the situation and in your recommended remedy.

Other problem-solving patterns

While the reflective thinking process is an excellent way to approach a problem, it is only one form a group can use. It is not a blueprint but a general framework that encourages *understanding* of a problem before members reach a solution. Research has been done on other patterns of problem solving to test the traditional Reflective Thinking format and to develop a better understanding of the decision-making process in small groups.

Larson compared the "single question form" of analysis with the "ideal solution form" of decision making with the reflective thinking pattern. Based on "reasoning characteristics of successful and unsuccessful problem-solvers," the single question form study administered problems to groups who were instructed to use the following outline for their discussion:[4]

1. What is the single question, the answer to which is all the group needs to know to accomplish its purpose?
2. What sub-questions must be answered before we can answer the single question we have formulated?
3. Do we have sufficient information to answer the sub-questions confidently?
4. What are the most reasonable answers to the sub-questions?
5. Assuming that our answers to the sub-questions are correct, what is the best solution to the problem?

The "ideal solution form" is a variation of a method suggested by Kepner and Tregoe.[5] When small groups used this method they followed the following pattern:

1. Are we all agreed on the nature of the problem?
2. What would be the ideal solution from the point-of-view of all parties involved in the problem?
3. What conditions within the problem could be changed so that the ideal solution might be achieved?
4. Of the solutions available to us, which one best approximates the ideal solution?

Larson found in his study that the single question form and ideal solution form "appear to be more productive than the traditional reflective thinking pattern." Persons who participate in small group decision making, then, should not only understand and practice the principles of reflective thinking, but also continue to search for better means of solving problems. A method that involves a group of persons is a highly complex event and must be continuously investigated. We hope the basic principles discussed in this chapter will be a sound beginning.

Activity

With three or four friends, study the problems below. Decide which method of problem-solution would be best for each. Try to solve each problem. Some answers are upside-down.

1. An army cook at a small and isolated outpost on limited rations baked his pies or cakes at night, finishing around 8:00 a.m. He could then sleep until the dinner meal. But his pies and cakes would disappear while he slept. He was certain the kitchen help was stealing the pastries, but he did not want to miss any sleep to guard the pastries or catch the thieves. What could he do?

2. A contractor wins a bid to redecorate the interior of a huge cathedral. In order to build scaffolding, he must quickly know the interior dimensions, including the height of the ceiling. How can the height of the ceiling be determined quickly and inexpensively?

3. You manage a supermarket. A "burr under your saddle" is an elderly lady who shops there who insists on going over the cash register tape minutely to make sure she was not charged for something she did not actually purchase (so far, she has never found herself to be overcharged). She is often a bottleneck in the checkout lane. You have pointed out time and again, with the finest of good manners, that she has never been overcharged, yet she persists. What can you do?

1. Bake blueberry pies one day. When they disappear, check among the kitchen help for black tongues.

2. Let a helium-filled balloon rise to the ceiling on a string. Measure the string.

3. Deliberately fail to ring up one day, say, a 33-cent can of beans; catch your "error," and add it on when she insists on checking the tape. Next time, "miss," a 44-cent loaf of bread. Keep undercharging until she feels motivated to desist from the *expense* of correcting you. On the one day when she decides this, it might cost you the price of an item, but should be well worth the expense.

Small group theories

Various theories have been advanced to explain small group behavior. Although no single theory can fully explain the small group, each of the major theories has merits depending upon what assumptions one wishes to make about the small group. The three major theories examined here are those of George Homans, Kurt Lewin, and Robert Bales.

George Homans

George Homans, in his attempt to analyze groups, presents a framework broad enough to encompass group life in urban gangs, factory teams, and many other social situations.[6] The four major elements in Homans's system are (1) activity (the operations people perform), (2) sentiment (the feelings people have), (3) interaction (communication between people), and (4) norms (the standards people hold).

By examining these four dimensions of any group, Homans is able to make certain evaluations about the group. In a series of studies, Homans used his system to make the following generalizations about group behavior:

1. The more frequently people interact with one another, the stronger their sentiments of friendship for one another will be.

2. Persons who interact with each other frequently are more like each other in their activities than they are like other persons with whom they interact less frequently.

3. To the degree that activities of the other individual in a reciprocal role relationship conform to the norms of one's own group, one will like the person.

4. The higher a member's rank, the more often he or she originates interaction and receives it.

5. The closer a member comes to realizing the norms of the group, the more interactions this person will receive from and give to other members of the group.

The above statements are only illustrative of Homans's system of analysis and his findings. The major criticism of Homans's approach is that it does not take us very far in explaining group behavior. His system does not carry us much beyond the idea that human behavior in its broadest sense somehow hangs together. The system does little to help analyze the content of interaction.

Kurt Lewin

Lewin's *field theory,* or "group dynamics," as it is frequently called today, begins by developing a conceptual framework of the individual which is later applied to the small group.[7] Lewin's theory is based on five assumptions:

1. Each individual perceives in a unique way the environment, and this leads to the concept of the psychological field or life-space of the individual.
2. An individual occupies a position in this life-space; this life-space is in a certain relationship to physical reality.
3. An individual is oriented toward goals, which usually involve a change in the relative positions of the individual and the objects in the life-space.
4. An individual acts in certain ways to obtain these goals or engages in the process of moving toward these goals.
5. An individual in the process of moving toward these goals may encounter barriers that have to be circumvented or that may result in a change in goals or in life-space or both.

Field theory is applied to small groups by substituting the term *group* for *individual.* A group has a life-space, is oriented toward goals; it moves toward these goals and may encounter barriers. In relating field theory to groups, Lewin and his followers introduce some new concepts to deal with certain group dimensions. The most important of these concepts are *norms,* meaning the rules governing behavior of members; *roles,* referring to the relative status and prestige of group members; and *cohesion,* the degree of attachment or involvement that members have for the group.

In applying field theory to the small group, researchers have become primarily concerned with cohesion and its relationship to leadership, interaction, productivity, and other aspects of group behavior. The concept of cohesion refers to the forces that bind members of a group together. These forces include the degree of closeness members feel for each other, individual satisfaction from being a part of the group, and a willingness for group members to be honest in their communication with each other. Advocates of field theory suggest that cohesiveness can be increased by the following conditions: cooperation rather than competition in the group, democratic rather than authoritarian group atmosphere, and the existence of previous organization in the group.[8]

The basic idea behind the group dynamics approach is that the greater degree of cohesion in a group, the more efficiently it moves toward its goal. Occasionally, one member may not go along with the majority of the group. When this happens, research indicates that communication in the group tends to be directed to the person disagreeing in an attempt to get him or her to change.[9]

Robert Bales

A third small group theory is advanced by Robert F. Bales.[10] Bales's major contribution is an observational scheme for small group communication. Bales maintains that the process of group interaction may be thought of as a continual stream of acts, words, gestures, and reactions. This stream may flow slowly or quickly. At times it includes only part of the group and at other times all of the group.

In an attempt to examine the interaction of groups, Bales developed his *Interaction Process Analysis* (IPA). IPA involves the use of a trained observer behind a one-way mirror to record group process. The observer records group process in terms of twelve categories:[11]

1. Shows solidarity (raises other's status, gives help).
2. Shows tension release (jokes, laughs, shows satisfaction).
3. Agrees (shows passive acceptance, understands, concurs).
4. Gives suggestion (direction).
5. Gives opinion (evaluation, analysis, expresses feeling).
6. Gives orientation (information, repeats, clarifies, confirms).
7. Asks for orientation (information, repetition, confirmation).
8. Asks for opinion (evaluation, analysis, expression of feeling).
9. Asks for suggestion (direction, possible ways of action).

10. Disagrees (shows passive rejection, formality, with-holds help).
11. Shows tension (asks for help, withdraws out of field).
12. Shows antagonism (deflates other's status, defends or asserts self).

The IPA recording procedure rests on the assumption that an observer can judge the dominant function or meaning of an act and that in the long run the true tendencies of individual and group behavior will be portrayed with accuracy. Bales and his associates maintain that the agreement between different observers using the twelve-category method is adequate for most purposes.[12]

In brief, Interaction Process Analysis is a systematically conceived set of observational categories useful in the analysis of any sort of discussion group. It has been frequently employed by Bales and others to provide much data about group behavior and group communication.

Other studies

These theories by Homan, Lewin, and Bales illustrate the kinds of studies done in the area of small groups and demonstrate some of the factors important in small group work. Many additional studies have been made in recent years. For descriptions and evaluations of these studies, read the following articles: Ernest G. Bormann, "The Paradox and Promise of Small Group Research," *Speech Monographs,* 37 (August 1970); a Response to Bormann in the same journal: Carl E. Larson, "Speech Communication Research on Small Groups," *Speech Teacher,* 20 (March 1971); and Dennis S. Gouran, "Group Communication: Perspectives and Priorities for Future Research," *Quarterly Journal of Speech,* 59 (February 1973). Some of the findings mentioned in studies evaluated by these authors are quoted in this chapter.

Leadership in small group communication

What is leadership? Many researchers, such as Stogdill, have spent much time and energy trying to find what traits or characteristics of people are associated with leadership.[13] But recent researchers, such as Cartwright and Zander, observe that leader characteristics useful in one situation are not so useful in others.[14] Recent research has tended to focus on what *functions* group leaders perform rather than what *traits* they possess. This type of research asks the question, What does the leader do in the group setting?

Functions of leadership

There appear to be two major functions performed by the leader of a small group: the task function and the group maintenance function. The *task function* is composed of leader behavior that is designed to accomplish a task or to find the answer to a problem the group is discussing. Some group task functions are:

1. Defining the problem to be discussed.
2. Ordering the sequence of topics.
3. Asking for information about the problem.
4. Clarifying the contributions of group members.
5. Asking for evaluation of information.
6. Asking for solutions.
7. Asking for evaluation of solutions.

The *group maintenance* function is composed of leader behavior to promote group cohesiveness and group harmony. Some group maintenance functions are:

1. Encouraging participation by all members.
2. Developing permissive and informal group atmosphere.
3. Seeking to make group members feel secure.
4. Providing for contrasting views to be presented.
5. Providing for tension release.
6. Resolving differences between group members.

The two major leadership functions may conflict. A small group leader may get so involved with solving a problem that group maintenance is neglected. As a result, a group may accomplish the task but in the process destroy group cohesiveness necessary to implement the solution. The leader can also err in the other direction, devoting so much time and attention to group maintenance that, though there is good group harmony, the group is inefficient in accomplishing the task. The ideal leader, of course, is one who is good at both functions. How does a leader balance these two major functions of leadership? Different leaders employ different styles of leadership. The question of leadership style pertains to how much control the leader exercises over the group. Major leadership styles are discussed below.

Styles of leadership

Authoritarian leadership.   In authoritarian leadership, all policy is determined by the leader. The leader usually determines the specific task for each participant. This type of leader feels that group participants are limited in ability and need strict guidance and control. The style is rigid and inflexible. The authoritarian leader is usually reluctant to acknowledge those who disagree, and the leader dominates discussions. Authoritarian leaders discourage member participation and, usually early in the discussion, members resign themselves to the fact that the leader will make all decisions no matter what anyone else may have to contribute.

When a leader employs the authoritarian style, the solution may be reached quickly, but the costs in terms of group morale are very high, and the emotional consequences of authoritarian leadership are serious. Why would any group leader use this style? In many situations leaders want group members to know beyond any doubt that they are in control. Many times, however, leaders may not be aware that their actions in the group are perceived by group members as authoritarian.

Supervisory leadership.   This style of leadership, which stops far short of autocratic control, is useful when efficiency is critical. The supervisory leader almost always introduces the problem for discussion with a lengthy description. The leader usually decides what problems will be discussed in the meeting and frequently summarizes what has taken place in the group. This type of leader is not as formal and rigid as the authoritarian leader; however, this leader is so concerned with procedure and accomplishing the task that little attention is devoted to the group maintenance function.

Democratic or participatory leadership.   In discussing the two previous styles, we found that both authoritarian and supervisory leaders depend on methods that limit the participation and freedom of other group members. The two previous styles are employed because leaders feel superior to other members of the group and as a result restrict the participation of group members.

Democratic or participatory leadership, on the other hand, emphasizes cooperative or participative leadership. Group members are encouraged to participate actively in the discussion process. Rather than restricting group members, this style of leadership has a positive effect. A democratic leader seeks to accomplish the following:

1. All members of the group should participate freely.
2. Communication should be directed to all members, not just to the leader.
3. Group decisions should be perceived as group achievements.
4. Group members should be able to satisfy some personal needs in the group environment.
5. Group members should be able to identify with the group.

This style of leadership is a difficult assignment. The democratic leader must have the ability to coordinate both the task and the group maintenance functions. This type of leadership is frequently employed because it promotes a high degree of group cohesiveness and at the same time the group moves toward accomplishing a task.

Laissez-faire or group-centered leadership. In this type of group, members are expected to be self-directive. A leader in this type of group refrains from structuring the group in any way. The leader listens but does not show approval or disapproval. This leader may clarify on occasion but is careful not to inject his or her own thoughts. The atmosphere is extremely permissive. The leader of a group-centered group always tries to view the discussion from the frame of reference of the member who is speaking.

Leaderless group. Finally, we briefly consider the leaderless group, which is not a style of leadership but the absence of a formal leader. In this group, leadership acts are assumed alternately by various members. Frequently members in a leaderless group cannot agree on the rights and responsibilities of members. At present, there is considerable disagreement over whether leaderless groups can be effective in problem-solving discussions.

Conclusions on leadership styles

The styles of leadership we have been talking about can be seen in perspective on the following continuum:

Leaderless Group	Group-Centered Leadership	Participative Leadership	Supervisory Leadership	Authoritarian Leadership

MINIMUM CONTROL ——————————————————————— MAXIMUM CONTROL
BY LEADER   BY LEADER

As we have suggested earlier in this discussion, participative leadership style is desirable the majority of the time. A study by Fox indicates that participative leadership usually takes longer before the group reaches consensus; however, member satisfaction is highest with this style of leadership.[15] Although we have suggested that participative leadership is usually desirable, each group leader will want to select a style that is in keeping with his or her own personality and the needs of the particular group.

Planning for small group communication

Discussion of small group communication would not be complete without some consideration of planning. The methods of group leadership and group participation are of little use unless careful attention is given to planning. Several areas should be considered in planning for small group communication.

Selecting the topic

When selecting a topic for a problem-solving assignment in the classroom, pick a topic that is timely. It is much easier to get members interested in a current topic. The topic should also be controversial; there should be at least two sides to the issue. The topic should be significant—it should concern a major issue. Finally, the topic should be capable of making the class feel involved.

Limiting the topic

Do not select topics for discussion that are so broad they cannot be covered in the time available for the group discussion. For example, "What should be the U.S. policy toward intervening in the internal affairs of other nations?" might take days to discuss. But the question, "What can the U.S. do for Central America earthquake victims?" can be handled in a much shorter time.

Wording the topic

The topic question needs to be worded so it is open to alternative answers. The question should usually be phrased so it cannot be answered yes or no. Usually topics that have several sides are best for discussion. Following are some good discussion topics that are worded to allow several points of view: What should be done about the parking problem on campus? Under what circumstances, if any, should the National Guard be used to control campus disorder? To what extent, if any, should students determine faculty promotions? What can be done to alleviate pollution in the community? What should be done to guarantee equal job opportunities for all United States citizens? How can we handle the problem of overpopulation? How can poverty be alleviated in the United States? What should be done to educate American youth about sex?

Planning the agenda

Usually it is helpful for the leader and one or two others to draw up an outline of the major points to be covered prior to group discussion. This outline should be given to group members ahead of time so they can do some thinking about the topic. Suggestions for constructing the outline will come to mind by reviewing the standard agenda for a problem-solving group discussed earlier in this chapter. The standard agenda is helpful in allocating time so the group does not spend all its time on one aspect of the topic. The agenda should cover these areas:

1. Definition of the terms, scope, and limits of the problem.
2. Analysis of the factual and nature of the problem and its causes.
3. Proposing and evaluating possible solutions.
4. Selection of a single final solution.
5. Suggestions for putting the solution into operation.

A word of caution is needed here. While planning is a vital phase of small group communication, do not overstructure the group situation and as a result stifle creative thinking. A group that operates mechanically does not usually come up with fresh approaches to problems.

Participation in small group communication

As we have discussed, the leader of a small group performs a vital function. The success of small group communication, however, also depends on effective participation by the rest of the members. People frequently have the idea that participants in a group can perform adequately with a minimum of preparation. A group member sometimes assumes that because several others are present, the group will perform effectively. To be an effective member of the problem-solving group, each member must have extensive knowledge of the problem being discussed. One obtains this knowledge through careful research and preparation on the topic being discussed. In addition to being well prepared, the effective group participant needs a wide variety of skills conducive to group productivity. The group participant needs to contribute to group leadership, to group productivity, and to group cohesiveness.

Earlier, we discussed leadership as the primary function of one member of the small group. In most groups, a single person takes primary responsibility for leading the group. Occasionally, a weak leader may have difficulty, and other group members should help perform the leadership function without completely trying to take over the leader's position. Group participants would do well to familiarize themselves with our previous discussion of leadership even though they may not be assigned the job of leader.

Participants can also make the group leader's job easier. Group members should try to follow the agenda set forth by the leader. Group members should follow the flow of the discussion and be sensitive to how the subject being discussed relates to the progress of the entire discussion. Each member needs to know where the group is and where it is going. Group members should be aware of critical questions that need to be covered and should attempt to move the group toward these key questions if the leader fails to do so. The effective group member is always ready to perform the leadership function but usually provides ample opportunity for the designated leader to do so first.

Although each should be able to perform the leadership function, the major responsibilities of the group member are really two-fold: to work toward group productivity (task function) and to work toward group cohesiveness (group maintenance function).

Participant task functions

Whatever the task or goal of the group, each participant will want to help accomplish it. There are several ways each group member can help accomplish the task.

Contributing information. The problem-solving group needs information to reach decisions. The effective group member gathers and brings information on the topic to the meeting. Some participants tend to contribute all their information the first time they have the opportunity to speak. The participant needs to develop the ability to see where his or her information on the topic applies and to realize that timing is critical in the presentation of information.

Evaluating information. The participant needs to bring several critical skills to the problem-solving situation. One of the most important is the ability to carefully examine all information presented to the group. The participant should offer additional supporting evidence or contradictory evidence when it is available. Fallacious reasoning and unsupported assertions should be exposed. Good reasoning and accurate information are essential to the group problem-solving process. Resist the tendency to accept everything that is said during the discussion.

Asking questions. The group participant performs an important function by asking pertinent questions at appropriate times. The use of questions is helpful in exposing inaccurate information or in clarifying a point one of the other members is attempting to make. The use of questions encourages feedback and aids everyone's understanding. Questions are also useful in keeping participants on the main subject of discussion. A proper question can focus the attention of the entire group upon the central issue.

Empathetic listening. Chapter 3 stressed the importance of listening. The effective group participant listens to what other members are saying and is alert to what is said "between the lines." The empathetic listener tries to see the topic from the frame of reference of other members who speak and is sensitive to the attitudes and feelings of the other members in the group.

Group thinking. Group thinking is different from individual thinking. Participants need to relate their comments to the thinking of the group. Make reference to what other members have said and what has already been agreed upon. Usually the longer you participate in a group the more skilled you become in group thinking. Group members must be wary of trying to move ahead too quickly. In order for the group to function effectively, members must work together.

After summarizing articles written on the effects of interaction on member attitudes in a group, Larson concludes that "considerable convergence of attitude might be expected as a result of group communication, that individuals might be expected to be more committed to their positions after discussion, that most of the influence is exerted by majorities, but that minorities might be expected to have appreciable effects upon majority attitudes, that frequently the final position arrived at through discussion is markedly different from either the majority or minority pre-discussion positions, and that discussants might be expected to be more critical of the issues forming the base for their attitudes after having discussed these issues."[16]

Participant maintenance functions

Up to this point, we have mostly talked about how an individual behaves to accomplish a task in the small group setting. Now we look at participant behavior that contributes to group maintenance. Good interpersonal relations in the group make the group more effective in problem-solving and make the task more rewarding for members. Good interpersonal relations increase group cohesiveness, and participants in a cohesive group have a strong desire to see the group succeed in its task.[17] The following considerations are some of the more important conditions that contribute toward group cohesiveness.

Equal status. All of us have been in groups where we find it difficult to identify with the group because there are members of much higher status. Greater unity and cohesiveness can be attained when the group members are of approximately the same status. Group leaders can do much to make participants feel they have equal status by the way they direct the interaction of the group. It is difficult to have group cohesiveness unless members feel they have equal status with other members.

Sensitivity to others. An effective participant is pleasant. Other group members are pleased that he or she is in the group. A sensitive group member is interested in understanding fellow members rather than in trying to prove them wrong. A sensitive member is quick to give those expressing minority viewpoints a fair hearing.

Previous experience with other members.   Previous experience with the other group members puts one in a better position to evaluate their contributions. We can much more accurately assess the attitudes and feelings of others when we have had previous contact with them in other small group situations.

Managing conflict and controversy in small groups

You may be thinking that cohesiveness is to be achieved at the expense of any other principle. Cooperation and pleasantness among group members seem to be the end-all of communication behavior in interpersonal communication. Conversely, it is implied that conflict and controversy should be shunned as activities that negate cooperation and cohesiveness, thus making it difficult to obtain quality decisions from group discussion. But this is far from the truth. We now look into how conflict and controversy can add to the effectiveness of group decisions.

There exists today an active and growing scientific body of studies on the management of conflict in small group communication. Although it has been criticized for a number of theoretical and methodological reasons,[18] this research and practical experience by experts with working groups have established a considerable number of principles about the effective resolution of conflicts.

The values of conflict

Disagreement can be of definite value in group decision-making. Disagreement occurs when two or more people have conflicting views, evaluations, values, attitudes, perceptions, goals, strategies, or interests. Some writers prefer to refer to such disagreement as "conflict";[19] others prefer the term "controversy."[20] Whatever you call it, it is almost inevitable in any seriously undertaken problem-solution task.

Given the diversity of individuals' psychological selectivity (see Chapters 2 and 3), it is nearly certain that any member of a group is bound to be a minority of *one* on at least one aspect of attitude or behavior. In other words, if six or seven people sat down in a problem-solving conference and found that they all agreed on every single point raised, it would be statistically amazing, to say the least!

Of course, controversy can disrupt and demoralize a problem-solving group. Disagreement is only valuable if it is properly managed or resolved. Researchers generally agree that there are values to be gained from properly managed conflict and there are detriments to conflict that is suppressed. As Johnson and Johnson warn us,[21]

> Unfortunately, most groups seem [to] . . . encourage group members to suppress conflicts, to agree without commitment, and to stifle their creativity. It is characteristic of ineffective groups that they suppress and withdraw from controversy. Compromise in order to avert controversy is their rule. They often agree quickly, and believe that relationships among members are so fragile that they cannot stand the strain of prolonged differences. Norms in groups like these have to be changed if they are to develop and improve their problem-solving effectiveness.

Johnson and Johnson seem to be echoing the sentiment of the late French writer, Joseph Joubert: "It is better to debate a question without settling it than to settle it without debating it." While Johnson and Johnson devote less space (under two pages) to the value of controversy than does Filley, the more comprehensive list of values from properly managed disagreement comes from the former.[22] Paraphrased, they are:

1. Creative, higher-quality decisions.
2. Commitment among group members to implement a decision that is reached.
3. Improved problem-solving ability.
4. Encouraging of inquiry, objectivity, sharpened analysis, stimulated interest, heightened curiosity, and increased involvement in and commitment to the group.
5. Increase in members' motivation and energy to work.
6. Greater understanding of oneself and one's motives.
7. Greater fun and interest.

Properly managing conflict

Properly managed conflict or controversy can be highly *constructive,* whereas improperly managed it can be *destructive.* Any conflict or

Solving problems through small groups

controversy can be classified as managed either in a constructive or destructive manner on the basis of (1) the *process* by which it is managed and (2) the *outcome* of the disagreement. Below we paraphrase and summarize the contrasting process management techniques and outcomes of constructive and destructive disagreements.

TABLE 11–1. **Contrasting Management Techniques Resulting in Constructive or Destructive Controversy[23]**

CONSTRUCTIVE TECHNIQUES	DESTRUCTIVE TECHNIQUES
The conflict is defined as a mutual problem.	The conflict is defined as a win-or-lose proposition.
All, or nearly all, group members participate in the conflict.	Only a few members participate; some withdraw deliberately.
Ideas and feelings are expressed honestly and openly.	Ideas and feelings are either suppressed or expressed deceitfully.
Each person's contribution is given serious attention, is valued and respected.	The contributions of at least some members are ignored, devalued, not respected.
Effective, empathic communication takes place.	Empathic communication does not take place.
Differences in opinions, attitudes, and ideas are brought out into the open deliberately and are clarified.	Differences in opinions, attitudes, and ideas are ignored or suppressed.
Different underlying assumptions and frames of reference are brought out into the open and discussed.	Different underlying assumptions and frames of references are not brought out, so are not discussed.
Disagreement is considered one of *ideas* and not *personalities;* it is not taken as personal rejection.	Disagreement is considered one of *personalities,* not of *ideas;* it is taken as personal rejection.
Different positions are understood clearly.	Different positions are not understood clearly.
Similarities of positions are perceived adequately so they can be combined in a creative synthesis.	Similarities of positions are not perceived, so they cannot be combined in a creative synthesis.
Emotions are answered by emotions.	Emotions are answered by tolerant but uninvolved "understanding."
Group members are relatively equal in power, authority.	Group members are widely divergent in power, authority.
Tension is at a moderate level.	Tension level is too low or too high.
Members' incentives are for creative resolution through problem solving.	Members' incentives are for domination and "winning" over other members.
A mutually satisfying solution is worked for and arrived at by problem-solving methods.	Conflict-reducing or -ending procedures (flipping a coin, voting, etc.) are used.

TABLE 11–2. Contrasting Outcomes of Constructive and Destructive Controversy

CONSTRUCTIVE OUTCOMES	DESTRUCTIVE OUTCOMES
Decisions are correct and of high quality.	Decisions are incorrect and of low quality.
Decisions are highly creative.	Decisions are relatively lacking in creativity.
Members are satisfied that they have been listened to and understood.	Members feel they have been ignored or misunderstood.
Members feel they have had a positive influence on the group.	Members feel they have had little or no influence on the group.
Members feel part of the decision and are committed to its implementation.	Some members do not feel part of the decision, so are not committed to its implementation.
Members are highly satisfied, personally, with their participation and the process of work the group went through.	Members are not personally satisfied with their participation or the process of work the group went through.
Group cohesion is enhanced by members' feeling liked by and liking other members, feeling acceptance for and by other members, and feeling trust for and from other members.	Group divisiveness is heightened by members' mutual dislike, nonacceptance, and distrust.
Positive feelings result from release and dissipation of emotional feelings and tension.	Negative feelings dominate because emotions and tension have been repressed or suppressed.
Members learn, through the experience, to better manage future controversy.	Experience lowers members' ability/motivation for future controversy management.
Members learn much about the issue under discussion.	Members learn little about the issue under discussion.

Summary

We examined several small group theories and found that in order to function effectively in a small group, participants need to be aware of the responsibilities of leadership and participation.

Both the leader and participant have two major functions: the task function and the group maintenance function. Both leader and participant must contribute to the achievement of both functions. If a group member strives only to accomplish the group task, he or she may harm interpersonal relations within the group and make the group ineffective in the future. On the other hand, if too much attention is devoted to the group maintenance function, the group may have trouble solving the task.

Some planning is necessary for small group communication. However, planning should not be carried to such an extreme that it stifles the creativity of the group. Small group communication plays a vital role in our society, and a basic knowledge of how the small group functions is impotrant to all of us.

QUESTIONS FOR THOUGHT
AND DISCUSSION
CHAPTER 11

1. How can reflective thinking be used in day-to-day decisions?
2. What should be achieved during the analysis of a problem?
3. How does one's understanding of the causes of a problem influence what one will recommend to solve the problem?
4. What is meant by *criteria* to be used in helping determine the solution to a problem?
5. What methods of decision-making might one consider in addition to reflective thinking? What are the strengths and weaknesses of each?
6. What are the traits of a good leader?
7. Distinguish between task and group maintenance functions in small group decision making.
8. Define several styles of leadership and illustrate each from actual situations.
9. What should you do when planning for small group communication?
10. What is meant by *empathetic listening?*
11. In what ways does conflict in groups have value?

EXERCISES · ASSIGNMENTS | CHAPTER 11

1. Prepare a three- to five-minue report in which you briefly apply the group discussion steps of analysis in reflective thinking to a topic in the news. For example, define terms inherent in the topic, limit it, analyze the causes of the problem, and so on.
2. Observe a group involved in decision making, and evaluate that activity in a report.
3. Participate in a group outside of class in which you, without revealing your purpose, try to guide the group through the basic steps of analysis studied in Chapter 11. Prepare a report of this experience and share your reactions with the class.

4. Review the contributions of Homans, Lewin, and Bales to our understanding of how the small group functions. Select a particular group and discuss which theory provides the best insight into the operation of that group.

ENDNOTES | Chapter 11

1. John Dewey, *How We Think* (Boston: D. C. Heath, 1933).
2. Harry Sharp, Jr., and Joyce Millikin, "Reflective Thinking Ability and the Product of Problem-Solving Discussion," *Speech Monographs,* 31 (1964): 124–127; quoted in Carl E. Larson, "Speech Communication Research on Small Groups," *Speech Teacher,* 20 (March 1971): 92.
3. John K. Brilhart and Lurene M. Jochem, "Effects of Different Patterns on Outcomes of Problem-Solving Discussion," *Journal of Applied Psychology,* 48 (1964): 175–179; reported in Larson, *op. cit.,* pp. 93–94.
4. Carl E. Larson, "Forms of Analysis and Small Group Problem-Solving," *Speech Monographs,* 36 (November 1969): 452–455.
5. Charles H. Kepner and Benjamin B. Tregoe, *The Rational Manager: A Systematic Approach to Problem Solving and Decision Making* (New York: McGraw-Hill, 1965).
6. George Homans, *The Human Group* (New York: Harcourt, Brace, 1950).
7. Kurt Lewin, "Frontiers in Group Dynamics," *Human Relations,* 1 (1947): 5–41.
8. Morton Deutsh, "Field Theory in Social Psychology," *Handbook of Social Psychology,* vol. 1, edited by Calvin S. Hall and Gardner Lindzey (Reading, Mass.: Addison-Wesley, 1954), p. 215.
9. Leon Festinger and John Thibaut, "Interpersonal Communication in Small Groups," *Readings in Social Psychology,* rev. ed., edited by Guy Swanson, Theodore Newcomb, and Eugene Hartley (New York: Henry Holt, 1952), p. 134.
10. Robert F. Bales, *Interaction Process Analysis* (Reading, Mass.: Addison-Wesley, 1950).
11. *Ibid.,* p. 9.
12. Robert F. Bales, "Some Statistical Problems in Small Group Research," *Journal of the American Statistical Association,* 46 (1951): 311–322.
13. See R. M. Stogdill, "Personality Factors Associated with Leadership: A Survey of the Literature," *Journal of Psychology,* 25 (January 1948): 35–71.
14. See Dorwin Cartwright and Alvin Zander, *Group Dynamics: Research and Theory,* 2nd ed. (New York: Harper & Row, 1960), p. 491.
15. William M. Fox, "Group Reaction to Two Types of Conference Leadership," *Human Relations,* 10 (1957): 279–289.

16. Carl E. Larson, "Speech Communication Research on Small Groups," *op. cit.,* pp. 95–96. See also William E. Utterback, "The Influence of Conference on Opinion," *Quarterly Journal of Speech,* 36 (1950): 365–370; Utterback, "Measuring the Outcome of an Intercollegiate Conference," *Journal of Communication,* 6 (1956): 33–37; Ray H. Simpson, "Attitudinal Effects of Small Group Discussions: Shifts on Certainty-Uncertainty and Agreement-Disagreement Continua," *Quarterly Journal of Speech,* 46 (1960): 415–418.

17. Alvin Zander and Herman Medow, "Strength of Group and Desire for Attainable Group Aspirations," *Journal of Personality,* 33 (March 1965): 122–139.

18. David W. Johnson, "Communication and the Inducement of Cooperative Behavior in Conflicts," *Speech Monographs,* 41 (March 1974): 64–78.

19. Alan C. Filley, *Interpersonal Conflict Resolution* (Glenview, Ill.: Scott, Foresman, 1975).

20. David W. Johnson and Frank P. Johnson, *Joining Together: Group Theory and Group Skills* (Englewood Cliffs, N.J.: Prentice-Hall, 1975).

21. *Ibid.,* p. 149.

22. *Ibid.,* pp. 148–149.

23. *Ibid.,* pp. 157–158. Tables 11–1 and 11–2 reprinted by permission of Prentice-Hall.

APPENDIX A

EVALUATING SPEECHES

Each time a speech is given, it is evaluated, or criticized. The evaluation may be a rather formal or official matter and find its way onto national television via commentators such as Eric Sevareid, Walter Cronkite, or Howard K. Smith, or into print in a *New York Times* editorial or a doctoral dissertation by a speech communication scholar. It might be as informal as, "I sure did like that speech!" or, "What guff *he* put out!" Speech students generally expect their teachers to have informed and judicious opinions on contemporary speeches and speakers. They occasionally ask questions such as, "Professor, what do you think of the President as a speaker?" or, "How did you like the Governor's speech last night?"

When a critic makes an evaluation of a speech, he generally hopes that those who hear or read his evaluation will agree with that evaluation. That is, a speech critique in basic nature is not unlike that of a "speech to convince on an issue of value." As such, a matter of prime importance should be an explanation (and perhaps even a justification) of the critic's *criteria* for judging.

What are the criteria generally used for such an evaluation? There are several, and one should not be surprised to find that not all speech critics use the same ones. Let us look at those criteria, as summarized for us by William A. Linsley:

> The traditional standards for judging preferred by most critics who have expressed their impression of a "good" speech can be generalized in six theories. Speeches are "good," according to the *ethical* theory, if the speaker has demonstrated worthy motives. Honesty is applauded and deceit condemned. The theory neglects to explain how speaker motives are determined and if determined how they are to be judged. Speeches are "good," according to the *truth* theory, if they are in league with established fact. A man who speaks falsely delivers a "bad" speech. This theory neglects to explain how the critic is to know what is true, presumes speeches occur only when the truth can be known and assumes that because one speaks the truth he is blessed with the competence to deliver it. Speeches are "good," according to the *pragmatic,* or *results* theory, if the response occurs which the speaker seeks. If the cause is lost, the speech is deficient. This theory neglects

to account for those causal factors which influence the consequences but are extraneous to the speech, and it neglects to explain how speaker intent can be determined. Both the true cause of an audience response and the intended consequences may be unassessible. Thus, neither is the achievement of the "desired" response a sign that the speech is "good" nor does failure to realize the "intended" effect signal a "bad" speech. Another theory claims speeches are "good" because of their *artistic qualities.* This presumes certain accepted principles of speaking which when incorporated into a speech make it "good" and when omitted make it defective. The inability to ascertain truth, motives and results, encourages the critic to settle on the presence of principles as a standard of judgment. This theory, which is unmindful of audience response, is reminiscent of Plato's arguments against rhetoric, and the charge of indifference to truth and morality. Speeches are "good" according to the *contribution* theory when "good" is interpreted, not as opposed to "bad," but as "worthwhile" for their contribution to needed understanding. This theory reacts to bases for judgment which are too speaker-centered and do not consider how the speaker's ideas provide an index of the values and goals of society or add to the theory of how speeches are adapted to particular audiences. The *contribution* theory prefers the speech which provides material which under careful examination produces insight about ideas, society, history or speech theory. This theory neglects to consider that speakers do not prepare and present speeches so critics might study them. A sixth theory, and probably the most common, is *eclectic,* or *relativistic* and draws on the other five in an effort to take advantage of the strengths of each.[1]

But, as a student in a speech class, you are probably less interested in criteria for "rhetorical criticism" than in how you are likely to be *graded* on your speech work by your instructor. Grades, after all, seem to be a sort of "necessary evil" in classroom work, but are expected by students. As McKeachie says:

Whatever a student's motivation for being in college, grades are important to him. If he is genuinely interested in learning, grades represent an expert's appraisal of his success; if he is interested in getting into professional school, good grades will unlock graduate school doors; if he wants to play football, grades are necessary to maintain eligibility. Most students are motivated to get passing grades. . . .[2]

One must understand at the outset, of course, that the grading or otherwise evaluating of speeches is quite a bit less than an exact art. Just as people of intelligence and good will might differ in the evaluations of a movie, play, a beauty queen contestant, or an oil painting—trained and experienced teachers of speech communication can differ on the merits of a particular speech. However, their training and experience also lend some commonality to their judgments.

Many teachers of speech communication use some kind of a rating sheet or chart on which to evaluate students' speech work. This sheet often is filled out, augmented sometimes with written comments, and handed the student after he has finished an assignment. The rating form may be further augmented by the instructor's oral comments on the speech assignment, perhaps also by classroom discussion of same. The rating form used by an individual instructor is probably one he or she has come to rely upon through training and practice, and, although a considerable amount of research on rating scales has been done, no one seems to have come up with *the* one rating scale which is best for all raters and all speaking situations. Most of the scales used, however, rate what is usually called "general effectiveness" of the speech. The writers of this book feel that a speech's grade should reflect the instructor's reasoned judgment of how "generally effective" a speech has been—that is, how well the speech was constructed and presented so as to produce the audience response the speaker sought.

Two published studies furnish some measure of support for our judgment. One is a mail survey of what a national sample of speech communication instructors require for speeches of different "grades," and the other is a report of two experiments.

In 1960, Professor Robert T. Oliver of the Pennsylvania State University published a list of standards which the Penn State speech faculty try to use in the grading of all student speeches there.[3] These standards were rewritten to conform more closely to what educational experts call "behavioral objectives" and became the substance of the mail questionnaire study.[4]

The questionnaire was mailed to the 651 people listed in the Speech Communication Association's 1966–67 *Directory* as belonging to the association's Undergraduate Speech Instruction Interest Group. The questionnaire listed the 14 "behavioral objectives" and asked each teacher to check each objective as to whether he expected a student to achieve it for a "C," a "B," or an "A" grade on his speech. Instructors were informed that it was understood that, if achievement for an objective were expected for a "C," it would likewise be expected for a "B" and for an "A"; and a "B" objective would be expected of an "A" speech.

A total of 328 usable questionnaires were returned, and the results are shown in Table 1. If you read objectives 2–4, 7, 10, and 14, those the instructors overwhelmingly agreed should be expected for a "C," you should note that these six objectives denote criteria which are fairly easily determinable mechanics of a classroom assignment. They do not mention the achieving of measurable *results.* But: read the eight "B" and "A" objectives; these objectives denote either enriched (some would say, "artistic") style of speaking or else the achievement of the speaker's purpose.

If you look at the percentages of persons checking the "B" and "A" objectives, you might be struck with the apparent difficulty of separating the "B" speech from the "A" speech. One who is familiar with the research on the rating of human achievements would expect some such ambiguity, but might also expect more ambiguity than in fact is reflected by these data. But the main point to be emphasized here is: speech communication experts tend to rather clearly differentiate the "C" or "average" speech from the "B" or "A" speech; the "C" speech meets the "requirements of the assignment" without achieving its purpose, whereas the "B" and "A" speeches both meet the requirements of the assignment *and* tend to achieve their desired audience responses. The implication for the student should be clear: follow the instructions of this textbook and those of your instructor that will help you achieve the specific audience responses you seek, and grades will "take care of themselves."

The other study mentioned above involved the reporting of two experiments regarding the actual measurable effect of speeches.[5]

In the first experiment, one student who habitually received C's or less on his speeches in one class and another student who habitually received A's on his speeches in another class were compared for persuasive effectiveness. Each, without the knowledge of the other, was asked to give a speech on the same topic —the abolition of capital punishment. Each was given the same thesis to argue and the same main points to support in proving his thesis. And each was directed to identical sources from which to draw his evidence.

Each speaker gave his speech on the same day to his respective class. The class members then completed scales assessing their attitude toward capital pun-

TABLE 1. Respondents requiring "Behavioral Objectives" for different grades on classroom speeches (N = 328).

	Required for Grade of:		
	C	B	A
Behavioral Objective	No. (percent)	No. (percent)	No. (percent)
1. The speech style was distinguished by elements of vividness, such as analogies or comparisons, metaphor, specific instances, humor, concreteness, etc.	19(5.8)	177(54)	125(38.1)
2. The speech had a clear purpose in terms of auditor response sought, supported by main heads easy to identify (One respondent required item for a D).	227(69.2)	87(26.5)	9(2.7)
3. The speaker demonstrated reasonable directness and communicativeness in delivery.	287(87.5)	36(11)	3(.9)
4. The speaker did not detract from his message through gross errors of grammar, pronunciation, or articulation.	278(84.8)	37(11.3)	7(2.1)
5. The speaker made a genuinely individual contribution to the thinking of his audience.	17(5.2)	126(38.4)	170(51.8)
6. The speech was intellectually sound in developing a topic of real worth, using adequate and dependable evidence.	73(22.3)	221(67.4)	33(10.1)
7. The speech conformed reasonably to the assigned time limit (Two respondents required item for a D).	294(89.6)	17(5.2)	6(1.8)
8 The speaker made understandable an unusually difficult concept or process; OR he won *some* agreement from an audience initially inclined to disagree with him; OR he won *some* tendency to act from an audience initially inclined to not so act.	16(4.9)	136(41.5)	161(49.1)
9. The speaker achieved a variety and flexibility of mood and manner suited to the multiple differentiation of thinking and feeling demanded by the subject matter and by the speaker-audience relations.	19(5.8)	130(39.6)	159(48.5)

Reprinted from *The Speech Teacher,* XVII (September 1968), p. 208.

Appendix A

Behavioral Objective	Required for Grade of:		
	C No. (percent)	B No. (percent)	A No. (percent)
10. The speech was of the type assigned (to inform, to convince, to actuate, etc.) (Two respondents required item for a D).	313(95.4)	8(2.4)	5(1.5)
11. The speaker moved the audience progressively from initial uncertainty (of knowledge, belief, or tendency to act) toward the acceptance of the speaker's purpose, by orderly processes, toward a final resolution of the uncertainty in a conclusion that evolved naturally from the materials used by the speaker.	18(5.5)	138(42.1)	158(48.2)
12. The speech was better than most classroom speeches in *stimulative quality,* that is, in challenging the audience to think, or in arousing depth of response.	5(1.5)	230(70.1)	88(26.8)
13. The speaker established rapport of a high order with apt style and direct, extemporaneous delivery, achieving a genuinely communicative *circular response.*	10(3.0)	96(29.3)	212(64.6)
14. The speech was presented on the date for which it was assigned (Five respondents required item for a D).	286(87.2)	14(4.3)	5(1.5)

ishment, and the attitudes of the two classes were compared with one another and with those of a control group. The statistical analysis revealed that the "A" speaker changed the attitudes of his audience against capital punishment, whereas the "C" speaker did not.

Later, each speech—which had been tape recorded as it was given in the classroom—was played to a group of experts in speech communication, who were asked to rate it as they would a normal classroom speech they might hear. The speech by the successful speaker was rated as far superior to that of the unsuccessful speaker.

The second experiment involved two "good" and two "poor" speeches written and recorded by speech communication professionals. One good and one poor speech each was lauding "advertising" as beneficial to our everyday lives; also, one good and one poor speech each was written urging that capital punishment be abolished in the United States. A group of speech communication teachers heard these speeches played on a tape recorder, then graded them as they would had they heard them in speech communication classes. Each good speech received grades averaging "B+," and each poor speech received grades averaging "C" or "C−."

The attitudes of a large number of college students toward "advertising" and "capital punishment" were assessed before and after hearing one of the advertising and one of the capital punishment speeches. Statistical analysis of the results showed that each "good" speech changed the students' attitudes in the intended direction, but that neither "poor" speech did.

Again, this advice to the student seems pertinent: concern yourself less—on a conscious level at least—with "getting a good grade" on your speech and, instead, concentrate on those instructions and techniques which you are taught in your course that will most help you to be successful in achieving the specific purpose you select for each speech.

ENDNOTES APPENDIX A

1. William A. Linsley, *Speech Criticism: Methods and Materials* (Dubuque, Iowa: Wm. C. Brown Company Publishers, 1968), pp. 2–3.
2. W. J. McKeachie, "Research on Teaching at the College and University Level," in *Handbook of Research on Teaching,* ed. N. L. Gage (Chicago: American Educational Research Association, Rand McNally and Company, 1963), p. 1119.
3. Robert T. Oliver, "The Eternal (and Infernal) Problem of Grades," *The Speech Teacher,* IX (January, 1960), pp. 8–11.
4. Charles R. Gruner, "Behavioral Objectives for the Grading of Classroom Speeches," *The Speech Teacher,* XVII (September, 1968), pp. 207–210.
5. Charles R. Gruner, Marsha W. Gruner, and Donald O. Olson, "Is Classroom Evaluation Related to Actual Effectiveness of Classroom Speeches?" *Southern Speech Journal,* XXXIV (Fall, 1968), pp. 36–46.

APPENDIX B

FORMS FOR EVALUATING SPEECH COMMUNICATION

The evaluation of interviews, small group situations, and speeches is at best an inexact art. In this appendix, we have brought together several evaluation forms that should provide the interested student some additional insight into the basic principles of speech communication that are critical to interviewing, small group communication, and public speaking.

Post-meeting reactions

We can learn some things about a discussion by simply asking group members to report feelings, judgments, or reactions. This is generally a nonthreatening type of evaluation, and sometimes it is all that is needed for the first round of discussions in a class.

Reaction Questionnaire

Discussion Subject: _____

Group: _____ Date: _____

Check (√) or encircle the number which represents your reaction to the following eight questions.

1. *Understandability of Language:* To what extent were you getting the meaning of each other's statements?

1	2	3	4	5	6	7	8	9	10	11

We talked past each other, much misunderstanding   We communicated directly with each other

From William M. Sattler and N. Edd Miller, *Discussion and Conference,* 2d ed. (Prentice-Hall, Inc., 1968), pp. 473–475. Adapted and reprinted by permission of Holt, Rinehart and Winston, Inc.

2. *Opportunity to Communicate:* To what extent did you feel free to talk?

1	2	3	4	5	6	7	8	9	10	11

Never had oppor-
tunity to talk

Had every oppor-
tunity to talk

3. *Support and Acceptance:* How much support did the group members give each other?

1	2	3	4	5	6	7	8	9	10	11

The group was
highly critical
and punishing

The group was
permissive and
highly receptive

4. *Interpersonal Atmosphere:* How pleasant was the affective-interpersonal atmosphere of the group?

1	2	3	4	5	6	7	8	9	10	11

Very unpleasant,
quarrelsome,
unfriendly

Very pleasant,
personable,
enjoyable

5. *Acceptance by Leader:* If one person seemed to lead the discussion, to what extent do you feel you were accepted by him?

1	2	3	4	5	6	7	8	9	10	11

Completely
rejected

Somewhat
rejected

Fairly well
accepted

Completely
accepted

6. *Self-Satisfaction:* How satisfied are you with the part you played in this discussion?

1	2	3	4	5	6	7	8	9	10	11

Very
dissatisfied

Moderately
dissatisfied

Moderately
satisfied

Very
satisfied

7. *Value of Conclusions:* How satisfied are you with the decisions or conclusions reached in the discussion?

1	2	3	4	5	6	7	8	9	10	11

Very
dissatisfied

Moderately
dissatisfied

Moderately
satisfied

Very
satisfied

8. *Overall Rating:* How would you rate the discussion as a whole?

Evaluating the group

The next element to be evaluated is group operation as a unit or team. This evaluation is important, as it is related to high-quality productivity and also to the other discussion objectives of member satisfaction-commitment and group maintenance. Here, again, two types of evaluation are appropriate: a running record, and a final estimate of group functioning.

Running record of "groupness"

The questions to be answered concern such elements as these:

    I. To what extent does the group climate promote free, permissive talk?
       A. Is the atmosphere informal rather than rigidly stiff?
       B. Does every member participate?

C. Do members react to contributions in ways that encourage the communicator to talk again later?
D. Do high-power members react to contributions in ways that encourage lower-power members to talk again later?
E. Are the physical surroundings pleasant and conducive to enthusiastic talk?
F. Do members seem enthusiastic about the importance of discussing the problem and do they consider participation worthwhile?

II. To what extent are members compatible?
A. Are members friendly to each other?
B. Do members seem to like each other?
C. Do members seem to enjoy talking with each other?
D. Do members smile occasionally as they talk to others?
E. Do members behave in ways which generally minimize the threat to others' egos?

III. To what extent does the group operate as a cohesive unit?
A. Is there mutual helpfulness among members?
B. Do members seem to be dependent upon each other for support?
C. Do members seem eager to hear the group's reactions rather than proceeding on their own?
D. Is there effort to bring deviates back into agreement with the group?
E. Do members seem more concerned with group interests than self-interest?
F. Do members seem cooperative rather than competitive?
G. Do members seem pleased when other members are congratulated for superior contribution?

IV. To what extent is there efficient communicative interaction?
A. Which members contribute most and which least?
B. Which members' contributions are most helpful to the group?
C. What kinds of information-opinion are contributed by each member?
D. To which members are most communications directed?
E. What proportion of communications are directed to the whole group?
F. Are members attentive listeners?
G. Do contributions relate to and build upon earlier contributions?

Evaluating leadership

It is obvious that special scales must be designed for evaluating the designated leader or leaders. Here, too, the criteria are suggested by what has already been said about leadership.

Does the designated leader, or those carrying the leadership responsibility:

I. Have an adequate knowledge of group process?
A. Understand interaction?
B. Understand the influence of power relationships?
C. Understand the influence of interpersonal relations?
D. Understand the influence of group size?
E. Understand the nature and types of leadership?
F. Have ability to be impartial?

Adapted from *Discussion, Conference, and Group Process,* 2nd edition, by Halbert E. Gulley. Copyright © 1960, 1968 by Holt, Rinehart and Winston, Inc. Reprinted by permission of Holt, Rinehart and Winston, Inc.

II. Have an adequate knowledge of the problem?
  A. Have sufficient information?
  B. Recognize when a topic has been adequately discussed?

III. Have adequate reasoning abilities?
  A. Have the ability to think quickly?
  B. Check for fallacies?

IV. Have respect for others?
  A. Have social sensitivity?
  B. Display tact?

V. Have adequate language and speech skills?
  A. Express complex ideas swiftly and clearly?
  B. Summarize objectively, fairly, and quickly?
  C. Take all views into account?
  D. Listen adequately?

VI. Introduce the discussion adequately?
  A. Introduce participants skillfully?
  B. Introduce the problem skillfully?

VII. Guide the discussion adequately?
  A. Follow an orderly pattern systematically?
  B. Keep discussion on the track?
  C. Rebound from tangents skillfully?
  D. Clarify and restate to assist forward movement?
  E. Give transitional summaries to assist forward movement?
  F. Ask for definition?
  G. Ask the right questions?

VIII. Regulate the discussion adequately?
  A. Preserve order and prevent chaos?
  B. Restrain overeager participants and encourage low participators?
  C. Encourage cooperative attitudes?
  D. Build cohesiveness-solidarity?
  E. Encourage permissiveness-interaction?
  F. Minimize effects of power discrepancies?
  G. Resolve conflicts?
  H. Stress agreement?

Evaluating participants

In judging group productivity and "groupness," some evaluation of individual participants occurs. It is important some of the time, however, to concentrate on judging the effectiveness of each person, since it is the individual who must attempt to improve himself as a discusser. The criteria on which he should be evaluated are drawn from everything that has been said about participation:

I. Does he have cooperative attitudes?
  A. Does he display objectivity toward the problem?
  B. Does he display objectivity toward others?
  C. Does he cooperate as part of the group?
  D. Does he discuss enthusiastically?

Adapted from *Discussion, Conference, and Group Process*, 2nd edition, by Halbert E. Gulley. Copyright © 1960, 1968 by Holt, Rinehart and Winston, Inc. Reprinted by permission of Holt, Rinehart and Winston, Inc.

II. Does he make substantive contributions to the discussion?
   A. Is he well informed?
   B. Is he mentally alert?
   C. Does he answer rather than evade questions?
   D. Does he contribute information when needed?
   E. Does he reason adequately?
   F. Does he check for fallacies?
   G. Does he build on others' reasoning?
   H. Is he thorough?

III. Does he use language adequately?
   A. Is his language clear?
   B. Is his language accurate?
   C. Is his language appropriate?
   D. Is his language fair to others?

IV. Does he speak adequately?
   A. Does he speak intelligibly?
   B. Does he speak naturally?
   C. Does he speak interestingly?
   D. Does he speak efficiently?
   E. Does he listen "behind the statement"?

V. Does he help the leader?
   A. Does he heed the pattern?
   B. Does he help the group stay on track?
   C. Does he refrain from usurping the leader's functions?

VI. Is he ethical?
   A. Does he refrain from pretending to understand more than he really does?
   B. Does he refrain from distortion and deception?
   C. Does he refrain from channeling talk for his own purposes?
   D. Does he use language and reasoning fairly?

Interview Evaluation Form

Name _____

	0–1–2 very ineffective	2–3–4 moderately ineffective	4–5–6 average	6–7–8 moderately effective	8–9–10 very effective
	1	2 3	4 5	6 7	8 9 10
Introduction and establishment of rapport					
Use of questions to secure information					
Answers to questions					
Control of critical moments					
Listening					
Providing perspective (context)					
Organization					
Overall communication skill					
Closing					
Does the interview achieve its goal?					

Total Rating _____

COMMENTS:

Speech Critique

Name _____ Date _____ Rater _____

Project _____ Time _____

Subject _____ Grade _____

Criteria	Rate 1–5	Comments
CONTENT		
ORGANIZATION		
LANGUAGE		
AUDIENCE ADAPTATION		
SPEECH ATTITUDES AND ADJUSTMENTS		
BODILY ACTIVITY		
VOCAL ELEMENTS		
GENERAL EFFECTIVENESS		
TOTAL		

RANKING

1   2   3   4   5   6   7

AUTHOR AND NAME INDEX

Kilpatrick, James, 11, 67
Kissinger, Henry, 43
Klapper, Joseph, 232, 233, 235, 238
Knapp, Mark L., 71, 89, 90
Knower, Franklin H., 127
Koeppel, Fern, 127
Kruger, Arthur N., 152
Krugman, Herbert E., 231
Kumata, Kideya, 112, 127

Laird, Melvin, 226
Lardner, Ring, 61
Larson, Carl E., 251, 256, 264, 270, 271
Lazarus, Emma, 107
Lee, Robert E., 230
Lewin, Kurt, 253, 254, 270
Lewis, Richard B., 127
Liebert, Robert M., 238
Likert, Rensis, 140, 152
Lincoln, Abraham, 57
Linkugel, Wil A., 66
Lull, P. E., 126
Lyle, J., 238

MacArthur, Douglas, 59
McCarthy, Joseph, 202
McCloy, John J., 227
McCormick, Mary C., 127
McCroskey, James C., 99, 100, 125, 213, 217
McEwen, W. J., 237
McGregor, Douglas, 152
McLuhan, Marshall, 232, 238
McNaughton, Wayne L., 152
Maslow, Abraham H., 7, 11, 136, 152
Mead, Margaret, 58, 66
Medow, Herman, 271
Mehrabian, Albert, 72, 73, 90
Meyer, H. H., 152
Mill, John Stuart, 30
Miller, Gerald R., 127, 151
Millikin, Joyce, 243, 270
Mills, Judson, 186
Milton, John, 61
Minnick, Wayne C., 14
Mizner, Wilson, 39, 50
Monroe, Alan H., 207, 217

Napoleon, 56, 75
Newcomb, Theodore, 270
Newman, Edwin, 130, 151
Nichols, Ralph G., 40, 48, 51

Nilsen, Thomas R., 215, 217
Nixon, Richard M., 224

Oliphant, 228
Oliver, Robert, 133, 151
Overstreet, H. A., 207
Oswald, Lee Harvey, 113, 201

Paar, Jack, 231
Pace, R. Wayne, 237
Painter, Edith G., 106, 125
Pei, Mario, 231
Perkins, Frances, 56
Peterson, Brent D., 237
Petrie, Charles R., Jr., 51, 166, 186
Phillips, David, 127
Phillips, Kalman, 33, 50
Pierce, John R., 66
Plato, 186
Pokorny, Gary F., 126
Pope, Alexander, 63
Porter, Richard E., 11, 51, 151
Poulos, Rita Wicks, 238

Rankin, Paul T., 40, 50
Read, Jill, 90
Reagan, Ronald, 224
Reasoner, Harry, 86, 91
Reid, Ronald F., 14
Reston, James, 220, 221
Revesz, G., 151
Richards, K. E., 138, 152
Richardson, Glen A., 187
Rogers, Carl, 145
Rokeach, Milton, 238
Roosevelt, Franklin D., 56, 103, 221
Roosevelt, Theodore, 63
Rose, Pete, 113
Rubinstein, E. A., 238
Russell, Michael L., 90

Sahl, Mort, 112
Samovar, Larry A., 5, 10, 11, 51, 130, 151
Schalliol, Charles, 99, 100, 102, 125, 211, 217
Scheflen, A. E., 71, 72
Schramm, Wilbur, 29, 30, 50, 237
Schultz, Charles, 59
Sears, D. O., 50
Sevareid, Eric, 227
Shakespeare, William, 73, 124, 201
Sharp, Harry, Jr., 243
Shaw, Bernard, 84

Sheldon, W. H., 74, 90
Siegel, Bertram, 74, 90
Simpson, Ray H., 186, 271
Smith, Barbara Hernstein, 89
Smith, Kate, 37, 233
Snyder, J., 90
Steinberg, Mark, 151
Steiner, Gary A., 11, 14, 17, 19, 24, 37,
    191, 206, 216, 232, 238
Stephens, John C., Jr., 109
Stevenson, Adlai E., 62, 120
Stogdill, R. M., 256, 270
Summers, Harrison B., 228, 237
Surlin, Stuart H., 238
Swanson, Guy, 270
Sydiaha Daniel, 146, 152
Syrus, Publilius, 130
Szep, Paul, 228

Tannenbaum, Percy H., 186
Taylor, Pat M., 126
Thibaut, John, 270
Thomas, G. L., 67
Thompson, Ernest, 166, 186, 171, 187
Thornton, G., 91
Thurman, Wayne L., 90
Tomkins, S. S., 90

Tregoe, Benjamin H., 251, 270
Truman, Harry, 59, 119
Tubbs, Stewart L., 217
Twain, Mark, 57

Ulrich, Joan H., 127
Utterback, William E., 271

Vidmar, Neal, 238

Wallace, Karl R., 126
Walters, Barbara, 220
Weaver, Carl, 51
Welles, Orson, 228
Wells, William D., 74, 90
Wheeless, Lawrence R., 29, 50
Wilcox, Roger P., 156, 186
Wilke, W., 90
Wilson, Edward O., 11
Wilson, John F., 111, 126
Wilson, Woodrow, 61
Winchell, Constance M., 96

Young, Owen D., 99

Zander, Alvin, 256, 270, 271
Zimmerman, Ralph, 107, 125

SUBJECT INDEX

Counseling interview, 140
Credibility of speaker, 98–99
Criteria, for solving problems, 247

Deduction, 114ff.
Defining problems, 244
Definition, as proof, 109
Definitions, speech communication, 14ff.
Democratic leadership in small groups, 258ff.
Description:
  process, 14
  as proof, 110ff.
  state, 14
Dialect regions, 84
Directed interview, 144
Dissonance, 191

Ectomorph, 74
Effect, instrumental, 199
Empathy, 122
  in conversation, 133
  in group communication, 263
Employment interviews, 135ff.
Endomorph, 74
"Enlarged conversation," public speaking as, 86ff.
Environmental factors in communication, 86
Epiglottis, 79
Ethics, of persuasion, 214
Ethos, 213
"Even-if" case, 204–205
Evidence and speaker credibility, 98–99
Exaggeration, 62
Examples, as evidence, 101ff.
Exit interview, 141
Exposure, selective, 15ff.
Expression, 19
Extemporaneous speeches, preparation, 86ff.
Eye contact, 73ff.

Facial expression, 73
Fact, issues of, 201ff.
Factual information, 99ff.
"Fairness doctrine," 223ff.
Familiarity, for interest, 32
"Family Circus," 34–35
Federal Communications Commission (FCC), 223ff.
  fraud, 224

"Feedforward," 133
Field theory, 254
Figurative language, 60ff.
"Fraction of selection," 29
Frame of reference, 34ff.

"Gatekeeping," 227
Gestures, 72
Glottis, 79
Grievance interview, 141
Group dynamics, 254
Group maintenance functions, 257
Group thinking, 263
Group-centered leadership, 259
Guideposts, 171

Hair, 75
Height, of speaker, 74–75
Homeostasis, 205ff.
Homeostatic condition, 191
Homophily of source/audience, 30
Humor:
  for interest, 33
  in speech, 111ff.

"Ideal solution form," 251
Illustration:
  as introduction, 102
  as proof, 101ff.
    hypothetical, 101ff.
    literal, 101ff.
Indexes, for research, 95ff.
Induction, 114
Inflection, vocal, 81
Informative speech:
  induction/deduction order, 169
  model, 181ff.
  problem-solution order, 168
Instrumental effect and goal, 199
Intentional/unintentional communication, 8ff.
Interaction Process Analysis (IPA), 255
Interest:
  in conversation, 134
  factors of, 31
  novelty, 32
  suspense, 32
  vitalness, 31
  wit, 33
Interpersonal communication, 20ff.
Interview, 135ff.
  consulting, 139
  correction, 140
  counseling, 140